EXPLORE MISSOURI'S GERMAN HERITAGE

by W. Arthur Mehrhoff

Churches in the German Heritage Corridor frequently held pride of place. St. Paul United Church of Christ, completed in 1846, rises above the Missouri River at Hermann, Missouri.

EXPLORE MISSOURI'S GERMAN HERITAGE

by W. Arthur Mehrhoff

Missouri Life Inc., Rocheport, Missouri
In cooperation with the Missouri Humanities Council

Missouri Life Inc., PO Box 57, Rocheport, MO 65279

ISBN 978-0-9968058-3-4
Printed in the USA

Editor: Danita Allen Wood
Book and Cover Design: Kath Teoli
Photography and Photo Research: Edward Lang and Casey Vroman

MissouriLife
THE SPIRIT OF DISCOVERY

With appreciation to the Missouri Humanities Council for support

GERMAN HERITAGE CORRIDOR of Missouri

MH MISSOURI HUMANITIES

For the descendants of Missouri's German settlers and all Missourians who care about our heritage.

A hillside at Hermannhof Winery offers a view of the Tin Mill Brewing Company and historic downtown Hermann. The Gasconade County Courthouse dominates the background.

Contents

Geh und erforschel = Go and Explore

das Tagebuch = the Journal, by the author

Foreword from Dr. William S. Belko

SHORTLY AFTER TAKING OVER as the Executive Director of the Missouri Humanities Council at the beginning of 2015, I stopped with several of my staff at a local brewery in Hermann after a long day of meetings and touring. Obviously the German heritage of the region reigned above all other facets, yet it seemed somewhat distant, as if the predominant culture and society of that community stood on the brink of disappearing. Still, there existed so many connections to its German founding and its German American past that something, I thought, had be done to secure its resurgence, considering Missouri's German American heritage was—and is—a principal feature of this state's identity. I then thought of the numerous other communities situated along the Missouri River, north and south of its banks, winding far westward from St. Louis, that were as German as Hermann. As a Missourian, moreover, it struck me about my own German descent, as my family, both maternal and paternal, came overwhelmingly from German provinces. All of them emigrated to the United States well before there was a unified German nation arising in the 1870s—families with surnames such as Webber, Thimmes, Schillinger, Bonner, Myers, and Lasar, which we can trace back to several German states. In fact, many of my German ancestors arrived in the latter half of the 1700s, during periods of massive German migration to America, eventually becoming Americanized and migrating to my home state of Missouri, where they married into recently arrived German families following the 1848 Revolution in Germany. All of these factors quickly combined in my head, and I thought, "Why is there no trail, no extensive heritage area, no corridor dedicated to the rich German heritage of my home?" That did it, as right there and then, I embarked on a crusade to remedy this deficiency and to create Missouri's German Heritage Corridor.

Within the ensuing year, with steadfast work from my new staff (including a few hired solely to see this corridor to fruition), the MHC succeeded in getting state legislation passed officially recognizing the German Heritage Corridor of Missouri. Of course, we did not stop there, as this was only the beginning of a time-consuming, far-reaching, and long-overdue statewide venture. In 2017, the MHC created a nine-member steering committee, composed of scholars and professionals from within Missouri who are widely recognized for their knowledge of Missouri's rich German heritage. We subsequently convened on several occasions other scholars and professionals from Missouri and across the nation who are equally well-versed in German American history and culture. Through many day-long workshops and brainstorming sessions, facilitated by one of the nation's top interpretive planners, this esteemed group of individuals provided the theoretical underpinnings and formulated the essential content for a brilliant interpretive plan. Much of the substance of this volume can be credited to their diligent work.

This comprehensive interpretive plan outlines the foundation of a three-phase, ten-year implementation plan for all of the state, not just the designated German Heritage Corridor, as so many other communities across this state were—and still are—of majority German ancestry and still maintain distinct features of German culture. Numerous local and statewide projects are already underway as this volume is published. Stay tuned, for there is considerably more work to be done over the next decade. The Missouri Humanities Council—along with countless nonprofit organizations, government agencies, and local communities across this state partnering with us in this worthy endeavor—remain committed to reviving appreciation for our pervasive German heritage.

This seminal volume is crucial for providing the foundational review of where our state's rich German Heritage Corridor stands today, and provides the reader with the essential facts, ideas, and concepts—that is, the placemaking—for where the Corridor will go in the future.

Wir feiern und unterstützen unser Kulturerbe! (We celebrate and support our cultural heritage!)

Dr. William S. Belko
Executive Director
Missouri Humanities Council

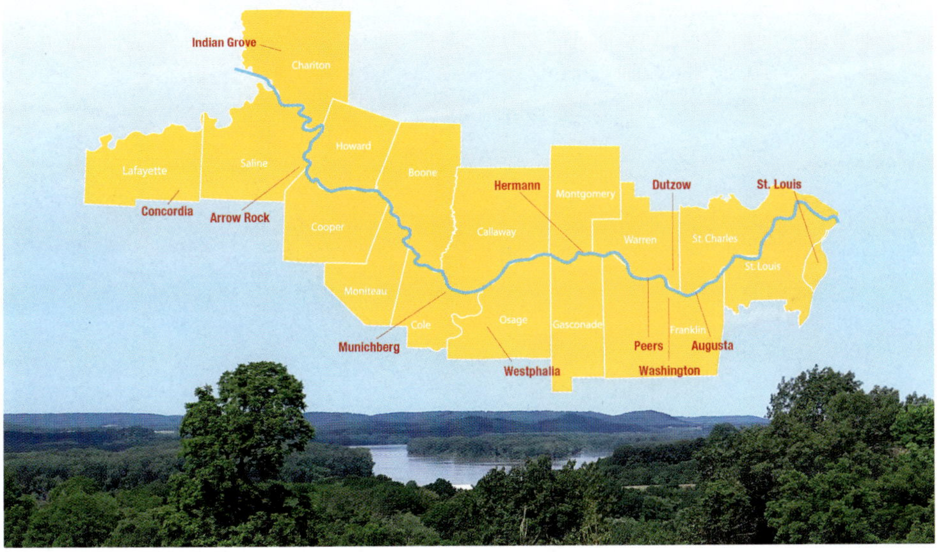

CORY DENNISON, MISSOURI HUMANITIES COUNCIL

Above: The Hermann riverfront is home to several historic brick buildings that now contain businesses that appeal to its many visitors. Hermann is at the heart of the German Heritage Corridor.
Left: On his sixth birthday, W. Arthur Mehrhoff chose his grandfather to practice oral history interviewing skills. These skills proved necessary in his later work as an ethnographer.

W. ARTHUR MEHRHOFF, MISSOURI DEPARTMENT OF CONSERVATION

IN THE EYE OF THE BEHOLDER

ein Bildungsroman

About Your Author

Geographic regions like the Chesapeake Bay, the Appalachian Trail, and California's celebrated Napa Valley glitter like rare gems in our increasingly standardized American landscape. Many Missourians will know at a glance that the photo at left shows the *Deutschheim* region of our state along the mighty Missouri River, with the landmark dome of the Gasconade County Courthouse at Hermann reaching through the wooded bluffs toward the sunlight. Special places like *Deutschheim* (home of the Germans), with its unique natural beauty and cultural heritage, help us better understand Missouri life, how Missourians at a certain time and place understood their world, and which artifacts belong in our heirloom collection.

That premise also underlies the German Heritage Corridor initiative of the Missouri Humanities Council. The German Heritage Corridor includes Deutschheim as well as other sections throughout Missouri where immigrants of German descent clearly demonstrated the special ways they made this new world their home, through their wineries, breweries, masonry, gardening, music-making, social organization and, of course, *Deutsches* language.

This major programming effort by the Missouri Humanities Council focuses an array of expert lenses on one of our state's most distinctive cultural regions. It aims to enlighten local citizens, Missourians, the nation, and even the world about this distinctive heritage, as well as to encourage new interpretive efforts that help interested communities use that heritage in shaping their own futures. Think *Antiques Roadshow* with a distinctively German accent. This book is one such interpretive effort, or lens, focused upon Missouri's German heritage.

Just like the photo at left, it's more enthusiastic than encyclopedic, taken from a particular vantage point. If you are considering touring this cultural region with an interpreter, then you probably want to conduct due diligence regarding the vantage of your tour guide. First of all, I'm in the game, so to speak, as an active participant in the Missouri Humanities Council German Heritage Corridor initiative, as well as a longtime *Missouri Life* magazine writer about our special places. I have also

W. Arthur Mehrhoff
Author

worked as a museum educator at the Jefferson National Expansion Memorial and, more recently, at the Museum of Art and Archaeology at the University of Missouri. I have consulted extensively with communities about heritage tourism and preservation through my work for the Governor's DREAM Initiative throughout Missouri, and before that, for more than a decade with the Minnesota Design Team.

On a personal note, I earned a doctorate from Saint Louis University in American Studies with an emphasis in material culture and was a 2014 Research Fellow in the Historic Landscape Institute at Thomas Jefferson's Monticello. In 1986, I guest lectured about Missouri's German heritage at the University of Tubingen *Abteilung fur Amerikanistik* (Department of American Studies); culture becomes much clearer when trying to explain it to outsiders from a distance. Writing about Missouri's German heritage also grows out of my genealogical research dating way back to the time of the American Bicentennial, a childhood spent in neighborhood schools with Schumachers, Krauses, and Fischers, as well as more than a little nostalgia for delicious sauerbraten, *Senfgerken*, and rolled oats bread prepared by *meine Grossmuttern*.

However, nostalgia is history without the pain. Winemakers like Missouri's legendary George Husmann clearly understood the need to balance sweetness with acidity in order to create complex wines of distinction. To better understand Missouri's German heritage, then, we also need to recall the immigrants' painful uprooting from traditional German village life, dangerous trans-Atlantic crossings with burials at sea, challenges of pioneer life in 19th-century Missouri, the intolerance often directed toward immigrant populations, and the personal and cultural burdens associated with three major military conflicts.

As Missouri wine pioneer George Husmann clearly showed with his vital horticultural work on grape vines, hybridization of European and Missouri rootstock produced a much healthier varietal. Perhaps we, too, can conduct an intercultural transfer, grafting the rootstock of our Missouri German heritage into our present to help us become award-winning vintners of a rich and healthy future vintage of Missouri life.

Above: Author W. Arthur Mehrhoff presented on April 13, 2014, at the University of Missouri's 175th anniversary celebration. Right: Mehrhoff (center), Austin Skinner (left), and Caitlin Yager, both with the Missouri Humanities Council, attended an inaugural event for the German Heritage Corridor initiative.

GERMAN
HERITAG
CORRIDO
of Missouri

Tower Grove Park

THE MONUMENT of Alexander von Humboldt sits within a park that was donated to St. Louis by Henry Shaw, the son of an English iron manufacturer. A successful merchant in the city, Henry established the Missouri Botanical Garden in St. Louis in 1858 and donated Tower Grove Park ten years later. The park's fountains and artistic replicas of ruins, pergolas, and other Victorian design elements earned the park a National Historic Landmark designation. Families and other groups can reserve pavilions for special events and celebrations. A summer concert series for children, other band concerts, a farmers' market, lectures, and art exhibits also attract visitors. Trails, tennis courts, athletic fields, and a wading pool provide recreation. Tower Grove Park is bounded by Magnolia Avenue and Arsenal Street, between Kingshighway Boulevard and Grand Avenue.

geh und erforsche!

MARKING THE SPIRIT OF THE TIMES

die Zeitgeist

At Ground Zero of a Monumental Journey

das Tagebuch:
From my vantage, the Alexander von Humboldt monument is the ideal place to begin exploring Missouri's German heritage. The word "monument" derives from the Latin "monere" (to bring to mind). When we visited the monument, my wife succinctly observed that von Humboldt went from "wonder of the world" to "wonder who he is?" But he's still important, as you will see.

Our exploration of Missouri's German heritage begins appropriately enough in St. Louis at the monument in Tower Grove Park to legendary 19th-century German naturalist and explorer Alexander von Humboldt (1769-1859). The Smithsonian American Art Museum described it as a "full-length standing portrait of Alexander von Humboldt, leaning against a stump with his coat draped over it, his left foot forward and hands clasped in front of his waist."

This 11-foot-high statue was designed and cast at the Royal Bronze Foundry in Munich by master German sculptor Ferdinand von Miller, who created many leading examples of 19th-century American public art. The statue depicts a reflective von Humboldt wearing a period traveling costume of knee-high boots and a typical short waistcoat.

The statue stands atop a 13-foot-tall Missouri red granite pedestal designed by noted St. Louis architect George I. Barnett, who also designed Henry Shaw's nearby Tower Grove House. Four bronze panels mark the granite pedestal: a title identifying von Humboldt; a view of Ecuador's Mount Chimborazo, the volcano that von Humboldt was the first to scale; an image of the Amazon River valley that he explored to its source; and a likeness of statue donor Henry Shaw, with his quote honoring von Humboldt as "the most accomplished traveler of this or any age." Not surprisingly, Missouri's German immigrants and their *Vereins* (associations) thronged to the statue's 1879 dedication.

As his prominent place in Tower Grove Park directly opposite the Shakespeare statue clearly indicates, von Humboldt strongly influenced 19th-century America. His scientific expeditions across South America provided a model for American explorers such as Meriwether Lewis and William Clark, as well as English naturalist Charles Darwin. His breathtaking adventures, combined with his curiosity about the relationships between nature and culture, earned him international scientific acclaim and the sincere admiration of world citizens such as Johann Wolfgang von Goethe and Thomas Jefferson, with whom he frequently corresponded.

In a 2009 book, *Passage to Kosmos: Alexander von Humboldt and the Shaping of America*,

Oil painting of Alexander von Humboldt by Joseph Karl Stieler, 1843

University of Notre Dame English professor Laura Dassow Walls shows how his ideas about natural history and geography, like the ocean current named for him, coursed into all streams of American culture. Writer Ralph Waldo Emerson called von Humboldt the "universal man," and his influence can be found in works as diverse as those by Henry David Thoreau, Walt Whitman, the Hudson River School of Art, and American naturalist John Muir. Mountain ranges, exotic animal species, universities, American counties, towns, and streets were named for him. In his five-volume lifework entitled *Kosmos*, von Humboldt showed how nature affected humans and how humans shaped, for better or worse, the surface of the planet.

A century after its dedication, von Humboldt's monument and his legend had both fallen into disrepair. The Amazon River plaque on the base was stolen in 1974 but recovered in 1995. The Henry Shaw medallion, originally part of a larger plaque on the east side of the pedestal, was removed and stored in 1952. The lower portion of the plaque, thought to be lost, was found in 1996, and the entire Shaw plaque was restored, reinstalled, and rededicated on October 26, 1997. Today the monument once again shows clear pride of place.

The German Cultural Society of St. Louis

THIS NOT-FOR-PROFIT organization intends to foster educational and benevolent activities that preserve and advance German customs, language, and music. It began as the St. Louis Chapter of the American Aid Society, founded in 1945 to aid German refugees from Eastern Europe. When immigration to the United States became possible, many of these immigrants joined the society, along with other immigrants from Germany and Austria. Anyone interested in the Society's mission is welcome. One of the largest of the German societies in the St. Louis area, it features a multipurpose building and hall on Jefferson Avenue as well as a facility in Jefferson County used for outdoor events. The German Cultural Society is located at 3652 Jefferson Avenue in south St. Louis.

geh und erforsche!

A Search for Cultural Authenticity

Like the Humboldt monument in the heart of Tower Grove Park, Missouri's enormously influential German heritage also fell into disrepair during the 20th century. Two world wars, Prohibition, and modern mass society tarnished its luster, its *pluribus* nearly dissolving in the melting pot of the *unum*.

However, we in the 21st century have finally begun to remember, reclaim, and restore some long-forgotten pieces of our heritage. Globalization has generated strong reactions and resistance, including a deepening search for personal and cultural authenticity. This trend (economists now talk about an Experience Economy) has catalyzed unique markets, niches, and associations (think of Cosplay), especially in the field of tourism. Perhaps it's appropriate that the German American Heritage Society paid for the restoration and reinstallation of the recovered plaque.

This book, then, invites readers on a 21st-century journey of exploration to recover the not quite lost world of Missouri's German cultural heritage. Like its role model Alexander von Humboldt, it will carefully observe this region, draw upon a wide variety of sources and approaches, and enthusiastically (maybe even lyrically on special occasions) interpret this heritage for "accomplished travelers" who share the romance of time travel and know that the past is a foreign country.

Perhaps even more importantly, von Humboldt was also the first modern writer to speak of Earth as a "web of life," a living tapestry of cultural regions like Missouri's German Heritage Corridor. That's an even more timely message for us today, so this book will try to *weven zusammen* (weave together) a new understanding of this unique heritage and bring to mind its enduring place in Missouri life.

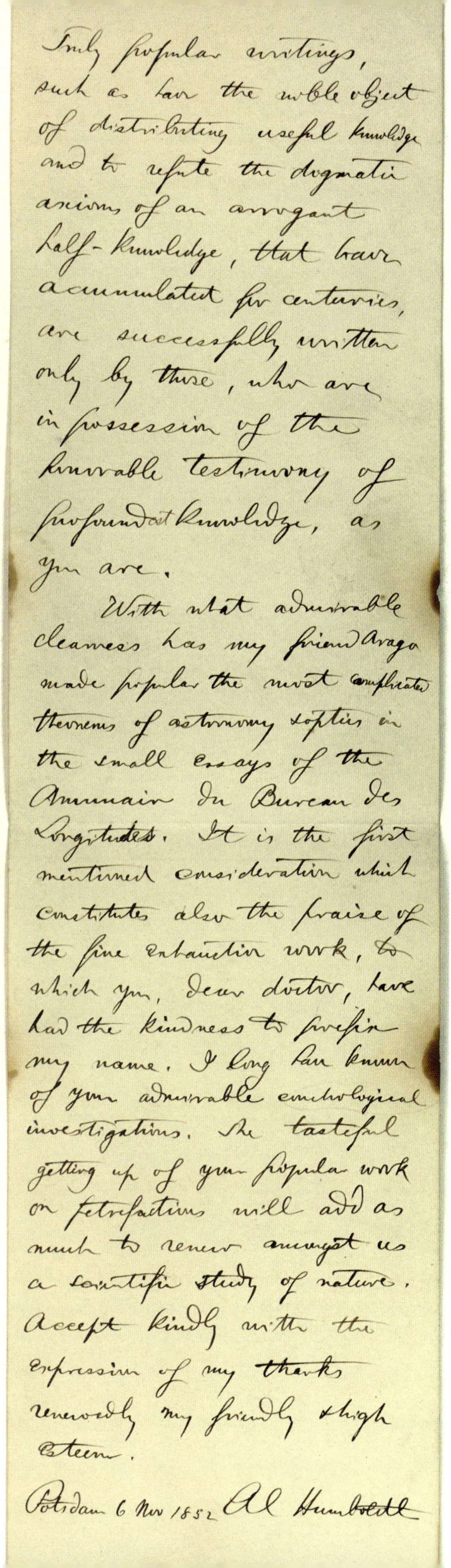

Truly popular writings, such as have the noble object of distributing useful knowledge and to refute the dogmatic axioms of an arrogant half-knowledge, that have accumulated for centuries, are successfully written only by those, who are in possession of the favorable testimony of profoundest knowledge, as you are.

With what admirable clearness has my friend Arago made popular the most complicated theorems of astronomy & optics in the small essays of the Annuaire du Bureau des Longitudes. It is the first mentioned consideration which constitutes also the praise of the fine [illegible] work, to which you, dear doctor, have had the kindness to prefix my name. I long have known of your admirable [illegible] investigations. The tasteful getting up of your popular work on petrefactions will add as much to renew amongst us a [illegible] study of nature. Accept kindly with the expression of my thanks renewedly my friendly & high esteem.

Potsdam 6 Nov 1852 Al Humboldt

Correspondence from Alexander von Humboldt to Emil Adolf Rossmässler, 1852

"Truly popular writings, such as for the noble object of distributing useful knowledge and to refute the dogmatic axioms of an arrogant half-knowledge, that have accumulated for centuries, are successfully written only by these, who are in possession of the favorable testimony of profoundest knowledge, as you are."

This print of Union soldiers with a flag shows them fighting back against a mob of attacking civilians. "Terrible Tragedy at St. Louis, Mo" ran in the *New York Illustrated News*, May 25, 1861.

The Incident at Camp Jackson

One of cultural geographer Peirce Lewis's famous 1979 *Axioms for Reading the Landscape* is that the ordinary, run-of-the-mill things that humans have placed upon the face of the earth provide strong evidence of the kind of people we were, are, and are in process of becoming. Whether defined as a group's entire way of life or simply how it views the world, culture, such as Missouri's German heritage, is unintentionally reflected in the ordinary landscape.

However, Lewis also reminds us that reading the ordinary American landscape is not as easy as reading history books. Like books, landscapes can be viewed as signs and deciphered, but unlike books, they were not really meant to be read. Our ordinary American landscape often reads like a book in bad condition with many pages missing, edited, and re-edited over time by many different people with really bad handwriting. Every now and then, though,

The interpretive sign explains to passersby the Civil War incident that happened here. German troops were involved.

we can find a bookmark in the ordinary landscape that opens another important chapter in Missouri's German heritage. The Camp Jackson interpretive sign just east of Grand Boulevard between Olive Street and Laclede Avenue is just such a bookmark.

At various times in its long history, the intersection of Grand and Olive has been a streetcar hub for visiting doctors and dentists, the city's Great White Way movie theater district, the focal point of major urban redevelopment efforts, and now, the attractive site of the Saint Louis University campus. However, in 1861 the intersection of Olive and Grand at the western edge of the city was called Lindell Grove when a militia of Confederate sympathizers led by Brigadier General Daniel M. Frost was captured there by Union army soldiers, mainly volunteers of German descent, led by US Army Captain Nathaniel Lyon.

das Tagebuch

Like many native St. Louisans, I visited midtown St. Louis many times over the decades, from going to movies like Ben-Hur during the 1950s to studying for my doctoral work at Saint Louis University during the '80s. Also like many native St. Louisans, I walked across the site of Camp Jackson many times without noticing this history underfoot. Now I feel my footsteps across this intersection echoing even more deeply.

Opposition to Slavery

Many leaders of St. Louis's German community, like Henry Boernstein, editor of the German language newspaper *Anzeiger des Westens*, radically opposed slavery and rallied Missouri Germans against the institution. Many German immigrants across all social classes compared Southern plantation owners to despised German feudal barons.

As historian Andrew Wanko of the Missouri History Museum noted, German immigrants made up many Union volunteer regiments. Some consisted almost entirely of *Turnverein* (a German American social and gymnastic society). The 17th Missouri Regiment was one such regiment that became popularly known as the "Western Turners." Another group, the St. Louis Turnverein, announced at the beginning of 1861 that it was halting all social activity at the central *Turnhalle* downtown to become "a military organization for the defense and liberty of the Union."

Abraham Lincoln's political rival and later Secretary of State William H. Seward celebrated the prominent antislavery views of Missouri's Germans in a campaign speech in St. Louis:

> *Everywhere I go in Missouri it has been said to me that the Republican Party of this state consists principally of the German population. I am pleased that it is so. For wherever the Germans come, it is their mission to create a way for freedom. Whoever defends right against injustice is in the right place, wherever he might have been born. So let us happily permit Missouri to be Germanized.*

Not all Missourians shared Seward's opposition to slavery or his welcoming attitude toward German immigrants. Letters and other reports at the time indicated that the Missouri state government planned to seize the federal

Right: Camp Jackson was photographed in May 1861 during the Missouri militia's drills. Below: An illustrated map from the same year shows how Camp Jackson was surveyed and staked out under instructions from Confederate sympathizers.

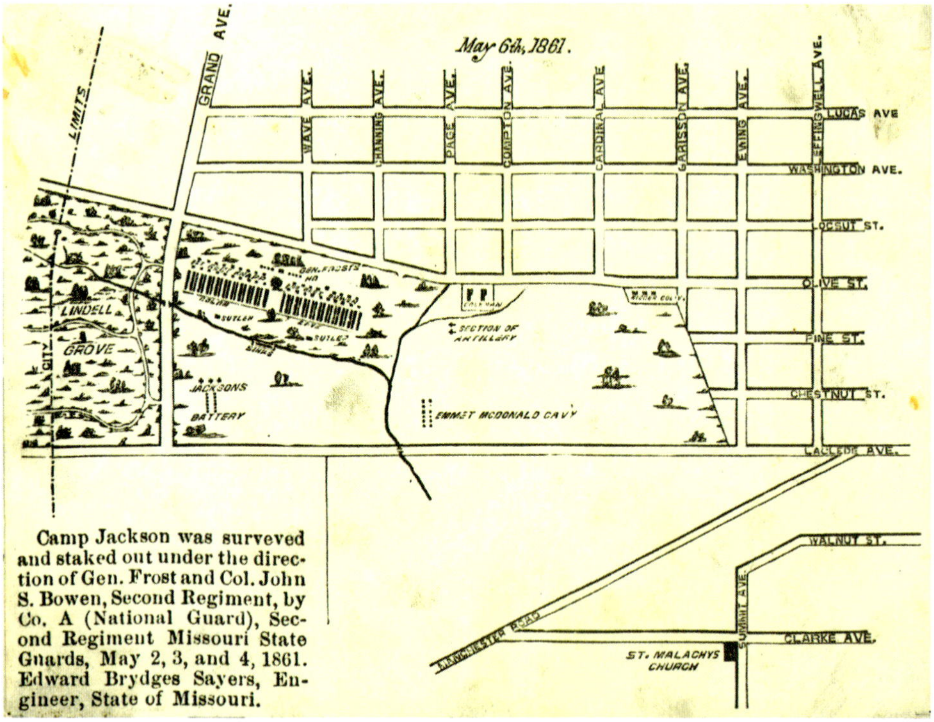

MISSOURI HISTORY MUSEUM

arsenal near the Anheuser-Busch Brewery. The Missouri Volunteer State Militia met at Camp Jackson, just north of St. Louis. Here Governor Claiborne Jackson's forces received weapons from the Confederate government—many from the federal arsenal at Baton Rouge, Louisiana.

In early May, 1861, Captain Nathaniel Lyon rallied his forces, composed of ten regiments of primarily German American volunteers, an artillery battery, and two companies of US Infantry. This force of approximately ten thousand men surrounded and captured approximately seven hundred Missouri state forces at Camp Jackson.

While Captain Lyon's troops were marching prisoners to the arsenal, an angry mob of Southern sympathizers gathered along the route. The *Civil War Muse* reports:

> *As the crowd magnified in size, it became increasingly belligerent. They first hurled epithets at the 'damned Dutch,'* [or Deutsch (German)], *then clods of dirt, stones, and brickbats. Soon after the column of* [Union] *troops and their prisoners began to march down Olive Street, shots rang out and Capt. Constantin Blandovski* [a leader of the Turners] *fell mortally wounded. In response, the Union volunteers fired into the crowd.*

The resulting stampede that took place in the crowd of onlookers resulted in the death of 28 spectators, including many children, and numerous others wounded. "This is basically the event that ended up keeping Missouri in the Union," noted Pam Sanfilippo, historian at the Ulysses S. Grant National Historic Site, but more than ever as a house bitterly divided.

Captain Nathaniel Lyon led German volunteer regiments to defend the federal arsenal at St. Louis.

Jefferson Barracks Park

JEFFERSON BARRACKS, located on 1,700 acres, contains a historic site, a national cemetery, and a still active military installation with a Veterans Affairs hospital complex. It is the oldest operational military installation west of the Mississippi River. Established in 1826 as an infantry school, it was named after Thomas Jefferson, who had died earlier that year.

Many prominent leaders in the Civil War had been through Jefferson Barracks by the time the war erupted in 1861. Union Generals Ulysses S. Grant, William T. Sherman, Philip Sheridan, Winfield Scott Hancock, and Montgomery Meigs had duty here, as did Confederate Generals Robert E. Lee, James Longstreet, Albert Sidney Johnston, Joseph E. Johnson, and Braxton Bragg. President Zachary Taylor and Confederate President Jefferson Davis had also served here.

The incident at Camp Jackson ensured that Jefferson Barracks remained under Union control. During the Civil War, Jefferson Barracks served as a military hospital for both sides as well as a recruitment depot for the North.

Today, the 426-acre Jefferson Barracks Park has a visitors center, trails, picnic shelters, and archery ranges, and visitors can tour the Old Ordnance Room, the Laborers House and Ordnance Stable, the Powder Magazine Museum, and the Jefferson Barracks Telephone Museum.

The active military base serves the Army and the Air National Guard, and the Veterans Affairs healthcare campus also serves as the Veterans Canteen Service.

geh und erforsche!

The park is at 345 North Road, St. Louis.

Without German Missourians' help in fighting, Lincoln's efforts in cutting the Confederacy in half along the Mississippi River would have been a failure, and perhaps, even a Confederate victory.

Missouri Civil War Museum

THE MISSOURI CIVIL WAR MUSEUM is located at Jefferson Barracks. Michael Weeks, a historian and author of *The Civil War Roadtrip Guide*, calls it "the most impartial and balanced site I've seen that covers that contentious period in detail." The museum has more than a thousand artifacts and several films in seven different galleries. The museum is housed in the 1905 Jefferson Barracks Post Exchange & Gymnasium Building. The building was used as a barracks in World War I and as both an athletic facility and an overflow ward for the Jefferson Barracks hospital during World War II. It became vacant in 1946. The museum saved the building and opened in 2013.

geh und erforsche!

The Consequences of Camp Jackson

Historical events like the Camp Jackson affair remain alive in political culture for a very long time. An immigrant population that challenges the dominant surrounding culture often may find its challenge accepted.

Maintaining Missouri in the Union to capitalize on St. Louis's strategic location proved crucial to eventual Union military success. The incident at Camp Jackson enabled Jefferson Barracks to muster Union troops and the arsenal to arm them, Gratiot Street Prison to hold Confederate POWs, and James B. Eads's shipyards to build Union ironclad vessels. St. Louis's vital transportation networks of river and rail served the Union on the cutting edge of the conflict. In an article for the Missouri Civil War Museum website entitled "The Role of German Emigrants in Civil War Missouri," historian Scott Williams concluded:

> *Without the help of Missouri's German community in the Civil War, the state would have never provided support to the Lincoln administration in its war with the Confederacy. At best, Missouri would have instituted 'armed neutrality,' confiscated federal property and purged all US Army installations from the borders of the state. Missouri then would have rejected President Lincoln's request for troops, [and] not allowed the state's industry and resources to be used in the war. Without German Missourians' help in fighting, Lincoln's efforts in cutting the Confederacy in half along the Mississippi River would have been a failure, and perhaps, even a Confederate victory.*

Missouri's German Heritage Corridor covers a great deal of the state, but perhaps none as culturally significant as this little plot of earth.

Five German streets in St. Louis whose names were changed during World War I have been given honorary designations, identified by yellow street signs.

Sign of the Times

das Tagebuch

While working at the Museum of Art and Archaeology, I learned about the concept of damnatio memoriae, which in classical antiquity meant cursing the memory of someone, for example, Roman emperor Nero, or a people, while removing all references to their name and image. It was considered the ultimate death penalty. The question for cultural studies like this one is whether damnatio memoriae is really a thing of the past.

A February 3, 2014, *St. Louis Post-Dispatch* article reported how some city residents hoped to reclaim the name of the former Berlin Avenue by having it appear as an honorary designation alongside its official Pershing Avenue title in the city's Skinker/DeBaliviere neighborhood. "We're not trying to wipe out Pershing," said Jim Merkel, a local author who wrote *Beer, Brats, and Baseball* about St. Louis's German heritage. "We just want to remind people that there was something before Pershing." Pershing was renamed in honor of General John "Black Jack" Pershing, General of the Armies, during World War I.

The proposition, pushed largely by city residents of German heritage, failed to attract much support from those who live there. Not everyone shared Merkel's enthusiasm for this significant part of Missouri's German heritage. "This wasn't a German section of town," said Mark Jaffe, president of the DeBaliviere Place Association. Jaffe also pointed out there may be other reasons against honoring Berlin with a sign: "We've got Holocaust survivors who live in the neighborhood."

That incident highlighted how people can interpret the same sign in very different ways. The distinguished anthropologist Clifford Geertz wrote in his 1973 book, *The Interpretation of Cultures*, that human culture is really a system of symbols. "[I believe] with [German sociologist] Max Weber that man is an animal suspended in webs of significance he himself has spun. ... I take culture to be those webs and the analysis of it to be … an interpretive one in search of meaning."

Holocaust Museum & Learning Center

THE MUSEUM OPENED in 1995, and its mission is: "Through the lessons of the Holocaust, we inspire all people to confront hatred, promote human dignity, and prevent genocide." The museum gives the life stories of survivors who live or lived in the St. Louis area through the St. Louis Memory Project, a series of workshops that has helped survivors write their stories. An introductory room contains pre-World War II photographs of Holocaust survivors who immigrated to St. Louis and relatives of St. Louisans who perished or suffered under Nazi oppression. Other exhibit areas show Jewish life before the Holocaust, the rise of Nazism in Germany, early World War II, the beginning of the Holocaust, the implementation of the Final Solution to murder all European Jews, liberation and rescue, and Jewish life after the Holocaust.

Find the museum at 12 Millstone Campus Drive, in the Kopolow Building, which is part of the Jewish Community Center complex near Creve Coeur, a St. Louis suburb.

geh und erforsche!

These webs of significance can assume monumental proportions, as the controversies currently raging over Civil War artifacts and monuments clearly reveal. The Camp Jackson historical marker, the Alexander von Humboldt statue, and the Pershing Avenue sign all suggest that Missouri's German heritage is indeed suspended in webs of significance spun over time, and that the First World War remains the most tangled web of them all.

Cultural Diversity in the Beginning

Having a street named after the leading German city indicates that Missouri Germans in the early 20th century signified what we would today call cultural diversity. A diverse mix of German Americans had dwelt in this country since colonial times; Missouri's Germans had emigrated from many different, even rival, regions during the tumultuous 19th century. Germans were the largest non-English-speaking minority group in both the United States and Missouri.

Missouri Germans occupied all social classes, especially a working class that strongly supported the labor movement. In the early part of the 20th century, they also displayed considerable religious diversity, including Catholics, Lutherans, Amish, Mennonites, Jews, and free thinkers who challenged the worldviews and attitudes of American and Missouri Protestantism.

Despite these enormous differences among Missouri Germans, seen from another perspective, they displayed some key themes of *Deutsches Kultur* (German culture). Social drinking played an important role in much of Missouri German culture, often involving entire families and musical performances in convivial settings even on Sundays.

Unfortunately, according to Professor Thomas Welskopp of the University of Bielefeld in Germany, such *Bier-* and *Weingartens* fundamentally clashed with the Christian temperance movement, which advocated totally prohibiting alcohol consumption to achieve a "100 percent pure" American culture.

The Turnverein fraternal organizations found in St. Louis and many larger Missouri German towns, such as Hermann, Washington, and Boonville, added gymnastics and physical culture to social drinking, but the prominent role of the Turnverein as volunteer militia during the Civil War still intensely threatened some Missourians.

Prominent German leader Dr. George Engelmann was the first president of the forerunner of the Saint Louis Science Center.

As the Alexander von Humboldt statue in Tower Grove Park suggests, Missouri Germans also placed considerable emphasis upon *Bildung* (education) for both personal and cultural renewal. For example, the beloved Saint Louis Science Center traces its roots to the Academy of Science of St. Louis, the first scientific organization west of the Mississippi.

Several prominent Missouri German leaders played roles in the academy: Dr. George Engelmann, the Academy's first president and a prominent amateur botanist, helped plan the Missouri Botanical Garden; physician Frederick Adolphus Wislizenus, a keen observer of Western natural history, helped found the Missouri Historical Society; naturalist Karl Andreas Geyer also exerted strong influence. Susan Blow, although not of German descent, observed German classrooms inspired by the work of early education pioneer Friedrich Froebel, learning all she needed to know about *Kindergarten* to show Missouri and the nation.

Most importantly, the German language in its many regional dialects and variations set Missouri Germans apart. Linguists view languages not simply as a collection of words but as complex systems of cultural symbols and connections, as living, breathing organisms.

"Up until World War I, everything was done in German around here," said Dennis Rathert, archivist and historian for Trinity Lutheran Church in Soulard, the last church in St. Louis to hold regular services in German. "The services were done in German. The school classes all day were done in German. Meetings were held in German. All of the records were kept in German." Many Missouri German children studied the language in both private and public schools, while several *Zeitungen* (German-language newspapers) kept the conversation alive among Missouri German communities and connected them with the larger *Kultur*.

Toward a Pure American Culture

Renaming Berlin Avenue in honor of General Pershing, the Missourian who led the American Expeditionary Forces over there, clearly indicates that an epic cultural shift took place. Like some highly volatile universal solvent, the First World War catalyzed major changes in American and Missouri life that nearly dissolved the distinctive German heritage. Although the United States officially declared neutrality at the outset of the conflict, American commerce and industry strongly favored the Allies. German American communities quickly condemned massive loans and arms sales to the Allies as

Naked Truth Monument

THIS BRONZE MONUMENT in Compton Hill Reservoir Park, at the corner of Grand and Russell Avenues in St. Louis, was built as a memorial to Dr. Emil Preetorius, Carl Schurz, and Carl Daenzer, the German American editors of the St. Louis *Anzeiger Des Westens* and *Westliche Post* newspapers. Adolphus Busch of brewery fame was the major donor. The memorial, unveiled in 1914, was a gift to St. Louis from the German American Alliance, whose leaders aimed to show their commitment to their adopted land. The nude woman symbolized truth, and the torches symbolized the enlightenment of Germany and the United States.

geh und erforsche!

neutrality violations and demanded an embargo on munitions shipments to belligerents. The Wilson administration, however, argued that wartime contracts with participating nations fell within the scope of American neutrality.

Banker J. P. Morgan openly supported Great Britain and France and soon became the leading financier of the war effort by providing Britain, France, and Russia with loans while convincing other bankers to do the same. Opponents of the war and even the Wilson administration suspected Morgan of trying to draw the United States into the war to rescue his bank, his loans, and his debt that was too big to fail.

Aggressive German attempts to halt American maritime trade with the Allies, such as sinking the *Lusitania*, played a major role in leading to America's declaration of war on April 6, 1917. After war was declared, the widening web of cultural significance demanded subscribing to liberty loans, donating to the Red Cross, enthusiastically participating in parades, and even joining the armed forces.

G.A. Buder, president of the *Westliche Post* in St. Louis, thought it wise to publicly declare that his newspaper bought $50,000 in Liberty Bonds, in case anyone should miss the point. Missourians now considered any form of dissent unpatriotic and pro-German.

New laws restricted the rights of speech, publication, and trade with Germany. The Espionage Act and the Trading with the Enemy Act, both passed in 1917, and the Sedition Act of 1918 decreed that any criticism of the government, the draft, or any aspect of the war could be punished by a fine of up to $10,000 and/or imprisonment for up to twenty years. Everyone needed to get in step.

The Wilson administration began a pioneering campaign in domestic propaganda to "engineer consent" for American involvement in the war. The government's Committee on

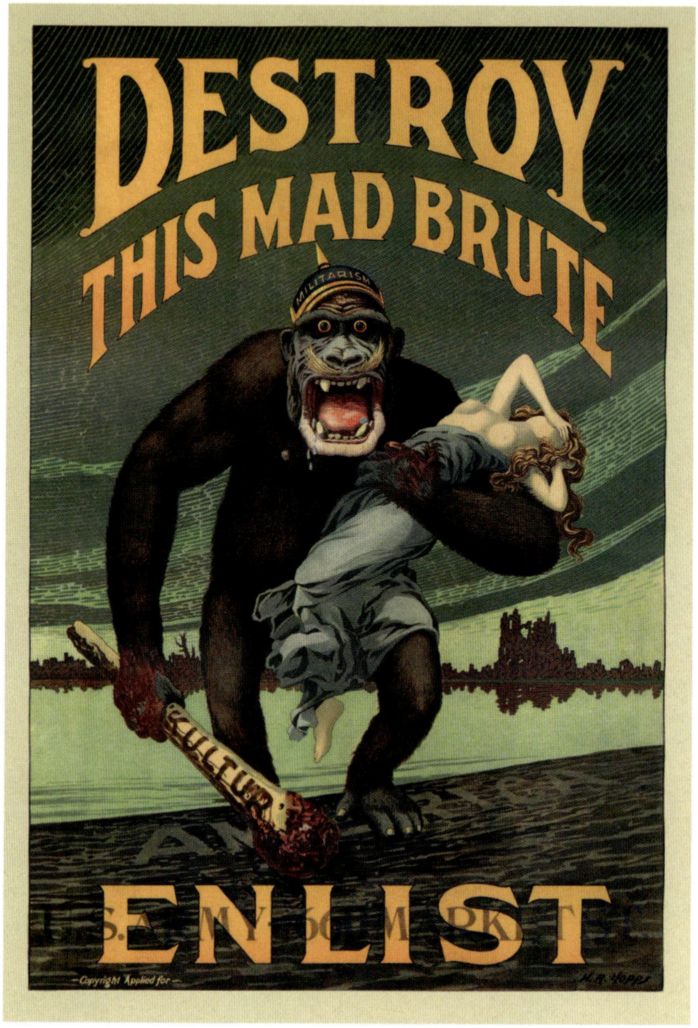

Propaganda posters during World War I contributed to anti-German sentiment.

Public Information (CPI) placed advertisements in magazines ("I Want You for the US Army" remains a classic) and distributed 75 million pamphlets defending America's role in the war. It also launched a massive advertising campaign to promote and sell war bonds, sending some 75,000 "Four-Minute Men" to rally rowdy audiences in popular theaters that were showing movies like *The Kaiser: Beast of Berlin*, loyally and profitably produced by Hollywood's emerging film industry with CPI's support.

Leaders of America's social elites also whipped up anti-German sentiment. Former President Theodore Roosevelt thundered that "those hyphenated Americans who terrorize American politicians by threats of the foreign vote are engaged in treason to the American Republic" and warned of a German invasion.

Did the memory of how Missouri Germans rallied to arms and played a leading role in the Union cause remain after half a century? Rolla Wells, the former St. Louis mayor and head of the Federal Reserve Bank, said during a promotional speech for Liberty Bonds at the influential St. Louis Club of business leaders, "I am glad to see the agitation now sweeping the country antagonistic to German-language newspapers, sermons in German, and German textbooks." He asked the cheering St. Louis crowd, "Why should such a custom be permitted?"

The Missouri legislature charged Governor Frederick D. Gardner and the Missouri Council of Defense, appointed by him under the National Council of Defense, with mobilizing the state for war. Gardner appealed for "one people, one sentiment, and one flag; ready to

During World War I, Trinity Lutheran Church in St. Louis changed its German name in a stained glass window after rocks were thrown.

cooperate, ready to sacrifice, ready to suffer" on one hand, but warned in April 1917 that "this is no time for slackers. … It is our duty to drive them out and brand them as traitors." One year later he called any pro-German a spy and threatened to establish martial law in Missouri if he discovered "these traitorous wretches." Both the governor and the state council instructed county and township councils to meet their mobilization quotas and control dissent.

Dissolution of German culture now received official sanction. The Trading with the Enemy Act required editors of foreign language newspapers, including the *Westliche Post* in St. Louis and *Missouri Volksfreund* in Jefferson City, to file translations of articles related to the government and war with local postmasters, increasing their costs. Editors who refused lost their mailing privileges and sometimes had to close, including the Osage County *Volksblatt*. The Cass and Linn County Councils of Defense banned the use of German on the telephone; the Franklin County Council of Defense merely pointed out that publicly conversing in German would be "unwise and unpatriotic."

The St. Louis School Board abolished new courses in the German language on April 27, 1918. The school board allowed students already taking advanced German to finish but cited "the public mind in St. Louis ... since the war began" to justify canceling introductory instruction. The board also banned three German textbooks, while some American cities burned German books.

Efforts then began to erase Missouri's German heritage. "They had to change the name of the church in the stained glass above the front door, which was *Die Dreieinigkeits Kirche* in German, but rocks started coming at the window," said Trinity Lutheran Church historian Dennis Rathert. Luxemburg, Missouri, became known as Lemay. In St. Louis, Kaiser Street became Gresham Avenue, while Hapsburger Avenue was renamed Cecil Place after British statesman Lord Cecil. In 1918, St. Louis Mayor Henry Kiel signed the bill stripping Berlin Avenue of its name. It was a sign of the times.

A Chain Reaction

The removal of Missouri's German heritage did not end on Armistice Day in 1918 at "the eleventh hour of the eleventh day of the eleventh month." During the war, the Anti-Saloon League Christian temperance movement had

Weldon Spring Conservation Area And Interpretive Site

THREE PICTURESQUE German towns in St. Charles County were evacuated between 1940 and 1941. Hamburg, Howell, and Toonerville, all farming communities, gave way to the world's largest TNT factory. The US Army purchased 17,000 acres in the county so a massive factory could be built to supply TNT and DNT to Allied troops in World War II. The Weldon Spring Ordnance Works employed 5,000 people and contained more than 1,000 buildings. It had produced more than 700 million pounds of TNT by the time the Japanese surrendered in August 1945.

After the war, the Army sold 7,000 acres to the state and 8,000 acres to the University of Missouri, which was later sold to the Conservation Department. Today, these properties are the August A. Busch Memorial Conservation Area and the Weldon Spring Conservation Area. In the 1980s, the US Department of Energy began decontamination of the area. Today, the Weldon Spring Site Remedial Action Project covers 45 acres. An enormous mound entombs tons of hazardous waste and provides an unusual attraction. Thousands of visitors a year climb stairs to the top of the 75-foot-tall dome at the Weldon Spring Interpretive Site to read about the history of the three lost towns. An interpretive center is housed in a building once used to check workers for radioactivity.

The conservation areas offer hiking trails, fishing, camping, hunting, bicycling, wildlife viewing, birdwatching, and more.

geh und erforsche!

generated a considerable amount of wartime anti-German sentiment by depicting Germans as drunken, anti-American gluttons, whose goal in producing beer was to corrupt American culture. The Anti-Saloon League's propaganda effectively connected beer and leading brewers like Anheuser-Busch with support for Germany, portraying beer consumption as treason. The anti-German hysteria generated by the propaganda helped ratify the 18th Amendment to the US Constitution in January of 1919, severely damaging major German economic activities like brewing and winemaking.

Public policy then got personal. In *King's Row,* Missouri novelist Henry (formerly Heinrich) Bellamann bitterly repaid the intense and subtle social pressures placed upon German descendants in Fulton, Missouri, with his descriptions of small-town treachery, cruelty, and corruption. The 1942 movie became Ronald Reagan's most celebrated film role.

Following the First World War, wartime propaganda techniques found important new applications in mass society through advertising. The genie of propaganda had escaped from the bottle.

But it was Joseph Goebbels who most ably

But do the signs tell us everything we need, or have we perhaps forgotten some important meaning?

exploited public information and advertising to the fullest as minister of propaganda for the Third Reich during World War II. Goebbels consciously pulled the wires of the "Führer cult" around Adolph Hitler to manipulate the organized habits and opinions of the German people.

Descendants of 19th-century Mehrhoffs, Sieckmanns, and Hirschausens in Missouri fought long and honorably as American GIs against a Germany manipulated into madness. Those battle-weary GIs then dragged their battered duffel bags home to start booming families in a rapidly suburbanizing postwar America that bore little resemblance to those Missouri German communities before the war.

President Eisenhower, who witnessed first hand the smoldering rubble of German cities like Dresden, promoted the Dwight D. Eisenhower National System of Interstate and Defense Highways (aka Interstate Highway System) to help move the American public out of crowded cities like St. Louis, now threatened by Soviet atomic and hydrogen bombs.

Mad Men of the 1950s and '60s shaped the booming American consumer society that the new mobility made possible. Advertising slogans ("See the USA in your Chevrolet;" "You deserve a break today") galvanized American popular culture. Products and propaganda now thoroughly and seamlessly spin through American and Missouri life 24/7/365. But do the signs tell us everything we need, or have we perhaps forgotten some important meaning?

Pershing Avenue started its life as Berlin Avenue, in 1871. In 1918 it was renamed in honor of World War I General John J. Pershing.

das Tagebuch

As a teenager, I often gazed without a second thought at the Pershing Avenue street sign while riding the Union Avenue bus to Lutheran Central High School, but I don't want to remain a teenager in my historical understanding of Missouri's German heritage.

Looking for a Sign

We've seen the tangled webs of significance enveloping the Pershing Avenue street sign, but the original question of how to remember Missouri's German heritage remains. Perhaps we need an *Antiques Roadshow* for all this old German stuff lying around—perhaps experts can tell us whether it holds any value or helps us better understand what we have. Maybe it's a treasure trove.

Because the Missouri Humanities Council sponsored the German Heritage Corridor initiative, we should consider the humanities for expertise on how to remember. In *The Heart of the Matter*, the June 2013 Report of the American Academy of Arts & Science's Commission on the Humanities and Social Sciences to the US Congress, humanities are defined as follows:

> *The humanities—including the study of languages, literature, history, jurisprudence, philosophy, comparative religion, ethics, and the arts—are disciplines of memory and imagination, telling us where we have been and helping us envision where we are going.*

Within that broad spectrum of "disciplines of memory and imagination," literature remains one of the best ways to help us better remember the meaning of Missouri's German heritage. According to novelist Kurt Vonnegut, an Iowan of German descent, the classic Cinderella story represents a fundamental literary archetype. It chronicles a rags-to-riches story, such as the 19th-century German immigration to Missouri, followed by a dizzying fall from the heights (such as the vandalism of the Alexander von Humboldt statue or the World War I suspicion of all things German), before finally being restored to a state of grace. The *Bildungsroman* (formation novel) offers a variation on the classic Cinderella story, as well as a major German contribution to world literature. *Bildungsromane* recount literal or figurative voyages of discovery (for example, Germans emigrate from their troubled old country to Missouri). That voyage of discovery typically involves a life-altering question (Can German immigrants find genuine freedom in the New World?) followed by a trial (What will happen to our German heritage because of demands for a pure American culture?). The voyage of discovery in a Bildungsroman typically results in the formation of a unique sense of identity and purpose.

While not a novel in the usual sense, the life journey of Alexander von Humboldt through his epic adventures to his great but uncompleted work *Kosmos* seems to take that search for meaning and purpose to a whole new level. In the words of German poet Rainer Maria Rilke, von Humboldt "lived his life in growing orbits which moved out over the things of the world," the epitome of the Bildungsroman.

But what's the conclusion of Missouri's German heritage story hidden by the Pershing Avenue street sign? We need to remember that Missouri's German heritage is thoroughly woven into many webs of significance, both unique and universal to Missouri and American life, and we are still spinning out those stories. This book considers a variety of cultural artifacts, signs if you will, that suggest we could still find some identity and purpose in that heritage if we weave our stories together.

Friedrich Hecker Monument

THE MONUMENT IN BENTON PARK in St. Louis was donated by the Hecker Monument Association. Friedrich Franz Karl Hecker was born in 1811 in Baden and became a German lawyer, politician, and a popular speaker and agitator during the 1848 German Revolution. As one of the leaders of a failed April 1848 uprising to establish a republic, Hecker was accused of treason and fled to Switzerland. He traveled to New York in early October 1848 and arrived in St. Louis on October 31, 1848. As a leader of the Revolution, he received a hero's welcome from German Americans in New York and St. Louis.

Hecker bought a farm near St. Louis, on the Illinois side of the river near Belleville, and became active in the Republican Party there. He also wrote a foreword to the German translation of Thomas Paine's *The Rights of Man*, published in Leipzig in 1851. Along with Abraham Lincoln, Hecker was selected to be one of two Republican electors-at-large if John Fremont were to win Illinois in the presidential election.

Hecker and other German American leaders were seen as critical to keeping the Republican Party unified around important principles, such as opposition to slavery. Once President Lincoln called for volunteers after the Battle of Fort Sumter, by then Colonel Hecker commanded the 24th Illinois Infantry Regiment, also known as Hecker's Rifles. He resigned that command in December 1861, but it continued to be known informally as Hecker's Old Regiment. In October 1862, he became a colonel of the 82nd Illinois Infantry Regiment, and he was badly wounded at Chancellorsville in May 1863. After recovering from his wounds, he later served at the Battle of Missionary Ridge and in capturing Chattanooga and Knoxville. He resigned this command in March 1864, and the regiment became known as Hecker's Second Regiment.

Hecker died in 1881, and the monument was dedicated in 1882. The streets that bound Benton Park are South Jefferson, Arsenal, Wyoming, and Illinois.

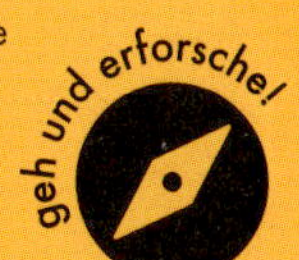

Above: Everyone arriving in St. Louis in the first part of the 19th century came in at this riverfront. No matter where they came from—Hamburg, Bremen, or other cities or villages—German immigrants arrived daily by steamboats from New Orleans or from Cincinnati, depending on where they entered the country. This sketch was drawn by Charles Graham and published by *Harper's Weekly Supplement* on June 6, 1888. Left: Gottfried Duden's *Report on a Journey to the Western States of North America* was published in 1829.

O BRAVE NEW WORLD

die Auswanderung

Whoa, Duden

Just as it helps us to better understand an individual by considering that person's origins and upbringing, peeking into their diary in a sense, so also understanding the meaning of a cultural heritage like that of the German Heritage Corridor benefits from looking carefully at its origins and underlying family stories. In that regard, then, Gottfried Duden's famous 1829 *Bericht über eine Reise nach den westlichen Staaten Nordamerikas* (*Report on a Journey to the Western States of North America*) represents the perfect artifact for beginning to develop a better understanding of Missouri's German heritage.

The Language of Travel

Emigration literature such as Duden's *Report* represents an extremely valuable type of cultural artifact: self-conscious writing about travel and immigration by those directly involved and aware of its significance. Travelers writing about their experiences in the New World became a popular literary genre in the 1800s. *Democracy in America*, by the French jurist Alexis de Tocqueville, is probably the most famous example of this genre, but Gottfried Duden's *Report* compares in some key respects to de Tocqueville's analysis of the new American republic and its open, energetic society.

German readers responded enthusiastically to such travel accounts; more than 150 examples of the genre were published in Germany between 1827 and 1856. Germans, who gave us such terms as *Wanderlust* and *Wanderjahr* (wander year, or "gap year" to be current) seem especially culturally predisposed to travel and travel writing. Travel writer Thomas Swick notes in his delightful *The Joys of Travel*, published in 2016, "If French is the language of love, then German is the language of travel."

Duden's enthusiastic audience, however, extended well beyond romantic young wanderers with knapsacks on their backs. Germany had been both crossroads and battlegrounds during the Napoleonic Wars, conflicts which affected all levels of society. By the 1820s, German farmers had escaped from many of the feudal obligations and dues owed to their traditional landowning barons but were often earning barely enough to survive.

German industrialization after the Napoleonic Wars undermined the strong economic position of artisans, skilled workers in handicrafts and trades, who belonged to the traditional guilds. A young Karl Marx now turned his revolutionary gaze upon factory conditions in his native Prussia and the Ruhr region. The *Auswanderung* (out-wandering) rapidly became a tidal wave cresting on the shores of America.

das Tagebuch

The genesis of my explorations into the meaning of Missouri's German immigrant experience first took place during the early 1980s in Dr. Helen Mandeville's wonderful Immigrant Experience Literature graduate course. Her course, part of Saint Louis University's doctoral program in American Studies, helped send me on a quest in search of Missouri's German heritage, with adventures along the way, such as giving a guest lecture on Missouri's German immigrant experience at the University of Tubingen in Germany and now, some thirty years later, this book.

The O'Fallon Historical Society and Log Cabin Museum

THE O'FALLON HISTORICAL SOCIETY operates the Log Cabin Museum at Civic Park in O'Fallon. The museum has many 1800s furnishings and artifacts, including a cabinet from the print shop of O'Fallon's first newspaper, *Der Katholische Hausfreund*. The log cabin was discovered in 1972 when the demolition of an old clapboard-sided farmhouse revealed the log cabin within. The Historical Society got permission to take the cabin down and rebuild it in Civic Park.

O'Fallon was named for railroad president John O'Fallon, whose railroad contributed to its growth, but it was founded in 1856 when Nicholas Krekel built a log home and established a post office, railroad depot, and general store on land owned by his brother, Arnold. The two brothers had immigrated to the United States in 1832, when Arnold was 17 and Nicholas was 10. The family settled first near Augusta. Arnold served as a justice of the peace, a lawyer, a German newspaper founder, and a state representative in St. Charles.

geh und erforsche!

die Auswanderung

In important ways, the *Auswanderung* represented a deeply conservative response by rural *Volk* (people) and urban artisans to rapid social change and dislocation. In the words of noted immigration historian Mack Walker: "These were people who relied upon their own skills and wished to do so in the future. … People that had something to lose, and were losing it, squeezed out by interacting social and economic forces."

Not surprisingly, Duden's 1829 *Report on a Journey to the Western States of North America* became one of the most influential examples of 19th-century emigration literature. Duden presented his *Report* to his eager readers in the form of highly readable and believable personal letters. The timing of Duden's *Report*, combined with its optimistic, sympathetic, and conversational style, made it a bestseller in Germany; we might even say it went viral. The book helped to attract thousands of German immigrants to the Midwest, particularly to the rapidly growing frontier state of Missouri. Of the 160,541 foreign-born residents of Missouri by the time of the Civil War, 88,487 came from the German states. The book both created a demand for and mirrored immigration and became a kind of Auswanderung creation myth. Consider this brief excerpt from the *Report*:

How often I have thought of the poor people of Germany. What abundance and success would the industry of a few hands bring to whole families, whose condition in their own country an American-born farmer cannot imagine to be possible. There is still room for millions of fine farms along the Missouri River, not to mention the other rivers.

The great fertility of the soil, its immense area, the mild climate, the splendid river connections, the completely unhindered communication in an area of several thousand miles, the perfect safety of person and property, together with very low taxes—all these must be considered as the real foundations for the fortunate situation of Americans. In what other country is all this combined?

The Missouri River valley in which Duden settled during the 1820s reminded him of his native Rhineland: abundantly fertile river-bottom soil criss-crossed by navigable rivers—depending upon the steamboat captain's skill—that offered industrious German farmers market opportunities for their crop surpluses at major urban centers like St. Louis or New Orleans. Although he included detailed descriptions of essential farming tasks such as clearing, fencing, and harvesting in his *Report*, the prosperous Duden had literally been able to farm out much of the hard manual labor on his own Missouri farm to German immigrant farmer Ludwig Eversmann, probably coloring Duden's enthusiastic, perhaps rosy, view of Missouri farm life.

Of the 160,541 foreign-born residents of Missouri by the time of the Civil War, 88,487 came from the German states.

Many eager German immigrants, inspired by Duden's *Report* to establish one of those "fine farms" in Missouri, found pioneer farming much more challenging than they expected, as anyone who has worked outside in Missouri's humid summers or freezing winters can attest. One group of *Auswanderers* inspired by Duden's *Report* was called the Berlin Society, which settled in what is now Warren County. The Berlin Society consisted of educated Germans, often called The Latin Farmers because of their fluency with that language and their incompetence at hard farm labor. The society almost seemed like a parody of the romantic nature worship widespread in early 19th-century Germany. One Latin Farmer described greeting the sunrise from a Missouri hilltop on New Year's morning:

There was the awe-inspiring nature, the glory of the rising sun which flooded with its rays the wild beauty of our surroundings, a splendid panorama before our feet, all held in the icy grip of death. We thought of our lonely situation far from our dear relatives and friends—a sweet melancholy filled our souls.

However sweet and abundant their melancholy may have been, it could not sustain a permanent settlement on the western frontier that was Missouri. Little remained of the Berlin Society by 1860.

Bethel Colony

BETHEL was founded 45 miles west of Hannibal in 1844, by German immigrants who believed the Bible taught that property should be held communally. By 1860, the population of 600 jointly farmed about 3,500 acres and owned large herds of cattle, horses, and sheep. The colony also supported a tannery, blacksmith shop, sawmill, grist mill, tailor, distillery, and textile mills. In 1855, however, the leader, Prussian-born Dr. William (or Wilhelm) Keil, departed by wagon train on the Oregon Trail, to found another colony, Aurora Mills, Oregon. Other community members followed him on later wagon trains. In 1880, the remaining members divided the property and ended what was perhaps Missouri's most successful communal experiment.

Today, Bethel, population 122, honors its heritage by preserving the Bethel Historic District, on the National Register of Historic Places. About 20 of the Bethel Colony's buildings still stand. You can follow a walking tour, visit shops, museums, and dine at the Fest Hall. The annual Youth Fiddle Camp can transport you back to the 1800s during a concert in the Performance Barn. Christmas in Bethel revives German Christmas traditions. Stay at Inn Harmony, built in 1847 and formerly known as the Colony Hotel.

geh und erforsche!

das Tagebuch

Gottfried Duden's vision recalls the last chapter of The Great Gatsby, in which "the inessential houses melt away" so that Nick Carraway experiences the primal power of the New World for its early explorers. However, Nick, unlike Jay Gatsby, realizes there is no perfect Eden, a good lesson for us to learn from the Auswanderung experience for shaping a healthier future.

This sign near Dutzow commemorates Gottfried Duden's promotion of emigration to the Lake Creek Valley area and also gives a timeline of area development, starting with Duden's 1824 arrival and ending with the 1873 building of the Friedrich Muench barn, shown on page 37.

Cultural Waymarking

Despite such misadventures, Duden's *Report* remains a significant contribution to US immigration history as well as a key artifact of Missouri's German heritage. Anthropologist Clyde Kluckhohn called culture a mirror for humans, in which they see the world as they have learned to see it, as well as seeing their own reflections in other cultures. English philosopher John Locke said that "in the beginning, all the world was America." America has always inspired big dreams and encouraged enormous projections. Thomas Jefferson envisioned America as a vast republic of small farms and farmers, while the 1840s saw utopian communities like the Shakers or Bethel Colony in northeast Missouri springing up everywhere.

Duden's *Report* represents a strongly accented German version of this very American habit of the heart:

> *If a little city could be founded for the purpose of making it the center of culture for the Germans in America, then there would arise a rejuvenated Germania, and the European Germans would then find in America a second Vaterland.*
>
> *No plan for the present time promises so much to the individual and to everyone as a plan of founding such a nursery for German culture in western North America, and especially in the lands west of the Mississippi River.*

Waymarking helps Auswanderers today locate and learn about unique geographic locations all over the world, so it's only fitting that a waymarking sign (N 38° 36.537 W 090° 59.349 15S E 675085 N 4275300 for your information) highlights this region of Missouri extolled by Duden nearly two hundred years ago. Here in this cultural mirror we see marked a kind of sacred landscape recalling Duden's vision of an abundant land with "room for millions of fine farms" to escape the troubles and even terrors of German history.

Duden's vision of a New Germany safely nestled in a Missouri Rhineland, with its natural beauty and German cultural heritage, still sets Missouri's German Heritage Corridor apart. However, other signs such as Camp Jackson and Pershing Avenue remind us that, romantic appearances to the contrary, the corridor is not set apart from history.

The Getty Foundation in Los Angeles, a major resource for museums and arts organizations, has conducted research about heritage conservation all across the country. The Foundation concluded that heritage conservation plays a definite, even essential, function throughout America, yet the concept of heritage conservation itself remains paradoxical. In the words of cultural geographer David Lowenthal: "Heritage is never merely conserved or protected; it is modified—both enhanced and degraded—by each new generation."

The paradox for us is that we need to continually recalibrate and revitalize our cultural heritage like Duden's heartfelt vision, to preserve its timeless qualities while shedding its cultural burdens. The Missouri Humanities Council created the German Heritage Corridor

Fort Zumwalt

FORT ZUMWALT PARK at O'Fallon sits on a portion of the original Spanish land grant in 1796 to Jacob Zumwalt. Jacob and his brother Christopher moved their immediate families to the area, and five more brothers followed them later. Jacob was a Revolutionary War veteran. The Zumwalt family originally came from Pennsylvania, via Kentucky. Jacob and his family built a log cabin using Pennsylvania German construction methods, with four big rooms, hewn log walls, a stone foundation, planed floors, a double fireplace, and other unique details related to the Pennsylvania Germans. The home may also have had a stockade fence and a nearby spring.

The home, large for its time, was called Zumwalt's Fort. It was a settler fort where neighbors would gather for protection against American Indian raids during the War of 1812.

Zumwalt's Fort was reconstructed and opened for tours in 2015, thanks to the O'Fallon Community Foundation. It is the only rebuilt War of 1812 settler fort in the state. Signs describe the construction and the people who lived there when it was still western frontier.

geh und erforsche!

initiative in 2015 to foster a stronger connection to our Missouri German heritage, a next generation "nursery" (with a tip of the tricornered cap to Duden) for that cultural heritage. The Council has brought together scholars and professionals to help fashion an interpretive plan for the Corridor and is now collecting oral histories, storytelling, and archival photographs on a website about the German Heritage Corridor cultural region.

A Common Heritage Grant through the National Endowment for the Humanities to the Missouri Humanities Council allows it to digitize publicly held artifacts, documents, and photographs related to Missouri's German heritage, again using new information technologies to deepen our awareness and appreciation of that heritage. Gottfried Duden's *Report* testifies not only to Duden himself and the Auswanderung but to us, its inheritors, not only to the spirit of the past but as a renewable resource for shaping the German Heritage Corridor in the future.

das Tagebuch

I have been honored to serve on the German Heritage Corridor advisory council. Conversations in groups and with individuals have greatly increased my own appreciation and, I hope, understanding of Missouri's German cultural heritage. These thoughtful and talented people will periodically show up throughout the pages of this publication, a "hotch-potch" as my German elders might have called it.

Trace Duden's footsteps with a day trip to Defiance, Missouri.

Borgmann's Mill

THIS NOTABLE MILL is in the village area at the Daniel Boone Home. Borgmann's Mill was built by German-born Frederich W. Borgmann between 1847 and 1850, five miles east of Marthasville. He also made wooden shoes, carpet looms, and other wooden tools and equipment. The mill was a one-and-a-half-story, timber-frame mill, powered by mule or oxen. At the time it was listed on the National Register of Historic Places in 1970, it was noted as perhaps the only "barley huller and corn grinder" constructed entirely of wood remaining in Missouri or the Midwest. An unusual Dutch door on the southeast corner of the east wall is where mill business was probably conducted. The mill's machinery, hand-carved from oak and apple-root wood, shows little wear, and it's possible that by 1854, another local mill, about a mile away and at a more favorable location at a crossroads, had converted to steam power. The National Register of Historic Places delisted the mill in 1994 because it was moved from its original location.

geh und erforsche!

MIKE MCCARTHY, WIKIMEDIA COMMONS

Daniel Boone Home

THE HISTORIC DANIEL BOONE HOME at Lindenwood Park, which sits on about three hundred acres at Defiance, showcases not only the legendary settler but also pioneer life. Gottfried Duden spent four days visiting with Nathan Boone here.

The home was built by Daniel Boone's son Nathan, and Daniel lived here toward the end of his life. The home overlooks the Femme Osage Valley and is next to a village that replicates a town from the same era in the early 1800s. The town contains more than a dozen buildings, and each building within the village came from within fifty miles of the Boone home property. The village includes a general store, schoolhouse, grist mill, and other buildings found in frontier towns.

Self-guided tours of the grounds are free, but guided tours of the home and village are also available. Many special events are held during the year, such as a candlelit evening tour during the Christmas holiday season. That can be an especially good time to visit, as you may see reenactors and extra activities.

geh und erforsche!

Friedrich Muench's contingent of the Giessen Emigration Society sailed for America on the *Medora*, shown in this lithograph. They settled across the Missouri River from present-day Washington.

Legacy

The lithograph at right depicts members of the Giessen Emigration Society greeting the trans-Atlantic sailing vessel, the *Medora*. Lithographs, like coins and stamps, may reveal many fascinating stories such as this one. In the wake of Gottfried Duden's famous 1829 *Report on a Journey to North America*, Friedrich Muench and Paul Follenius from Giessen, Germany, published a small pamphlet in 1833 proposing that a large, well-organized group of emigrants could establish a German state or colony in the far western United States, such as frontier Missouri.

Over a thousand people applied to join this daring company, risking everything they valued, including their lives. After perilous trans-Atlantic voyages to Baltimore and New Orleans in vessels like the *Medora*, many of the society's members eventually settled in St. Charles, Warren, and Franklin Counties.

By July 1834, the last members of the Giessen Emigration Society settled along Lake Creek, a small tributary on the north bank of the Missouri River across from Washington, fifty miles west of St. Louis. The story of the Giessen Emigration Society illustrates the heroic legacy of the Auswanderung, one befitting such a commemorative artifact as this lithograph.

Members of the Giessen Emigration Society came to Missouri from all across Germany, regions such as Coberg, Altenburg, Hesse, and Westfalia. They also ranged quite widely in occupation from farmers, blacksmiths, and carpenters to solid German burghers such as doctors, lawyers, and teachers. They displayed considerable diversity in their religious affiliations, including Catholic, Lutheran, Jewish, other Protestants, and so-called free-thinkers deeply skeptical of organized religion.

Some members of the Society had also participated in the widespread 1830 German political rebellions and faced political surveillance, even imprisonment, for their involvement. While members of the Giessen Emigration Society never established a permanent, separate German state in Missouri, these hardy survivors did firmly establish themselves and their imported German culture all along the German Heritage Corridor throughout the Missouri River valley.

Cultures and Heroes

A few years ago the Barron Prize for Young Heroes polled American teenagers and found that only half could name a personal hero. Students named comic book characters Superman and Spiderman twice as often as Gandhi, Martin Luther King, or Abraham Lincoln. Among the students who answered the survey, more than half named an athlete, a movie star, or a musician.

Popular culture now clutters our path with so much information about celebrities that we can no longer find our way to the rare book room of our cultural heritage, where the best and most valuable stories await us. Like the *Medora* lithograph, the stories of cultural heroes such as Friedrich Muench and Paul Follenius, who led contingents of settlers here, remind us

of our German heritage, especially the Giessen Emigration Society's enduring legacy, and can perhaps inspire our own cultural renewal.

Good friends and brothers-in-law Muench and Follenius both settled near the Missouri River in the Lake Creek region, but from that point onward their lives diverged significantly. Muench clearly demonstrated an important German cultural value known as *Bildung* (cultivating your unique character through careful reflection upon your meaningful life experiences).

Muench wrote extensively in German for newspapers and periodicals in both the United States and Germany as well as in English for the American market under his pseudonym "Far West," as Missouri was described at the time. Known affectionately as "Papa Muench" to Missouri Germans for his able leadership, he served admirably in Missouri politics throughout the 1800s, especially during the Civil War period when he served as a state senator in the Missouri legislature. Muench's fierce opposition to slavery, so consistent with his and Paul Follenius's revolutionary German idealism, angered many Missourians sympathetic to the Confederacy in this slave state, but also cemented his enduring legacy as a true leader of Missouri's Germans.

The legacy of Friedrich Muench's friend and in-law, Paul Follenius, has proven harder to weigh, although his contemporaries regarded the handsome, charismatic Follenius with more than a measure of awe. Muench wrote:

Paul was an attorney with an extensive practice in Giessen, where he enjoyed general esteem

Rare Book Room

THE WASHINGTON HISTORICAL SOCIETY has a Rare Book Room containing many hard-to-find volumes that relate to Washington, Missouri, and state history. Many of the books are in the German language, including family Bibles, some of which also contain genealogical and unpublished history by area citizens. The room is available to researchers.

geh und erforsche!

This barn was on the Friedrich Muench Farm at Dutzow. He first bought the farm in 1834. It was his home until he died in 1881.

das Tagebuch

Most likely my own father's death in his mid-forties closely attuned me to the story of Paul Follenius, so perhaps it is appropriate that a tune is particularly memorable to me. The final scene in the popular musical Hamilton entitled "Who Lives, Who Dies, Who Tells Your Story?" opens with a battlefield snare drum marking time's inevitable passage. Hamilton finally understands that he does not control his legacy and must rely on others, loved ones and even rivals, to tell his story. Although Hamilton "wrote like he was running out of time," in the playwright's own words, ultimately it is not Hamilton who tells his story.

and friendly contacts with the best people. There was every indication that an enviable life lay ahead of him. … Why did he suddenly renounce all this in order to risk the uncertainties of a course for whose success there was no possible guarantee? Because for him and for a few others the fiery ideas of freedom and nationhood that had inspired their student days were not to be quenched by the lure of personal comfort that life in Germany offered; because he could not gainsay the basic need to remain true to his inner self and his principles and to live his life accordingly; because he did not want to end his days as a placid German philistine. He chose the path of manly self-determination instead of ease and comfort.

However, farming on the Missouri frontier proved ill-fated for the idealistic young revolutionary, and his bold experiment in self-determination and cultural renewal claimed his life at an early age. Friedrich Muench wrote:

The year 1844 was in many ways the hardest that we experienced here. After a mild winter and favorable spring there followed a summer with such continuous drenching rain that the fields we had sowed were flooded and the rivers coming from the west rose to previously unknown marks. … The material damage was terrible but besides this a sickness spread throughout the countryside which few people escaped, and which snatched away many a human life. We suffered a terrible loss in the very premature death of our unforgettable brother, Paul Follenius. He died on the third of October at eleven o'clock at night of typhoid fever. I had spent four nights at his

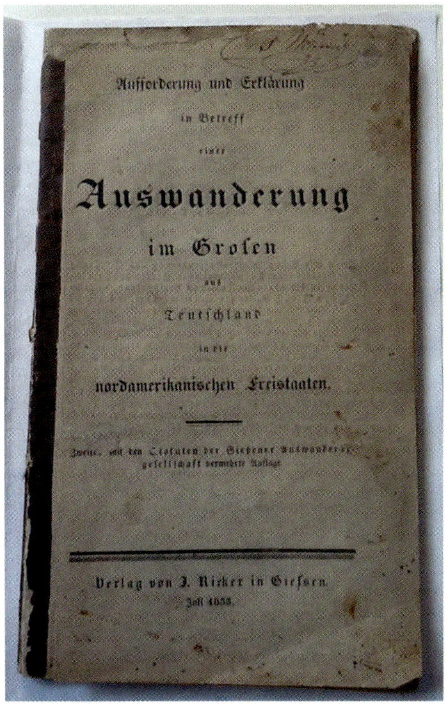

This pamphlet published in 1833 by Friedrich Muench and Paul Follenius declared their intent to start a "new and free German State in the great North American Republic."

bedside and was present when his life ended with a heavy sigh, a life of striving toward the noblest aims but fraught with many disappointments and heavy burdens. His noble and cultivated spirit, penetrating and sure judgment, great amount of energy, sensitivity and sure tact in his relations with others made him stand out among men. … He lived only forty-five years and four months, but his short existence outweighed many a life of long duration.

How can we weigh the measure of a life cut short like that of Paul Follenius? Ultimately, only those who live on can create the legacy.

Claiming the Legacy

However, a cultural legacy like Missouri's German heritage that is commemorated in the *Medora* lithograph is not just one thing. Even highly sympathetic interpreters who later create that legacy may, for a variety of reasons, not always understand its meaning in the same way. Consider the case of *Utopia: Revisiting a German State in America,* about the Giessen Emigration Society. This significant traveling exhibition featured video, texts, photographs, and other components and has now become a major documentary film. Organized by a collective of artists and intellectuals called the Traveling Summer Republic, *Utopia* appeared in two German cities, Giessen and Bremen, then in a smaller version at the German-American Heritage Museum in Washington, DC, before traveling in 2014 to the Missouri History Museum in St. Louis.

Peter Roloff, co-director of the project, noted that the exhibition's itinerary in Germany from Giessen to Bremen before coming to America reflected that of the Giessen Emigration Society. Roloff points out that, in the context of the exhibition, the word "utopia" simply refers to the Giessen emigrants' efforts to secure freedom for themselves and others. Their story intrigued him for its own sake, he said, but also because it related so well to contemporary controversies in Germany and America about immigration. The Giessen settlers to Missouri found themselves experiencing nativist sentiments that are once again strongly resurfacing in the wake of massive immigration.

"We tell the old story," Roloff said, "in a way that the visitors are getting their own ideas and creating, on their own, the bridge to today's issues." For Roloff and his colleagues, the story of the Giessen Emigration Society holds

German Immigration Exhibit

A FEW YEARS AGO, the Missouri History Museum had a notable photography exhibit relating to German immigration to Missouri. While the exhibit was temporary and is no longer displayed, you can find many items from the exhibit online by visiting MoHistory.org and then searching using these words: immigration, Germany, German, and utopia.

geh und erforsche!

up a valuable mirror, or a bridge, for our own culture.

Others may look in the same cultural mirror and see a very different legacy reflected. Although the exhibition certainly respected and even celebrated the epic quest of the Giessen Emigration Society, it also generated controversy here about the Society's legacy. James (Jim) Muench argued that his great-great-great grandfather, Friedrich Muench, was not a utopian and regarded such references to Friedrich Muench and his followers as inaccurate and inappropriate. "Missouri's German immigrants were not looking to build a utopia but were simply searching for freedom, just like the immigrants of today," he said.

Jim Muench collaborated with Missouri historians and museum educators Anita M. Mallinckrodt, Marc Houseman, and Cathie Schoppenhorst from the German Heritage Corridor towns of Augusta, Washington, and Marthasville to write *The Historic 1830s German Immigration to Missouri*. The authors drew on their own family histories and extensive curatorial experience to celebrate this key aspect of Missouri's German heritage, as well as to challenge what they considered the underlying, and potentially misleading, assumption (and the title, for that matter) of the *Utopia* exhibit. "Utopian is usually used to describe a religious movement," Muench observed, "like the Shakers or the Mormons, who went out and were forging their own little communities, away from the rest of the world. They were trying to get outside of the system. That's not what my ancestors were doing. They wanted to be part of the system."

Staking Our Claim

So what does that lithograph of members of the Giessen Emigration Society boarding the *Medora* really mean? We in America do usually associate

Mount Pleasant Winery

TWO BROTHERS from Germany, George and Friedrich Muench (or Münch) operated the Mount Pleasant Wine Company as a commercial wine business, starting sometime between 1834 and 1859. Cellars were built in 1881 using brick and limestone from the area. These same cellars are still used today to age Mount Pleasant's ports. The brothers shipped barrels of wine down the Missouri River to St. Louis and beyond. When Prohibition came in 1920, the winery closed, but it was revived in 1966. Mount Pleasant is a popular winery, located in the Augusta Appellation, the first appellation in America. The winery today grows nine grape varieties on 131 acres, and you can tour the historic cellars.

geh und erforsche!

utopianism with powerful religious movements like the Shakers because the communities they founded tended to endure the longest, but the origins of the term "utopia" itself may offer us another valuable humanities perspective on utopian thinking as we consider our own relationship with the Giessen Emigration Society and their charismatic young leaders.

Sir Thomas More, a gifted writer, churchman, and Lord High Chancellor of England, wrote *Utopia* (a Greek word meaning "nowhere" or "everywhere") in 1516 as his imaginative response to the highly destabilizing effects of the new woolen industry upon medieval English village life. His cultural vision in *Utopia* of an egalitarian island community looked backward to a simpler time but also forward to new possibilities then emerging from Renaissance discoveries of lands and knowledge. Similarly, German immigrants of the Giessen Emigration Society to the Far West of frontier Missouri sought to recreate something precious that was being lost, if not politically then culturally, within the abundant new American environment.

Thomas More was one of the most practical and celebrated statesmen of all time, who ultimately sacrificed his life for his ideals; *Utopia* provided a cultural astrolabe to help steer his course. Such a rich, imaginative cultural vision also guided the *Medora* and those passengers who made their way to the German Heritage Corridor.

Why should we even be concerned about our Missouri German origins and heritage? Through our deepened study and discussion of that legacy, we also participate in their epic journey. Clearer understanding of that legacy enables us to better understand the trajectory of our own lives.

Perhaps we could find our own new, imaginative vision, hidden somewhere in the Rare Book Room that is Missouri's German heritage.

das Tagebuch

I had the opportunity to study utopian communities with Sister Elizabeth Kolmer, former director of the American Studies program at Saint Louis University. She is widely regarded as one of America's leading experts on the topic. Her insight about the backward- and yet forward-looking quality of utopian thinking and the binding religious sentiments in such communities still resonates for me.

A statue of Hermann der Cherusker, a German hero for whom the town was named, appears to welcome people to the Hermann Visitor Center. The building was an old fire station before renovation.

Statue of Limitations

Hermann, Missouri is, literally and figuratively, a city on a hill for Missouri's German heritage. Its picturesque qualities attract visitors from all over the world and have garnered it many admiring travel articles, including one of my own, as well as and more importantly, a famous *New Yorker* piece by noted travel writer Berton Roueche. More than twenty blocks of Hermann are listed on the National Register of Historic Places. Hermann also takes urban design quite seriously, as the plaza at the Hermann Visitor Center clearly demonstrates, and the town has done so since its very beginnings during the great Missouri German migration of the 1830s.

The German Settlement Society

Organized settlement societies were sometimes established to facilitate group migration. One such group, the *Deutsche Ansiedlungs-Gesellschaf zu Pennsylvania* (German Settlement Society of Philadelphia) also caught Duden fever. A board of managers prepared a constitution in 1836 and established membership by selling shares of stock in the enterprise. Thousands of acres of Missouri land were purchased, and the town of Hermann was platted and founded in 1837. Members of the German Settlement Society mapped out a grand new city in this Far West, unconstrained by any detailed

This 1869 lithograph by A. Ruger shows Hermann as a busy river landing.

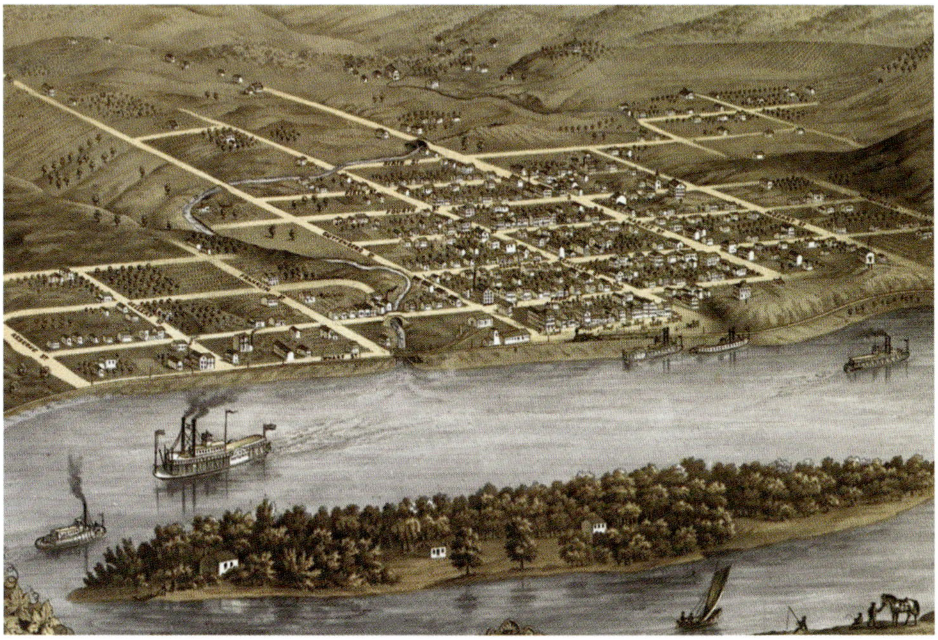

knowledge of its challenging topography. They designed Hermann with spacious market squares and sweeping boulevards, optimistically platting their city's main street ten feet wider than Philadelphia's bustling Market Street. The goal was to create a homogeneous, self-supporting German colony based upon farming, commerce, and industry, far removed from the assimilation challenges posed by a big American city like Philadelphia.

The society named the new town after Hermann der Cherusker, a legendary German tribal leader who defeated three Roman legions in the Battle of the Teutoburg Forest in the year AD 9. The City of Hermann celebrated the second millennium of the battle in 2009 and dedicated a bronze statue to their legendary cultural hero in Hermann Park at the ceremonial gateway to the city. While the statue of Hermann der Cherusker dominates the gateway to his namesake, a less prominent statue in the shady courtyard of the Gasconade County Historical Society brings to mind another no less heroic town founder.

More than 1,800 years after the Battle of Teutoburg Forest, George Bayer arrived in what is now called Hermann, Missouri, to fight some fierce battles of his own. In 1837 the

Historic Hermann Museum at the German School

THE GERMAN SCHOOL BUILDING, built in 1871, served as Hermann's elementary school until 1955. Classes were taught in both English and German for much of its history. Today, the building serves as the Historic Hermann Museum. The town clock atop the building tolls the time every hour. Volunteers wind the clock by hand twice a week, and the clockworks can be seen on the second floor. The museum has seven rooms of collections, including the Kinder Room, full of antique toys, a hand-made carousel, school desks, and old doll houses. The River Room has a replica of an early pilot house, models made by riverboat captains, and other Missouri River artifacts. The museum is at the corner of Fourth and Schiller Streets.

geh und erforsche!

German Settlement Society appointed this well-respected schoolteacher and gifted musician to serve as the society's agent. Bayer traveled to the Far West and purchased eleven thousand acres of the most rugged terrain anywhere on the Missouri River, a breathtaking (especially when walking its steep streets) site for a town, highly reminiscent of his native Karlsruhe in Baden-Wurttemburg in the Rhine River Valley.

When settlers arrived, they had to adjust the straight lines on the map that had been platted with no knowledge of the topography to the hilly terrain they found.

The Headaches of George Bayer

Despite his due diligence, Bayer experienced major setbacks while settling the Hermann community. Although he planned to come west with the first settlers in 1837, he contracted one of the many widespread public health scourges of that period, which kept him back in Philadelphia at the beginning of the trip. Unfortunately, the first 17 settlers, 9 adults and 8 children, began the trip without him.

Those first 17 settlers stepped off the last steamboat of the 1837 season into what one writer described as "a howling wilderness." Some howled that the orderly lots, as they appeared on the map and which they had purchased back in Philadelphia, were actually what today's Hermann residents jokingly refer to as "vertical acreage."

This disjointed beginning compounded his headaches. The first Hermann settlers were naturally eager to reach their Promised Land and start their new homes, but only the missing and delinquent (so they thought) Bayer possessed the legal authority to divide up the land and assign lots to the people. Bayer traveled to central Missouri with a second group, and they convened with the first settlers in the spring of

Wine Trail Weekends

ANNUAL WINE TRAILS hosted by the Hermann Vintners Association allow guests to sip and sample food and wine pairings at seven stops: Adam Puchta Winery, Bias Vineyards, Dierberg Star Lane Tasting Room, Hermannhof Winery, OakGlenn Vineyards, Röbller Vineyard, and Stone Hill Winery. The Hermann Wine Trail meanders through the scenic countryside that reminded settlers so much of home back in Germany.

Six different events include the Chocolate Wine Trail in February, a Berries & BarBQ Wine Trail in July, and the Say Cheese Wine Trail in December, among others.

geh und erforsche!

ꞏtone Hill Winery and Hermannhof Winery

OTH OF THESE WINERIES deserve a special mention.

Stone Hill Winery was established in 1847 and grew to be the second-largest inery in the United States. The wine produced there was known around the world nd won gold medals in eight world fairs, including one at Vienna, and by 1870, the inery was shipping 1.4 million gallons of wine per year. After Prohibition, the wine ellars were converted to produce mushrooms, until 1965 when Jim and Betty Held ought the winery. In fact, the Helds are often credited with reviving Missouri's wine dustry, to the point where today, Missouri has more than 130 wineries.

Today, Stone Hill's annual production is about 300,000 gallons of wine. Listed n the National Register of Historic Places, the winery offers free guided tours, which clude seeing the historic cellars (at right). You can also enjoy tastings or dining in e restored carriage house in a restaurant that specializes in German and American uisine paired with Stone Hill wine.

Hermannhof was built between 1848 and 1852 as a brewery, and its 10 stone ellars and brick building are on the National Register of Historic Places. ohibition brought a halt to this successful operation's beer making, but e Dierberg family bought the cellars in 1974 and began restoring the uilding. Today, all of the cellars hold premium wine. You can tour the ellars, located at the eastern edge of Hermann, on Highway 100.

geh und erforsche!

This 1888 engraving above shows Stone Hill Vineyards, and the historic cellars below can be seen during free guided tours at Stone Hill Winery, which also offers tastings.

The Gasconade County Historical Society in Hermann (building circa 1909) has an extensive Archives and Records Center for genealogical and general history research. It's at 315 Schiller Street. The Society also maintains a museum at Owensville. The bronze statue of George Bayer, the German Settlement Society's first agent at Hermann, stands in the Historical Society's courtyard.

1838. The marriage of the two groups was not a happy one.

The German Settlement Society had placed Bayer in charge of surveying all the land, assigning the residents their new lots, as well as supplying and distributing food, not to mention developing and running a new school for the children. Most school principals would probably say that would be enough. Complaints about Bayer's actions soon reached the German Settlement Society back in Philadelphia, and they released him from all his duties in a vote of no confidence. In scapegoating, individuals or communities project their uncomfortable feelings of anger, frustration, envy, or guilt onto another, usually vulnerable, person or group. Was Bayer made a scapegoat for the inevitable frustrations of settling a German colony on the Missouri frontier?

In 1839, at age 39, Bayer was buried in the Hermann Cemetery. Many local historians speculate that the excessive and often competing demands placed upon him dashed his romantic dream of a revitalized community for the Philadelphia German settlers and that a broken heart drove him to his grave. Purdue University psychologist Kipling D. Williams concluded that if you endure ostracism too long, you become depleted, depressed, helpless, and despairing. You can't cope any longer, so you finally give up. Perhaps Bayer gave up. Hermann lore holds that he was buried in the remotest part of the Hermann Cemetery and, supposedly, that no one could be buried within 75 feet of his grave. Buried, though, is not the same as laid to a peaceful rest; Bayer took the early community's blame and ostracism to his own early grave.

A Reprieve and Homecoming

Bayer's romantic vision may have simply been too far ahead of his time. Taking their cue from nature itself rather than superimposing a map upon unseen landscape, early Hermann settlers quickly planted vineyards on their steep, rocky hillsides where wild grapevines such as Cynthiana already sprawled abundantly.

By the late 1840s, tourists from St. Louis traveling via steamboat to Hermann's first *Weinfest* marveled at the grapevine-covered hills and the fine wine they now produced. By the end of the 1800s, the Hermann region had become renowned as a wine region. If not exactly the second coming of Philadelphia that people had envisioned, the steady development based upon river and rail traffic brought prosperity.

Sometimes, though, history is not what was but what people choose to say it was. Most communities, like most people, possess a shadow side that lies buried because we don't like that part of ourselves. During the bicentennial celebration of the 1970s, as Hermann residents reflected upon the less than ideal origins of their

White House Hotel

town as well as the increasing revitalization of its burgeoning wine industry, they boldly began to consider a new ending for one of their most basic cultural legends: that Bayer was derelict in his duty as a leader.

In 1986, for the sesquicentennial of the German Settlement Society, an unofficial local court of inquiry revisited the tragic case of Bayer and exonerated the overloaded young schoolteacher from blame. He later received the honor of his own statue in the courtyard of the Gasconade County Historical Society, a bronze bookend for legendary leader Hermann der Cherusker. Rest in peace, George Bayer.

OTHER GERMAN HERITAGE SITES IN HERMANN

- The White House Hotel at 232 Wharf Street was built in 1868. The three-story historic hotel is furnished with historically accurate furnishings from the 1880s and is open for tours as scheduled during some festivals.
- The Eitzen House, built in 1850 at 214 Wharf Street, is now the Kolbe Guest House. It faces the Missouri River and has all of the original woodwork, floors, and 12-foot ceilings. Fine German woodworking skills are on display here.
- The Concert Hall, built in 1878 by John Pfautsch and Phllip Kuhn, was the social site in early Hermann. Pfautsch had immigrated with his mother in 1847. The first floor contained a saloon, and the upstairs hall hosted concerts, plays, lectures, and dances. Today, the Concert Hall and Barrel Tavern make the building the oldest continually operating tavern west of the Mississippi. It's located at 206 East First Street.

geh und erforsche!

Concert Hall

Kolbe Guest House

das Tagebuch

Is it possible that we sometimes judge people on the basis of some impossible ideal image, or even project our own shortcomings and failures onto others?

The abundant woods, rolling hills, rivers, and creeks reminded the early 1800s immigrants of their homes in Germany.

Femme Osage

THIS CHARMING SMALL VILLAGE takes its name from the Femme Osage Creek on whose banks it was built. Like many German villages, a church was the heart of this unincorporated town. The Femme Osage United Church of Christ, founded in 1833, was the first Evangelical congregation west of the Mississippi. There are two cemeteries on the church grounds; one next to the church school dates back to 1830s.

geh und erforsch

SHAPING THE LANDSCAPE

die Landschaften

Sense of Place

Canadian geographer Edward Relph coined the term "placelessness" to describe the rising tide of undistinguished urban development now found in all parts of the country and, increasingly, the world. Reaction to this growing placelessness of modern life underlies much of the interest in cultural heritage tourism such as that offered by Missouri's German Heritage Corridor. Perhaps not surprisingly, then, people typically describe Missouri's German Heritage Corridor as having a strong "sense of place." That key concept focused much of the lively discussion among participants working in 2017 to fashion an interpretive plan for heritage tourism throughout the German Heritage Corridor. Sense of place is essential.

It is not particularly easy, though. History considers change over time, sociology explores human communities, and geography studies place. The key question geographers sooner or later have to ask, however, is "What exactly is place?" Is it the same as your GPS coordinates, is it some unique blend of nature and culture, or something even more complex and important?

Beginning in the early 1970s, so-called humanistic geographers like Relph rejected what they considered an anemic, academic definition of place and started to explore the integral role of human experience underlying sense of place. The *Oxford English Dictionary* prefaced its entry for place with the comment that its "senses are very numerous and difficult to arrange," then provided 69 entries arranged in 29 categories. Sense of place is also elusive.

Nevertheless, a working definition for "sense of place" in Missouri's German Heritage Corridor has gradually evolved, although it probably differs somewhat from one person to the next. Most probably agree that the natural beauty of its hilly, wooded Missouri River valley landscape provides the living canvas for its strong sense of place. The "townscapes" of small communities throughout the German Heritage Corridor also contribute mightily to its distinctive sense of place. Highly visible church steeples and their tolling bells anchor those townscapes. Like those tolling bells, sense of place involves history and tradition, some continuity that binds people to one another across time. For many, wineries represent important markers for this strong sense of place, as well as symbols of continued care for Missouri's German cultural heritage.

An Old World Village

As if defining "sense of place" isn't challenging enough, choosing a place that epitomizes a

das Tagebuch

I recall the tolling bells from the steeple of majestic Zion Lutheran church sounding at 6 pm on a fading Saturday evening in my old north St. Louis neighborhood. That was a clear urban example of creating a sense of place.

St. Joseph Catholic Church dominated the Westphalia scene on this vintage 1920s postcard and still does today, at right.

sense of place among the sixteen counties of the vast German Heritage Corridor is an exercise fraught with problems. Luckily, the Missouri Humanities Council has brought together many people with strong interests, experience, and expertise in Missouri's German heritage. For example, Gary Kremer, the Executive Director of the State Historical Society of Missouri, actively participates in the German Heritage Corridor initiative. Kremer, a native of Osage County, had mentioned the little town of Westphalia as a notable example of sense of place during one of our discussions. Several web sites identify Westphalia as the geographic center of Missouri's population, twenty miles southwest from Jefferson City, the capital city. Finally, an archival image of a vintage Westphalia postcard, labeled "Gateway of the Ozarks," provides the perfect artifact to explore the role of place in Missouri's German heritage.

The little town of Westphalia, Missouri, population 389, according to the last census, nestles within a bend of the winding Marais River just south of the Osage River and in a hilly, wooded landscape with impressive limestone bluffs. Its narrow, winding street pattern climbs a hill to Main Street, whose street sign features its German language counterpart *Hauptstrasse*. Atop the hill, venerable St. Joseph Catholic Church, with its complex of rectory, convent, and school, reigns over the townscape.

The nomination for St. Joseph Catholic Church to the National Register of Historic

Rhineland

WHILE THE COMMUNITY OF RHINELAND was devastated by the Great Flood of 1993 and most town residents accepted federal funds to move or rebuild their homes on a nearby hill, a few structures still stand and hint at its German forebears. German immigrants named the area after the picturesque Rhine River in Germany, and the town has had a post office since 1853.

St. Joseph Church at Rhineland, built in 1914, still serves the Rhineland area. This parish merged with that of St. Martin's Church at Starkenburg, built in 1874, to become the Church of the Risen Savior at Rhineland in 1979.

The nearby Heinrich Gloe House was listed on the National Register of Historic Places in 2007. The one-and-a-half-story dog trot frontier cabin was originally three separate buildings, built between 1852 and 1855. It sits on a stacked flagstone foundation.

geh und erforsc

Shrine of Our Lady of Sorrows

GERMAN SETTLERS FROM HERMANN moved to the Rhineland and Starkenburg area in 1847, and townspeople held special services together when missionaries came, using a white statue of Mary, named *Wiesse Dame* (White Lady). This historic Roman Catholic shrine, built by German immigrants and their descendants at Starkenburg, consists of the Gothic-style St. Martin's Church, whose steeple dominates that site and which was consecrated in 1874; the Log Chapel, built in 1883 to house the white statue of Mary; and the Chapel of our Lady of Sorrows, built in the Rhenish-Romanesque style in 1910, as well as several unique grottos, which include the Mount Olivet grotto, the Grotto of Lourdes—a replica of the one in France—and a Mount Calvary grotto. Fourteen stone Stations of the Cross stand behind the shrine.

St. Martin's parish was closed in 1970s and merged with the former St. Joseph's Church at Rhineland to become the Church of the Risen Savior at Rhineland, now the area parish. But annual outdoor pilgrimages here the third Sunday in May and the second Sunday in September feature Rosary Processions, the outdoor Stations of the Cross, dinner, reconciliation, benediction, and mass. The processions include the shrine's White Lady statuette, which has been replaced several times. Thanksgiving and Christmas concerts are also held. The shrine welcomes visitors.

geh und erforsche!

Places rose to eloquence:

> *From a distance outside of the town, the church spire can be seen towering above everything around it. The Romanesque-Gothic building provides a forceful orientation point as it is situated prominently on a hill. Surrounded by a school, convent, and German-influenced 19th-century houses, the church can be seen from any point in what seems to be an Old World village transplanted to the middle of the American continent.*

This "Old World village" depicted in the archival postcard and described so vividly in the National Register nomination offers a case study of the elusive yet essential "sense of place" that distinguishes Missouri's German heritage.

Sense of Place as History

Sense of place, as previously noted, rests upon continuity over time. The National Register nomination of St. Joseph Catholic Church noted that historically, it has much to offer. Not only does it literally tower over everything around it, but it also underlies much of Westphalia's history. A colony of Catholic Westphalians and Rhinelanders from Northern Germany founded the Low German community of Westphalia in 1835. According to the National Register nomination, "The settlement of seven families initiated Osage County to German immigrants."

In his book *The Westfalians*, noted immigration historian Walter Kamphoefner used Westphalia as an important example of chain migration, which he contrasted positively to the more celebrated emigration societies such as the Giessen Emigration Society. In Kamphoefner's words, "Transplanted Westfalians have seldom found a place in the historical record," perhaps because they were not as highly literate. Chain migration like Kamphoefner discovered operating in Westphalia involved complex networks of ordinary families, neighbors, and institutions helping recent immigrants, especially their kin and neighbors, successfully adapt to the Far West of Missouri. "Chance could not have produced the kind of homogeneous clusters my study discovered in rural Missouri," he wrote. "The trek to America was anything but a leap into the dark for chain migrants." A large settlement from Westphalia and neighboring areas in Germany—practically a transplanted village—had sprung up fifty miles west of St. Louis along the Missouri River.

Then as now, St. Joseph Catholic Church beat at the heart of that transplanted village. According to the National Register of Historic Places nomination:

> *The central location of a church, even the mere presence of one in a town, in this area and in this era, was significant. Early urban promoters realized that the presence of a church attracted settlers and often offered the church land and money to build with if they would locate in their town. It was in 1838, under the*

Kamphoefner House

THE KAMPHOEFNER HOUSE at New Melle is a history museum run by the Boone-Duden Historical Society in St. Charles County. The brick house, built in 1871 by John Friedrich Kamphoefner and his wife Wilhelmina, is one of the oldest houses in New Melle, made from brick fired in the town. Twelve children were born in the house. John was a blacksmith and wagon maker, and one of their sons carried these businesses on until 1941. John died in 1912 at age 65, but Wilhelmina lived in the house until her death in 1946 at age 94.

The house was bought and restored by Fred Weber Inc., a construction company, which has made it available for use by the historical society since the early 1990s. The Boone-Duden Historical Society displays old photographs from the area's towns, some all but gone, along with other artifacts, such as a late 1800s German-style dollhouse, a big bass drum from Femme Osage, and a mounted golden eagle. The Society also has old maps, books, census, tax, marriage, and cemetery records for those doing genealogical research.

The Penial Methodist Church School, a one-room schoolhouse, has also been moved to the site. The museum is open Sunday afternoons except holidays, but you can make appointments to tour weekday evenings or Saturdays by calling 636-798-2136.

geh und erforsche!

direction of Father Ferdinand Benedict Helias de Huddeghem, that Westphalia was made the resident headquarters of the Central Missouri Mission. Westphalia's St. Joseph was picked as the headquarters because of its strategic location in central Missouri where much missionary work was being done. It was also a stepping stone to the long contemplated Indian mission.

St. Joseph Catholic Church remained the mother-church of the Central Missouri Mission from 1838 until 1883, when the Jesuits departed and it became a parish church.

Sense of Place as Landscape

The statement of significance in the 1972 nomination to the National Register also noted that the church "is significant as a visual … landmark in Westphalia, Missouri."

In a Summer 1992 *Ozarks Watch* article, entitled "The German Presence in the Ozarks," Missouri geographer Russel Gerlach described how German cultural landscapes in the Ozarks, such as Westphalia, reflected their Old World heritage in both obvious and subtle ways, bringing some distinctly German settlement features to the Ozarks. According to Gerlach, Old World *Strassendoffer* (string or linear villages) are found in several Ozarks locales such as Westphalia, Altenburg, and Frohna. While most Germans abandoned traditional Old World architectural styles, he cited numerous examples of half-timbering, combination house-barns, and side-opening threshing barns in the German-settled areas.

These Missouri Germans in the Ozarks were known as outstanding farmers who cared for the land. Grain farms with carefully fenced fields, in a region better known for its livestock, reflected this emphasis. Their large buildings were often constructed of brick or native stone, suggesting a desire for permanence. In fact, many of their original structures remain occupied to this day, along with farms owned by the same family for more than a century. Their landscapes reflected order, long-term investment, and a neatness that Gerlach said appeared to be lacking in the region as a whole.

Sense of Place as Community

The vintage postcard also reveals the crucial link between community and sense of place. As the National Register nomination notes:

The church is also noteworthy for its role in the development of the community. [Urban historian] Lewis Mumford states that a town's physical environment becomes a symbol of its citizens' social relatedness. … Social facts are primary; the physical organization of the town, its industries, and its markets, its lines of communication and traffic, revolve around social functions. Even the alterations done in 1883 and 1905 reflect the changing needs of the people of Westphalia, if for no other reason than that a larger church was needed.

The idea and the reality of *Landschaft* in German culture had inspired thinking for centuries about what we now call community. *Schaft* is related to the German verb *schaffen*, to create or shape, similar to our English suffixes "ship," (such as township) and "scape" (such as landscape or townscape). Customs, institutions, and the people are fundamentally linked to the land in *Landschaft*. When powerful Prussia turned its *Landschaft* of Eiderstedt in Schleswig, near the border with Denmark, into a mere administrative district after 1864, the culture shock inspired German sociologist Ferdinand Tönnies to write his classic sociological treatise

Gemeinschaft und Gesellschaft (*Community and Association*), the source of much modern thinking about the concept of community and the forces transforming it today.

St. Joseph Catholic Church depicted in the postcard has certainly linked customs, institutions, and the people of the Westphalia *Gemeinschaft*. The National Register nomination noted:

> *Religion, being the center of community life, gave the Jesuit priests an opportunity to exercise a great amount of influence over the type of education and social activities the settlers participated in. The first school, built in 1835, was built by a Jesuit priest. The priests were well educated, the majority having received their training in the universities of Germany and Belgium. For more than a century, all of Westphalia's pastors were conversant in German. A bilingual teaching program was thus introduced in the school system as early as 1835. By the time the child was graduated from the elementary grades, he could speak High and Low German as well as English. The priests encouraged the writing of German poetry, which was heavily influenced by German Romanticism and traditions. For all occasions—festivals, commemorations, at births and deaths—German poetry, folk songs, and stories were sung and recited. The Church, by emphasizing the importance of bilingual training and German literature and customs, functioned to preserve the values and myths, which otherwise would have been lost through assimilation.*

The German word *Hauptstrasse* (road or street) on the Westphalia street signs also reminds visitors of the important role language plays in shaping a culture, as well as of Westphalia's distinctive sense of place.

Sense of Place as Living Heritage

Nevertheless, a good question for us today is whether Westphalia's strong sense of place is still alive or whether it has withered on the vine since that vintage postcard.

Winemaker Terry Neuner of Westphalia Vineyards reported that seeing a historic photo of Missouri Riesling grapes during a presentation by none other than Gary Kremer of the State Historical Society of Missouri inspired him to explore and resurrect that heirloom varietal grape. Terry and Mary Neuner have now revitalized the cultivation of the Missouri Riesling grape, and it appears that the "Old World village" atmosphere of Westphalia contributes to their efforts. Not only do they consciously draw inspiration from Westphalia's sense of place, but they are continually adding to it in innovative new ways.

Westphalia's sense of place offers a living heritage to the Neuners. They purchased farmland from Mary's aunt that had long been in her family. Mary placed a statue of The Blessed Virgin in an old limestone cave grotto on the gravel road leading to their home and vineyards. The Neuners have restored a historic house that was prominently cited in Charles van Ravenswaay's iconic book *The Arts and Architecture of German Settlements in Missouri: A Survey of a Vanishing Culture*. He wrote, "The Porth-Even-Fechtel farmhouse near Westphalia, with dimensions of about 45 feet by 35 feet, was probably built

Emmaus Homes

A GROUP OF PASTORS and lay people from churches in the Evangelical Synod of the West in the surrounding area founded the Emmaus Institution at Marthasville in 1893. They started with a vacated seminary building and served people with epilepsy and developmental disabilities. The name changed to Emmaus Homes in the 1960s, and today, the faith-based nonprofit still serves more than three hundred adults in eighty-five homes in Franklin, St. Charles, St. Louis, and Warren Counties.

geh und erforsche!

das Tagebuch

One of my colleagues with the German Heritage Corridor initiative, Dr. Cathie Schoppenhorst, presented a paper on the Emmaus Homes at the March 2018 Missouri Conference on History. The homes were noted for their success in treatment of epilepsy, and its sense of place was frequently noted as one important reason. Hospitals and many health professionals today consider sense of place, especially natural light and surroundings, important factors in promoting healing.

in the 1840s. It is one of the great early farmhouses in the area whose construction required skilled joiners, carpenters, and masons."

The Neuners have also restored a historic log cabin on site that was originally used as the schoolhouse at St. Joseph's Catholic parish in Westphalia. They display numerous cultural artifacts and heirlooms inside their historic home, such as an old oxen yoke passed down through Terry's family, which was used when they moved by wagon to Missouri in the 1830s.

That strong Westphalia sense of place also creates important new economic value and social values. For example, local Scout troops use their wages from harvesting grapes to support their scouting activities. The Neuners commissioned noted regional artist Jim Dyke to create a sweeping dining room mural of Westphalia; they also employed local artisan Kathy Johannesmeyer to craft a stained-glass window depicting the Marais River, the land, and their vineyards for the entrance to their wine-tasting room. McGinnis Wood Products of Cuba, Missouri, makes the oak harvested at the Neuner's farm into their wine barrels. The Kobe beef they raise strongly appeals to a new generation keenly interested in food and husbandry of the land. Mary also displays an heirloom watercolor painting that belonged to her father; it looks similar to that archival postcard shown earlier. The painting became their Reisling wine label.

A Parochial Ecology

Whether as beautiful backdrop or genuine benediction, its unique sense of place continues to shape Westphalia. At its richest and complex best, you can even taste hints of that elusive sense of place in a glass of wine. Theologian Michael Northcott's 2015 book, *Place, Ecology and the Sacred,* argues that the loss of sense of place, which he thinks began about 1800 with industrialization and industrial agriculture—processes similar to those that prompted German emigration to places like Westphalia—underlies our modern ecological crisis. He calls the sense of the sacred that characterized local communities of faith in Christian and Jewish tradition a "parochial ecology." Northcott writes: "Places of dwelling become places, and indeed sacred places, as they are shaped by human experience in interaction with local and specific ecological qualities."

If we could rediscover some of the finest parochial ecology in many of these traditional communities, the special reserves, perhaps once again we could create places that are "politically just, economically productive, and ecologically sustainable." Perhaps some of Westphalia's parochial ecology, its distinctive sense of place, can offer us a Missouri German heirloom rootstock that could be grafted onto increasingly "placeless"—or characterless—towns and cities.

Old Dutch Hotel

THE OLD DUTCH HOTEL in Washington, Missouri, offers a rich German heritage. The building was originally built by the Nieburg family in 1922, and they ran a restaurant there, probably living above the restaurant, as was typical for many businesses of the time. They were in the sausage-making business and probably began a restaurant to add value to their meat. The business was sold sometime by the mid-1930s to Heinie (abbreviated form of Heinrich) Diestelhorst. People in the community called him "Old Dutch," related to Deutsch, which was what the immigrants called themselves. Diestelhorst went with the Dutch idea for marketing, incorporating a Dutch Wind Mill neon sign and naming the restaurant and bar The Wind Mill. It was probably Diestelhorst who first started renting rooms, said Marc Houseman, Executive Director of the Washington Historical Society Museum. Houseman also reports that people have told him they stayed there, at what was popularly called the Old Dutch Hotel, as late as the early 1980s. They described fire escapes consisting of coiled ropes attached to the floor that guests were expected to toss out the window and climb down in case of fire. Houseman also said it has been documented that Harry S. Truman, while he was serving as president, got off the train in Washington and walked down Elm Street to the hotel to have a beer with his friend Heinie; they had served together in World War I and remained friends. The hotel changed hands as well as purposes several times before being beautifully restored and reopened as the Old Dutch Hotel & Tavern in 2011. The hotel once again provides guests a place to dine and spend the night.

The church spire in the Old Munichburg neighborhood across the creek from Jefferson City's traditional downtown is toward the upper right-hand corner of this 1869 drawing.

The Once and Future Village

The Monk's Hill

This 1869 panoramic drawing of Jefferson City reveals (toward the upper right corner) the Old Munichburg neighborhood that developed alongside Jefferson City's traditional downtown. Darrell Strope from the Cole County Historical Society can point out Old Munichburg in the picture by its landmarks, such as Wears Creek and the steeple of the original Central German Evangelical Church (now Central United Church of Christ).

First separated by a hill but then eventually connected to Jefferson City by bridges spanning Wears Creek, Old Munichburg today is the historic core of Jefferson City's Southside district, about fourteen blocks located south of US 50/63, west of Monroe and Poplar Streets, north of Franklin Street, and east of US 54 West.

In his book *Southside Sketches*, Walter Schroeder reports how a Missouri River steamboat carrying German immigrants docked at Munichburg during the great flood of 1844, which backed up waters all the way to the German village. The little village rather than the larger city was home for most immigrants before the Civil War, but the story of Old Munichburg's German cultural heritage really involves the ebb and flow between the village and the city.

German settlement in the village accelerated as many Germans fled their *Vaterland* (fatherland) from growing Prussian repression in the late 1840s. Like other *Auswanderung*, these immigrants moved to the Far West of Missouri to retain the culture they feared was being lost to them in rapidly modernizing Germany. Many of these early immigrants emigrated from the town of Münchberg or Muenchberg (the Monk's Hill), in Bavaria, so they called their new home "Muenchberg" as well. Non-German residents of Jefferson City typically misunderstood it as "Munichburg"—and so it became Anglicized, more or less.

Like other *Auswanderung* immigrants to Missouri, those who came to Munichburg sought new opportunities to preserve their Old World ways. Many first- and second-generation family members lived and worked exclusively in Muenchburg, close by others who shared their ethnic background and cultural beliefs. By 1859 the Central German Evangelical Church members erected their first building at the corner of Washington and Ashley Streets.

The church, with its steeple visible throughout the neighborhood (and on the panoramic map), became the cultural and social center of this very self-contained German ethnic neighborhood; a geographic area of about six square blocks contained their church, school, retail establishments, and recreation. Honeycombed with caves within its limestone bluffs, the village not surprisingly contained its own brewery (named Gundelfinger's City Brewery) in the 100 block of Dunklin. To paraphrase, it takes a village to raise a brewery.

Glory Days

However, after 1869 the physical and cultural distance between the village and city signified by the map greatly narrowed. The outstanding 2002 National Register nomination for Old Munichburg chronicled how the neighborhood expanded with the city during the period between the Civil War and the First World War. For example, the need for a larger school building reflected both the rapid growth of the neighborhood during the Gilded Age as well as its Americanization. A new public school constructed in 1904 replaced the one that had long served the neighborhood at the corner of Broadway and Dunklin. Around that same time, the Evangelical Church discontinued its parochial school (where classes were conducted in German rather than English), and Muenchburg children enrolled in the neighborhood's public school.

The Hermann Tanner house in Old Munichburg was built by the second generation of Tanners, in 1887. The house showcases the adoption of popular Queen Anne details such as the dentils, a second-story balcony, and an asymmetrical facade.

The houses in this Historic District also demonstrate the geographic expansion of the Old Munichburg neighborhood during this second period of development. Sociologists might call this expansive exhibition of wealth by the neighborhood's families who prospered from the rapidly growing city a form of conspicuous consumption. Census data indicate that Old Munichburg residents held job titles such as retail store owner, insurance salesperson, builder, musician, photographer, and wagon maker. Middle-class business owners and tradespeople dominated the Old Munichburg district by the latter part of the 19th century, and its architecture reflected both their prosperity and willingness to adopt more Americanized styles of housing.

Such increasing cultural assimilation led to the adoption of popular American architectural styles, a significant change from the traditional vernacular styles of Munichburg before the Civil War. During this second period of development, construction methods emphasized Missouri German building traditions but in mainstream American architectural styles. For example, a strong preference for masonry construction and Missouri German craftsmanship clearly remained. Certain Missouri German vernacular building influences, such as the use of red brick and arched windows, continued to shape the district even when mainstream styles like the elaborate Queen Anne predominated. Access to building materials now delivered by railroad rather than steamboat allowed houses in the district to exhibit many more decorative elements, such as stained-glass windows, cornice brackets, turned porch posts, and spindlework, which otherwise would have been unavailable.

Several buildings from the Munichburg district reflect this new expansiveness. The Herman Tanner House, 630 Broadway, was built by the second generation of Tanners to live and work in Munichburg. You can see the Queen Anne influence in the elaborate brickwork on both the front and side of this house, the stained-glass windows, and iron balcony—details on this impressive building that seem to signify the family's success with their dry goods store two blocks away.

The Joseph Pope House, 222 West Dunklin Street, celebrates another successful Munichburg entrepreneur with citywide influence. Pope designed much more than his house; he constructed some of the first sidewalks, streets, and highways in Missouri. In Jefferson City alone, Pope laid the first macadam street and probably 75 percent of the sidewalks and

das Tagebuch

Dr. Walter Schroeder noted that Oktoberfest has been a major force in public and media recognition of the Southside/Old Munichburg area as a defined community in Jefferson City, perhaps the most recognized and best defined neighborhood of the city. Sometimes the influence of an annual festival can last much longer than a day.

Jefferson City's Oktoberfest

THIS IS the main fundraiser for the Old Munichburg Association. It is always held the last weekend of September, as it is in Munich. Find the association's Facebook page or visit OldMunichburg.com. You can also read a blog, *Munichburg Memories*, by Walter Schroeder, buy a book about the area, and learn more about the association there.

geh und erforsche!

90 percent of all the city's streets. In 1917 his company received the first state contract for an improved road between the Osage River Bridge and Centertown, and Pope later served as a director for the Central Missouri Trust Company. The rich architectural ornamentation of the Queen Anne style obviously appealed to this generation of residents and allowed Munichburg's very talented Missouri German masons to display their artistry.

Other key aspects of German culture established in the Munichburg neighborhood during its early settlement period continued to influence development of the district between the Civil War and the First World War. For example, families continued to live close to one another and to remain in Munichburg for decades. Caroline Tanner, wife of Herman Tanner, remained in their Queen Anne home at 630 Broadway until at least 1951, sixty-four years after they first moved into the house. Alex Kocher, a wagon manufacturer, lived next door at 620 Broadway from 1900 until about 1945. Similarly, Joseph Pope's wife, Louisa, was still living in their house in 1951, fifty-four years after he built it. Descendants of the Pope family sold the house in the 1990s, over one hundred years after its construction. Like the century farms located around Westphalia, a value of permanence characterized the Missouri German families and the substantial houses they occupied in Old Munichburg.

Die Landschaften in Old Munichburg also displays strong German cultural influences. The use of alleys typified Munichburg, and all of the lots in the district originally terminated at an alley. The development of secondary houses fronting the alleys, so unusual in American cities, resulted from an Old World cultural influence. The Broadway-Dunklin Historic District at one of the primary intersections in the Munichburg neighborhood also displays some strong German cultural influences. This key intersection possesses high visibility due to its originally isolated location at the top of the ridge, the visual dominance of Broadway and West Dunklin as major arteries into and through the neighborhood, the high quality of the architecture and its ongoing maintenance, plus the annual fall color display of maple trees here. This section of Broadway used to be known as the "Avenue of the Maples," perhaps recalling Berlin's famous *Unter den Linden* boulevard; new maple trees planted in the fall of 2001 helped replace much of this romantic landscape that had been lost over the years.

Old Munichburg historic district also reveals the frugal nature of Missouri Germans, which served them well during difficult financial periods like the Great Depression. Retaining

St. Thomas

ST. THOMAS IS ANOTHER COMMUNITY where German settlers joined previous American settlers. German immigrants built a small log church for families that lived in the general area, near today's parish cemetery. It was replaced by a frame church in St. Thomas, and then by the current St. Thomas Apostle Church, built in 1883. Names such as Buschjost, Heisler, Hoecker, Loethens, Lueckenottes, Luther, Meyerpeter, Schell, Schuler, Sommerhauser, Vetter, and Walther can be found within an 1876 business directory at the Cole County Historical Society.

geh und erforsche!

das Tagebuch

My aunt displayed the frugal nature of Missouri Germans, too. She had a collection of 'string too short to use.'

alley houses, outbuildings, and even main houses while altering the structures for other uses demonstrated this conservation ethos of Munichburg's residents. Numerous residential buildings and the former school were converted to commercial use, rather than being replaced by a new building. Old Munichburg continues to reflect the steady evolution of Missouri German building traditions for over a century. It is a time capsule that still suggests a uniquely Missouri German approach to shaping the urban landscape of Missouri.

Restoring a Heritage

By the middle of the 20th century, however, the village and the city had parted ways. Urbanist Witold Rybcyzinski observed that "what seemed exciting in one decade looks gaudy, if not downright embarrassing, in the next, or simply boring. When old buildings are torn down, the motive may be expediency or crass commercialism, but it may also be a desire for something new." In the second half of the 20th century, all the above took place. The Old Munichburg neighborhood grew old: older residents passed away, subsequent generations joined the post-war suburban migration, and the houses and neighborhood lost their appeal to shiny, new models. A century after that 1869 map was drawn, popular perspectives about ideal American communities had dramatically changed. It became fashionable and easy for those still living in Old Munichburg to venture well beyond Wears Creek.

However, the story of Old Munichburg is not just an interesting urban legend about the olden days. As its website announces:

The Old Munichburg Association was formed

in 2000. We are dedicated to the revitalization of Jefferson City's historic Southside. The Association is made up of homeowners, business owners, and others who share a love of the district and a desire to promote, preserve, and protect it.

Perhaps as has happened in many larger cities across the country, the Old Munichburg Association will spark a successful rebuilding of this neighborhood, which has declined in recent decades, upon the solid foundation of its German cultural heritage.

Pattern One: Sense of Place

The Old Munichburg Association has long supported history projects focusing on the longtime residents of Munichburg. This ongoing effort involves interviewing, recording, and transcribing oral histories, as well as digitizing and archiving historic photos. Along that line, Walter Schroeder's *Munichburg Memories* blog, sponsored by the Old Munichburg Association, celebrates the history of Jefferson City's German Southside.

Schroeder, like his wife and mother, was born and raised in Munichburg; his maternal grandparents were German immigrants who settled in this neighborhood. Now retired from teaching geography at the University of Missouri, his *Munichburg Memories* blog recalls the history of Jefferson City's German ethnic community as well as his own stories about growing up in the Southside. Schroeder correctly points out that many people have helped to revitalize Old Munichburg, but every neighborhood or small town interested in its German cultural heritage needs a keeper of the flame like *Doktor* Schroeder.

The blog and his historical research began as a side project for Schroeder to enliven his monthly meeting minutes for the Old Munichburg Association, but they have evolved into a collection of essays illuminating the Southside's organizations, people, and geography. His book, *Southside Sketches: Essays on Jefferson City's Old Munichburg*, draws upon personal memories like shopping at mom-and-pop grocery stores. Other stories came from interviews with his mother and other older Southside residents, who spoke of visits by gypsies and exploring the area's legendary tunnels and caves. Schroeder also gleaned several other interesting tales from archival sources, including the German-language newspapers favored by the Southside immigrants but which would be unreadable by most residents today.

Old Munichburg was also successful in creating a historic district around Broadway and Dunklin streets, including more than twenty buildings placed on the National Register of Historic Places in 2002. Such designation signifies the Old Munichburg district's historic importance on a national as well as a local level, while making it possible for property owners to capitalize on federal and state tax credits for certified restoration of their historic buildings. The historic district has expanded since 2002 to the 100 block of East Dunklin, and several businesses have benefited from the neighborhood's strong sense of place. The Riversong Spa and Salon website highlights its array of services:

> *... amidst elegant surroundings of a century-old German home in the heart of Old Munichburg Historic District. Unique, original stained-glass windows grace the front rooms and entrance. Grandma's lace doilies and antiques add charm to this state-of-the-art day spa.*

Busch's Florist is reconstructing its historic greenhouse on the northwest corner of Dunklin and Madison. Busch's has been at that location since 1890, and its predecessor was there way back in the 1870s. And the legendary ECCO Lounge near Jefferson and Dunklin continues a restaurant and bar tradition at that site that stretches back to 1860. Like Norm and Cliff from television's popular series, *Cheers*, there may be some patrons at ECCO Lounge who go back that far.

Cottleville

THIS MISSOURI TOWN provides another example of Germans building alongside and eventually becoming incorporated into an earlier settlement. As far back as 1800, a few houses had been built at this spot where the old Boone's Lick Road crossed Dardenne Creek. The Giessen Emigration Society contributed more settlers, and at one time before the Civil War, the town boasted two hotels, five hundred people, and eleven businesses. In 1846, the townspeople attempted to have the County Seat of Justice transferred there from St. Charles but failed.

geh und erforsche!

St. Mary of Victories Catholic Church

WHEN GERMAN IMMIGRANTS flooded into St. Louis, they found the population about half Catholic, as French Catholics had settled the area. Their diocese stretched from Canada to the lower Mississippi River and from the mouth of the Missouri River to the Rocky Mountains. This church was established so German families could have German-speaking priests and worship in their own language.

The church was founded in 1843, near Chouteau's Landing, south of where the Gateway Arch stands. The architect was German American Franz Saler. Notable architectural elements include eight-foot-tall stained-glass windows, the high arch of the sanctuary, and an Egyptian-style doorway framed by pillars that hold a heavy wooden cross above the entrance. The church is listed on the National Register of Historic Places.

The church was consecrated in 1866 at the direction of Pope Pius IX. All Catholic churches are blessed, but only a few are consecrated, meaning it can be used only for Catholic worship and for no other purpose. Brass wall sconces mark the location of special oil used during the consecration ritual. Its high altar contains hundreds of relics of saints, bestowed by Pope Leo XIII.

The church was also the home of the Sisters of St. Mary, who came from Germany in 1872 and began their health care ministry. Because they worked with the poor and the sick, they became known as the Smallpox Sisters, and they entered the church to worship on a special separate balcony. Eventually, a convent attached to the church was built, and today, their legacy, the SSM Health Care Systems, operates hospitals and medical facilities throughout the Midwest.

The German population began leaving this section in the mid-1900s. After the failed Hungarian Revolution and a large influx of new immigrants, the archdiocese reassigned the church in 1957, and it became known as St. Louis's Hungarian Catholic Church. Today, it remains a vital church for Hungarians but also non-Hungarians, as well.

geh und erforsche!

das Tagebuch

While looking around Central United Church of Christ in search of Dr. Walter Schroeder, I had a brief conversation with two women from the congregation who graciously helped me find my meeting place. I learned in passing that they had visited Münchberg, Bavaria, as part of an exchange program between Old Munichburg and its German partner city, and they spoke enthusiastically about how it helped them appreciate their German heritage, including finding distant relatives. That brief but happy encounter reminded me of what anthropologists call 'authenticity', a key factor in cultural heritage tourism that enables travelers to make meaningful connections between heritage sites and their own lives. It's certainly a goal of the German Heritage Corridor initiative and of this book, too.

Pattern Two: The Built Environment

If broken windows indicate that no one cares about a neighborhood, then beautification efforts send exactly the opposite signal. Almost since it began, the Old Munichburg neighborhood association has installed and maintained attractive neighborhood banners identifying the historic district. In 2009, it purchased decorative sign-post covers and had them installed on street signs throughout the district.

Old Munichburg Association members also plant and maintain special landscapes in the district, such as beautification of the 100 block of West Dunklin. Combining beautification and a sense of cultural heritage, the Dunklin Street murals grace storefront windows at 117 East Dunklin. Commissioned by the Old Munichburg Association and executed by local artist Jim Dyke, these murals commemorate the cars, buildings, and people of Old Munichburg's rich history. You can gaze at them from across the street while you sip your espresso at a coffee shop or browse at unique stores.

The Munichburg Corner down Dunklin from the mural might be described by anthropologists as a liminal, or transitional, place that bridges two worlds. It's a gateway with key buildings memorializing the neighborhood's heritage while also opening to the neighborhood's bright future. The Munichburg Corner wraps around the northeast corner of Dunklin and Jefferson.

Stone for the wall was salvaged from the former Nilges Grocery Store, which once stood at the southeast corner of Jefferson and Ashley. The memorial design commemorates the village's German artisans who worked in brick, stone, and wrought iron, as found in many other German districts throughout the German Heritage Corridor. The Old Munichburg Association helped fund the Munichburg Corner project by selling commemorative

Several special landscapes in Jefferson City, tended by Old Munichburg Association volunteers, demonstrate their pride and determination to preserve their German heritage.

bricks and pavers, literally encouraging people to "buy into" the project and what it signifies.

Pattern Three: Cultural Activities

In 2004, the Old Munichburg Association collaborated with city government to initiate a partner-city relationship with Muenchberg, Bavaria, from which many Munichburg (and Jefferson City) families immigrated before the Civil War. Since 2004, numerous visits have taken place involving people from both cities, including organized visits of Jefferson Citians to Muenchberg. In September 2006, the association cosponsored a German-style *Volkmarch* with the City of Jefferson to celebrate its renewed relationship with Muenchberg. The citizens of Muenchberg gave a plaque to Jefferson City that now graces the Munichburg Corner, further cementing this intercultural transfer.

Old Munichburg also sponsors the annual Oktoberfest celebration in the area centered around Dunklin and Washington Streets. Oktoberfest, always held the last Saturday in September in true Munich fashion, has captured the *gemutlichkeit* (a warm good feeling) of the entire city, which benefits from this extremely popular festival. Perhaps most importantly, though, such a festival reminds visitors and residents alike that Old Munichburg is a very special place within the city as a whole.

Gemeinschaft und Gesellschaft

Unlike that self-contained 19th-century Missouri German village geographically and culturally separated from the larger city, Old Munichburg has learned over time to balance *Gemeinschaft* (community life) and *Gesellschaft* (larger associations characteristic of city life). For example, the Old Munichburg Association (OMA) now works closely with the City of Jefferson and others interested in center city revitalization and historic preservation. Schroeder noted that OMA, which is also a German term of endearment for grandmother, has received excellent and enduring support from its City Council representatives.

OMA also developed a Neighborhood Watch program with the Jefferson City Police department to foster stronger community relations and discourage crime in this revitalizing center-city neighborhood by adding "more eyes on the street." It also works with the city to promote code enforcement, improve landlord responsibility, and provide financial incentives for home improvements. Literally building upon those efforts, Old Munichburg partnered with other organizations to sponsor a complete Habitat for Humanity rehab of one of the historic residences.

The Old Munichburg Association and the City Council first began discussions in 2005 to create a Community Improvement District (CID) to accelerate infrastructure improvements

das Tagebuch

The thought occurred to me that this new district and neighborhood development plan might even inspire a new Gundelfinger's City Brewery in this new/old village.

in the area. The Munichburg CID has expedited replacement of crumbling sidewalks and gutters on a number of highly visible streets in the district, improvements crucially important for a walking neighborhood such as Old Munichburg.

Such a collaboration helps ensure professional design and construction that meets city codes as well as a high level of design quality throughout the area, clearly indicating civic care and concern to interested observers. In true Missouri German fashion, OMA members and participants pride themselves on paying their own way and putting their money where their heritage is.

Finally, the Capital Region Medical Center, along with an advisory board of property owners, business owners, residents, Lincoln University, and community leaders, worked with H3 Studios of St. Louis to develop an Old Munichburg/Southside neighborhood revitalization plan. Like many urban hospitals and universities, the Capital Region Medical Center recognized that its future health greatly depended upon that of its surrounding neighborhoods. This highly collaborative planning and design process involving many public presentations and interactive forums successfully led to the development and formal adoption of the plan by Jefferson City in 2017.

The plan noted that the unique homes, remaining alley houses, portions of the Dunklin Business District, and the Central United Church of Christ represented distinctive community assets, which provide the Old Munichburg neighborhood with a unique sense of place. Not surprisingly, then, it called for building the heart of the community around a "revitalized, vibrant, mixed-use Dunklin Street/ Old Munichburg business district." It also recommended developing a distinctive community identity on Dunklin Street with festivals, the

This mural is on a Central Dairy warehouse at 117 East Dunklin Street. The mural depicts Dunklin Street from the intersection with Madison Street, the center of the historic Southside Business District. The large Capitol Brewery is in the background at right.

George Engelmann's portrait was found during a renovaion of the Missouri Botanical Garden's library in 2017.

celebration of history, cultural resources, and street improvements. Finally, the wheel comes full circle to that 1869 map as the plan recommends developing a community park along Wears Creek.

Like some hardy heirloom seed, Missouri's German heritage of *die Landschaft* seems to have found good soil once again in the limestone bluffs of Jefferson City. "Today, Munichburg is being revitalized," the plan announces, "building on its strengths—sturdy brick buildings, enduring business centers, attractive, hilly, tree-lined streets, and a strong neighborhood identity."

Although most residents don't speak German anymore, it remains a place where you can walk nearly everywhere you need to go—a solid neighborhood where ice cream cones, dining, and shopping are available a few blocks away. Old Munichburg is as solid as those limestone bluffs and the people who shaped them.

A Picture Worth a Thousand Words

Workers renovating the Missouri Botanical Garden's venerable 1859 library building near the tomb of its founder, Henry Shaw, uncovered a hidden mural of German American botanist George (Georg) Engelmann. Next to the battered Engelmann portrait, workers also uncovered one of the creator of botanical taxonomy, Carl Linneaus, and Asa Gray, a Harvard professor and one of the premier American botantists of the 19th century. These three were distinguished company, certainly, that inspires some rather obvious questions about this cultural artifact: Who was Engelmann, and what did he have to do with legendary Swedish botanist Linnaeus and Gray and the world-famous Missouri Botanical Garden? The new light now being shed on that crumbling mural helps bring to mind a legendary figure of Missouri's German heritage, whose ideas about the natural world continue to cultivate its scientific and aesthetic appreciation.

A Brief Biography

So who was Engelmann? The Archives of the Missouri Botanical Garden contain his personal papers, which in turn include a treasure trove of almost 5,000 letters from about 550 leading and amateur scientists in the United States and Europe in the middle decades of the 1800s. The collection also includes the various scientific notes and written works composed by Engelmann during his life as a medical doctor living in St. Louis. The archives offer considerable help in answering our questions and completing the picture.

Engelmann was born in Frankfort am Main on Feb. 2, 1809, just ten days before Charles Darwin and Abraham Lincoln, other shapers of the 19th century who were born on February 12. In 1828 he was compelled to leave his exemplary studies at the University of Heidelberg after having joined in a political demonstration, a widespread phenomenon of that time that recalls young Paul Follenius from page 35. He entered the University of Berlin for two years, then in 1831 earned his MD degree from the University of Würzburg.

His dissertation contained the seed kernel of his subsequent career. More closely related to botany than medicine, it was devoted to plant morphology, mainly what 19th-century botanists called "monstrosities" and other strange plant forms. It was illustrated by five plates of figures drawn and transferred to the lithographic stone by young Engelmann himself.

His treatise related so well to research by the legendary German philosopher and naturalist Johann Wolfgang von Goethe that the revered Goethe obtained a copy of Engelmann's treatise and inquired about its young author. Goethe observed that Engelmann had completely apprehended Goethe's ideas and had shown a peculiar genius for their development.

Goethe and his good friend Alexander von Humboldt both encouraged the search for unity in nature and society, as well as nourishing an aesthetic appreciation of nature, and in his dissertation, young Engelmann clearly demonstrated these key principles. Goethe offered to give young Engelmann his whole store of unpublished notes and sketches, another precursor of Engelmann's cultural legacy.

Engelmann then emigrated from his native Germany with his young family to Belleville, Illinois, in the early 1830s. He then moved to St. Louis and established a highly successful medical practice with fellow expatriate Friedrich Adolph Wislizenus. Engelmann's fluency in German, French, and English served him well in the mid-1800s gateway city of St. Louis, and his highly successful medical practice subsequently allowed him to pursue his primary interest of botany.

Linneaus Redux

How did Engelmann rate a mural in the oldest botanical library west of the Mississippi River alongside Carl Linneaus, the founder of botanical taxonomy, and Asa Gray, considered one of the most important American botanists of the 1800s? As an active and influential botanical researcher in mid-19th-century America, Engelmann extended Linneaus's scientific legacy in important new ways with his special focus on unique American plant forms. The famous Engelmann spruce *(Picea engelmannii)* is named after him, and his two major works on cactuses remain important botanical references even today.

Like Alexander von Humboldt, he explored the New World tirelessly and developed vital scientific networks to share his findings. In 1832 Engelmann became associated with celebrated Swiss biologist and Harvard professor Louis Agassiz, and in the 1840s, he began a lifelong correspondence with Harvard botanist Asa Gray. Despite lacking a Harvard pedigree, this Missouri German clearly shaped American science and education.

Engelmann and Gray arranged for collecting plants in the Southwest before, during, and after the Mexican American War through their respective networks. As his dissertation interest in unusual plant forms already hinted, not surprisingly, Engelmann became America's greatest authority on cactuses.

Missouri Botanical Garden

THE ST. LOUIS BOTANICAL GARDEN, founded in 1859 by Henry Shaw, is considered one of the top three botanical gardens in the world, along with the New York Botanical Garden and Kew Gardens in London. It is the oldest botanical garden still in continuous operation and offers 79 acres of beauty, including a 14-acre Japanese strolling garden, Henry Shaw's original 1849 estate home, and one of the world's largest collections of rare and endangered orchids. Dozens of events are held here, including a Japanese Festival, Chinese Culture Days, and Best of Missouri Market. The 2,441-acre Shaw Nature Reserve nearby was established in 1925 to protect plant collections from the smoke pollution of the 1920s.

Linnean House

das Tagebuch

George Engelmann first immigrated to Belleville, Illinois, which was also the hometown of my maternal grandmother, Clara Schrauth, who taught me to garden. I know this essay is about Missouri life, but here's a tip of my gardening hat to Belleville, Illinois.

George Engelmann illustrated saguaro cactus for William Emory's *Report on the United States and Mexican Boundary Survey.*

German Heritage at the Missouri Botanical Garden

- See the restored George Engelmann portrait at the Stephen and Peter Sachs Museum at the Garden (above).
- Visit the Strassenfest German Garden, next to the Lehmann Building at the south end of the Botanical Garden grounds. This garden incorporates native flora of Germany and central Europe, as well as plants hybridized or discovered by native Germans. The design is an informal woodland setting full of herbaceous perennials, as well as deciduous trees and shrubs. Plants in this garden include sweeps of grass, astilbes, ferns, columbine, yarrow, and many others. This garden also has a bronze bust of George Engelmann. Depicted in the statue are conifers and cactuses that were described by him or named for him.
- Find the Floyd Pfautch Bavarian Garden directly south of the Strassenfest German Garden. This garden features plants native to alpine regions around the world, including Europe.
- Explore some of Engelmann's correspondence, handwritten in the old German script, at BiodiverstiyLibrary.org.

geh und erforsche!

EDWARD LANG

Tower Grove House at Missouri Botanical Garden is the restored country residence of founder Henry Shaw.

When the western scientific surveys reached cactus country in the 1850s, they called upon him to describe them. In 1859, he wrote and illustrated the section on cactuses in William Emory's celebrated *Report on the United States and Mexican Boundary Survey* (1857-59); soon Engelmann's cactus section was being published separately and is best known for its beautiful first plate showing towering saguaro cactuses along the Gila River in New Mexico. His many impressive engravings of cactuses in the *Report* still remain important resources for the world scientific community.

Engelmann led the creation of the Western Academy of Natural Sciences and later the Academy of Science of St. Louis, which in turn formed the basis for today's Saint Louis Science Center. He was also a charter member of the National Academy of Science. At a commemoration ceremony for Engelmann at the National Academy of Science in April 1896, his memoirist Charles A. White recalled:

> *Although Dr. Engelmann never lost an iota of his inborn love and veneration for his fatherland, he was thoroughly American in all his feelings. He identified himself fully with American scientists and labored earnestly for the advancement of science in the country of his adoption. So widely had his fame extended and so highly was he esteemed by his American compeers that when it was proposed to establish our National Academy his name was one of the first to be enrolled among its founders.*

George Engelmann and Shaw's Garden

Engelmann's distinguished biography and botanical achievements still do not explain why this German immigrant to the Far West of Missouri achieved such pride of place as a mural in the matrix of one of the world's most famous botanical gardens, one that many native St. Louisans like myself still call Shaw's Garden. When wealthy St. Louis merchant Henry Shaw decided to establish a botanical garden at the very edge of the rapidly growing city, he called upon Sir William Hooker, director of the Kew Gardens in England. Hooker advised Shaw to consult Engelmann, right there in his own home town, and the rest is natural history.

Engelmann then recommended his old friend Asa Gray at Harvard, and with the assistance of Gray and Sir Hooker, Engelmann persuaded Shaw to include a collection of botanical specimens (a herbarium) and a library in his garden. Instead of only a pleasure garden (a role nearby Tower Grove Park still fills wonderfully), Shaw endowed St. Louis with one of the finest research gardens in the United States and indeed the world. Despite its world-class educational pedigree, the Missouri Botanical Garden nevertheless still manages to please hundreds of thousands of annual visitors, from amateurs to zoologists, who explore its scientific and aesthetic wonders.

According to the Garden's National Register nomination, by 1855 the grounds for the new Missouri Botanical Garden had been laid. Shaw then encouraged Engelmann to buy books and specimens in Europe for the new botanical garden. During the next two years, Engelmann acted as Shaw's ambassador in Europe seeking "proper accessories" for the garden. This role included forwarding seeds and specimens to Shaw as well as purchasing the renowned

George Engelmann, left, helped Henry Shaw establish one of the most impressive herbariums and botanical libraries in the world, as well as the gardens, at the Missouri Botanical Garden.

Bernhardi herbarium in Erfurth, Germany.

In 1909, *Popular Science Monthly* published *A Biographical History of Botany at St. Louis, Missouri*, by Perley Spaulding. He noted that Engelmann, who was visiting Europe in 1857, was commissioned by Henry Shaw to study botanical gardens for ideas and suggestions.

About this time Engelmann corresponded with Sir William Hooker, Director of Kew Gardens, who wrote on August 10, 1857, "Very few appendages to a garden of this kind are of more importance for instruction than a library and economic museum, and these gradually increase like a rolling snowball."

Spaulding noted that Shaw largely entrusted the selection of books to Engelmann in consultation with the famous Hooker and Engelmann's other botanical friends. Engelmann urged Shaw to purchase the herbarium of recently deceased Professor Johann J. Bernhardi, of Erfurth, Germany.

Bernhardi had served for nearly forty years as the director of the botanic garden at Gartenstraße in Erfurth, as well as professor of botany, zoology, mineralogy, and *materia medica* at the University of Erfurth. He had studied and described several species of orchids and a species of rose without thorns, *Rosa × francofurtana*, that were found in the celebrated garden of Johann Wolfgang von Goethe in Weimar.

Thanks to extensive interchanges and acquisitions with other botanists, over the course of his long career, Bernhardi had assembled one of the finest herbariums in the world of sixty thousand plants with specimens from North America, South America, Asia, and Africa. Hooker wrote to Shaw on January 1, 1858:

> *He [Engelmann] tells me of the herbarium of the late Dr. Bernhardi, of Erfurth, which he expects to buy for St. Louis. That ought to be a good commencement for the more scientific part of the establishment. The state ought to feel that it owes you much for so much public spirit, and so well directed.*

Engelmann purchased the first books for the garden library in 1857 and subsequently the Bernhardi herbarium for $600. Today the Missouri Botanical Garden herbarium contains nearly 7 million specimens and the library over 120,000 volumes. Now we're starting to get the picture about Engelmann.

Legacy

Restoration of George Engelmann's mural seems especially appropriate as Missouri begins to shed new light on Missouri's German heritage. *Doktor* Engelmann shaped and continues to shape the natural world in many healthy ways. Several plants commemorate his name, including Engelmann Oak *(Quercus engelmannii)*, Engelmann Spruce *(Picea engelmannii)*, Apache Pine *(Pinus engelmannii)*, and Engelmann's Prickly Pear *(Opuntia engelmannii)*.

William B. Ashworth Jr., a historian of science at the University of Missouri at Kansas City, noted that in addition to his successful medical practice, pioneering botanical research, and crucial influence upon the formation of the Missouri Botanical Garden, Engelmann was also an expert on Missouri wine grapes. He played an important role in supplying France with American grape root stock when a root aphid, phylloxera, attacked French vineyards in the late 1860s. The efforts of Engelmann and other Missouri Germans like Hermann's George Husmann helped save the French wine industry from disaster; a monument at Montpellier, France, recognizes the New World for its assistance.

But wait, there's more ...

After Engelmann died in 1884, his son donated the herbarium, containing the original specimens from which many western plants were named and described, and papers to the Missouri Botanical Garden. The Missouri Botanical Garden has now digitized the herbarium. Through its Tropicos research database, the Garden now provides online public access to a collection of previously unavailable historic specimens, such as the Engelmann herbarium, as well as innovative analytical interfaces into these data sets.

An international audience of scientists, students, and people use these irreplaceable resources to explore and increasingly conserve the historic distributions of species throughout the American landscape and now the world, just as Engelmann envisioned long ago.

Engelmann's bequest also led to the founding of the Henry Shaw School of Botany as a department of Washington University in St. Louis. Shaw established a George Engelmann Professorship of Botany in his honor. Missouri Botanical Garden Director Peter Wyse Jackson now fills that professorship, sharing George Engelmann's remarkable legacy with future leaders who share his fascination and reverence for the natural world.

The picture restored, now we know what Herr Goethe must have seen in that young man and why we see his mural in the Stephen and Peter Sachs Museum at the Missouri Botanical Garden in a place of honor next to that of Carl Linneaus and Asa Gray.

Saint Louis Science Center

THE CENTER HAS ITS ROOTS in the Academy of Science of St. Louis, founded in 1856 as the first scientific organization west of the Mississippi. About a century later, in 1959, the Academy created the Museum of Science and Natural History in Oak Knoll Park in Clayton. The museum became independent from the Academy, which still operates today, and it also outgrew its facilities and moved after it acquired the James S. McDonnell Planetarium from the City of St. Louis. After renovations, it reopened as the Saint Louis Science Center in 1991. After continuing expansion over the years, today, the Center includes an Omnimax Theater, seven hundred exhibits in ten galleries, and space for traveling exhibits. In 2016, it was named a Smithsonian Institution Affiliate, providing access to artifacts and exhibits that travel nationally.

geh und erforsche!

The Pelster Housebarn has four levels, with the lowest basement level built into the hillside. Livestock was stabled there. Note the porch on the front side.

GOOD WORK

das Arbeit

Barn Again

The historic Pelster Housebarn, a venerable artifact of Missouri's German cultural heritage, still stands half-hidden in the heart of the German Heritage Corridor, nestled into a hillside south of New Haven in rural Franklin County. It is a splendid survivor of an Old World building style that integrated house and barn into one structure.

In his 1986 article "The Pelster Housebarn: Endurance of Germanic Architecture on the Midwestern Frontier," noted Missouri folklorist Howard Wight Marshall concluded that "construction of [the Pelster Housebarn] was no accident but a purposeful re-establishment of a decidedly European architectural mode."

Constructed by German Lutheran immigrant Friedrich Wilhelm (William) Pelster (1825-1908), the housebarn sheltered the Pelster family, livestock, and its farm work all under one roof. The housebarn form clearly reflects Pelster's German cultural heritage, but adapted creatively to specific Missouri conditions, preferences, and building materials.

Approximately 60 feet wide by 53 feet deep, the superstructure rests in typically solid German fashion on a massive, mortared, 24-inch thick stone foundation, fully visible from the rear and almost completely banked into the hillside on the front. Weatherboarding masks its uniquely German *Fachwerk* (half-timbered) construction, in which the wooden wall framing—studs, cross beams, and braces—are exposed to the outside, while plaster, brick, or stone fill the spaces between the timbers. A steeply pitched gabled roof covers the structure. The roof, originally covered with wooden shingles, sloped down the front to shelter a porch on the house end and an enclosed storage area on the other.

Family history suggests that the front room of the second level served as the "parlor" to welcome visitors, while the middle room served as both family living space and bedroom. A back room served as a kitchen, cupboard, and storage space. A *Diele* (a broad central hallway) separated the house section from the grain and hay storage areas. Tongue and groove planks, originally fastened with handcrafted wooden pegs, covered the floor. Traditionally, the *Diele* would have been used for threshing as well as unloading hay from wagons.

According to the Missouri Agricultural Census, in 1870 Pelster owned six horses, five milk cows, four other cattle, twenty-four sheep, and eleven swine. In today's planning parlance, the Pelster Housebarn was the ultimate mixed-use development project.

die Familie

Pelster came to central Missouri in that wave of German immigrants seeking refuge or fortune, or both, in America between the 1830s until the Civil War. While the economic, political, social, and cultural upheavals following the Napoleonic Wars pushed them out of their

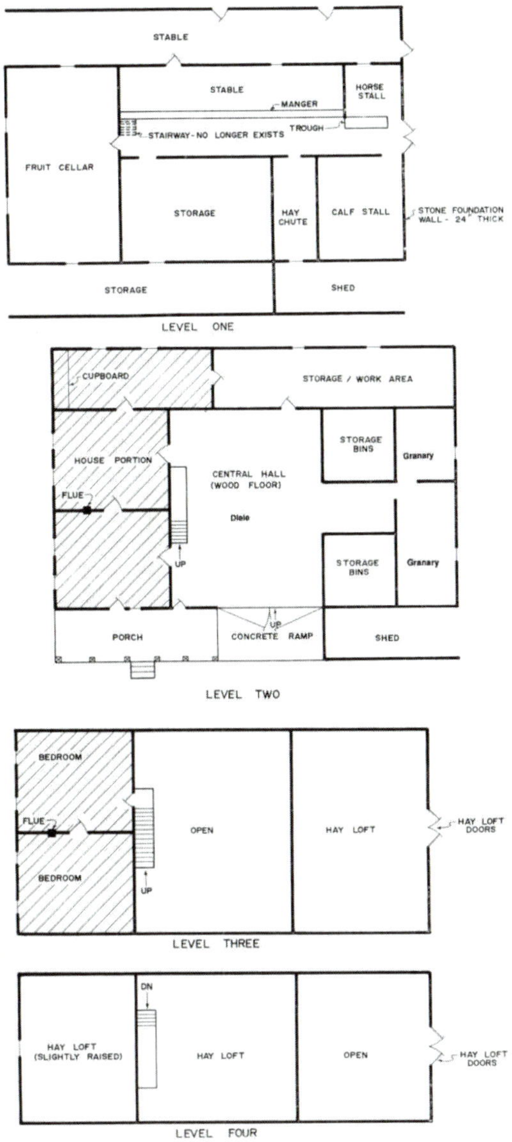

Starting with the basement level one, the diagrams show how space was allocated in the Pelster Housebarn.

traditional villages, travel literature published by Gottfried Duden and others pulled them toward a promised New Germania arising deep in the heart of America. Emigrating from the village of Dissen, near Osnabruck, Hannover, in northern Germany, Pelster arrived in Missouri in 1842 with his wife Maria Katherine and sons Rodolph and Wilhelm. Strikingly familiar, a hamlet named Dissen lay a few miles north of the Pelster farm.

Like many other German immigrants to rural Missouri, the Pelsters constructed a temporary log dwelling before constructing a more permanent (and more German) dwelling. Wilhelm, the son, undoubtedly participated in that early building project but left the home place in search of employment at a clay mine or brick factory in St. Louis. He eventually saved enough money to purchase his own land in Franklin County in 1856, about four miles west of his father's property, then set to work shaping a new life in Missouri.

While no written documentation clearly dates the Pelster Housebarn construction, family said it began on the eve of the Civil War but was delayed until after the war. Franklin County tax assessment records show Pelster's property value rose significantly in 1867, supporting the family legend. In true Missouri German custom, Pelster family members occupied the housebarn for more than sixty years.

Farm Life

Bäuerliches Leben (farm life) in the German Heritage Corridor changed very slowly during the period the Pelster family occupied the housebarn; many Missouri Century Farms, held in the same family for more than one hundred years, still belong to German families. Laurent Torno Jr., a preservation architect, architectural historian, conservator of Missouri German material culture, and adviser to the Missouri Humanities Council on the German Heritage Corridor, emphasized that with the exception of St. Louis and St. Charles proper, the German Heritage Corridor remained almost entirely rural and remote until well into the 1900s.

The Highway 19 bridge across the Missouri River did not open until 1931, while the bridge over the Missouri River at Washington did not open until 1936. The few state roads throughout the counties of the German Heritage Corridor consisted of gravel, while the county roads were dirt. Many properties were only accessible by two-track dirt trails for horses and wagons, and the trails frequently followed the creeks.

Torno noted that the typical rural household in the German Heritage Corridor tilled and toiled through a never-ending succession of long days. They planted, raised, and harvested their crops while also planting *gemusegarten* (kitchen gardens) for fruits and vegetables, preserving that which was not consumed fresh for later consumption. Many of them planted, raised, and harvested flax, which was then retted, broken, and combed with a succession of ever-finer combs to separate the linen fibers from the broken flax stalks, then spun the linen into thread, wove the thread into cloth, and made their own linens and clothing. They raised chickens, pigs, sheep, and cattle for meat, then butchered and cured their own meat or made their own sausage. They made their own soap, cut their own wood, built their own fences, and baked their own bread. In addition, many Missouri German families raised grapes and made wine, while many others practiced a trade such as furniture-maker, wheelwright, carpenter, blacksmith, cobbler, or shoemaker.

Like the Pelster Housebarn, Missouri German farm families integrated many activities into one household for self-reliant freedom. Torno

wrote, "This cycle of daily life prevailed even in the various small settlements, such as New Melle, Bay, Drake, Berger, and Dutzow, well into the 1900s."

Old World Traditions

The German immigrants often built their own buildings, as they were grounded in an ancient European vernacular building tradition. In 14th-century Holland and northern Germany, for example, such structures were built to shelter humans and livestock, often without partitions between living and stabling areas. Known in Holland as the *los hoes* and in Germany as the *Hallenhaus*, the house section occupied one end and the barn section the other of these long houses. Wagon doors on the gable end of the barn section would lead to a central threshing hall. This basic type, with its centuries of regional variations, was still being built in northern Europe into the 1900s.

In Switzerland and the southern Alpine region of Germany, housebarns were often banked into the slope of a hillside with the bottom level serving as a stable. While the hill insulated the rear wall of the stable, the front of the structure benefited from access to the sun and wind. The upper level contained the living quarters, storage areas, and threshing hall, reached by a ramp, while builders sometimes added a hayloft on the third level. Although the Pelster family hailed from northern Germany, their housebarn more closely reflects this southern Alpine vernacular architecture.

At the time of its 1978 National Register of Historic Places nomination, the Pelster Housebarn was one of only a dozen or so remaining housebarns in America. Wisconsin, Minnesota, Nebraska, North and South Dakota, and Texas all possessed some type of housebarns.

Some items remained in the parlor, at left, and the kitchen in the Pelster Housebarn. The photograph above was taken during a Historic American Buildings survey in 1983.

das Tagebuch

I still have my copy of "Object and Image: The German Housebarn in America" from the statewide celebration of the 1983 German American Tricentennial held at the University of Missouri in Columbia, as well as the memory of developing a friendship with the late Osmund (Ozzie) Overby, one of the heroes of historic preservation in Missouri and the United States. That copy and that memory continue to inspire my own preservation efforts.

As a cultural artifact, the Pelster Housebarn compared most closely to the Wisconsin examples, also built by German immigrants. However, the Pelster Housebarn was intended as a permanent dwelling, while the Wisconsin examples were later abandoned, probably intentionally, when replaced by detached dwellings.

Pelster's decision to build his permanent dwelling with heavy timbers seems much more predictable than his choice of the housebarn style. Many Missouri German settlers built temporary dwellings using horizontal log construction, but they typically selected masonry or half-timbering for their permanent homes. Known in Germany as *Fachwerkbau,* half-timbering was common there from medieval times until the 19th century, when it was introduced to America during the successive phases of German immigration. Mainstream American building traditions never really embraced Fachwerk, but it distinguished Missouri German structures.

The Pelster Housebarn exemplifies this unique Fachwerk construction. Massive white-oak timbers, hewn to desired size and shape with a broad axe, form the framing. All joints are expertly mortised, tenoned, and secured with wood pegs rather than nails. Noggings of limestone and plaster laid between the framing members provide insulation. In keeping with old-world traditions, each section of the frame bears a chiseled Roman numeral, designating its place in the structure. Pieces were laid out on the ground and assembled, then each section, or "bent," was raised and individually braced while the next one was assembled.

New World Adaptations

The housebarn tradition rarely survived the sea change of immigrant culture to America. While common in Europe, where high land and construction costs made consolidation of farm enterprises in one structure secure and economical, the Far West of Missouri posed an entirely different set of circumstances. Abundant land, timber, and popular tastes worked against the housebarn style. Missourians already here turned up their noses at this "foreign" peasant custom.

Although built in a German vernacular architectural tradition, the Pelster Housebarn also displays certain features adapted to the very un-German Missouri climate and way of life. For example, Germans rarely sheathed buildings with weatherboarding, primarily due to the shortage of lumber there. The practice was common enough in Missouri, though, probably due to its severe climate and ready availability of timber. The Pelster Housebarn was obviously built with the intention of weatherboarding, for nogging was not used between the timbers in the house section nor continued to the full height of the barn section.

The design and siting of the Pelster Housebarn also adapted to Missouri life. Rather than occupying valuable flat land, the lower level nestles into a hillside. The exterior of the house section incorporates a cut-out porch, sheltered under the main roof and supported by turned posts. This combination of hillside siting, weatherboarding, a visible porch, and gabled wagon entrance clearly distinguishes the Pelster Housebarn from the few other American housebarns. No wonder Howard Marshall called Pelster "the traditional builder with the creative spark."

A National Landmark

The Pelster Housebarn was nominated to the National Register of Historic Places in 1978, and it was officially listed in December of that year. In 1980 owners Harry and Jean Panhorst donated the housebarn to the Missouri Heritage Trust. The Trust received a loan from the

National Trust for Historic Preservation in the early 1980s to begin critical restoration and stabilization, such as roof repairs, replacement of missing weatherboards, restoration of wood windows, and exterior painting.

The Missouri Cultural Heritage Center of the University of Missouri then began a research project on the housebarn, culminating in a traveling exhibit for the 1983 German American Tricentennial celebration. Extensive interviews with 79-year-old Alfred Pelster, grandson of the housebarn builder, uncovered considerable family lore surrounding the history and occupation of the housebarn. The Vernacular Architecture Forum toured the site during its May 1989 annual national conference.

While the state of Missouri now owns the housebarn and the land it sits upon, it cannot be seen by the general public. Cindy Browne, site administrator of the Deutschheim State

das Tagebuch

My wife Sheryl and I renovated a 1910 brick house in the Fachwerk style from 1974 to 1988, a style which gave the house a great deal of its distinctive character. It's not an easy style to renovate, especially four stories above the city street, but that experience gave me some appreciation for what Wilhelm Pelster might have valued about his old housebarn.

Left: This photograph taken in 1983 shows the threshing floor and stairs that led up to bedrooms and a hayloft. Above: This detail of Fachwerk construction shows heavy timbers held with wooden pegs and marked with Roman numerals. Limestone nogging would have filled the spaces between the timbers.

Historic Site in Hermann, and others are working to preserve the housebarn, but the future of the Pelster Housebarn feels much less secure than its sturdy, traditional construction.

Our German Agricultural Heritage

Like the Pelster Housebarn, farmland and open space fill an important place in defining the special character of the German Heritage Corridor. However, that key piece of our cultural legacy can erode or even disappear. According to the American Farmland Trust, new development consumes around three thousand acres of productive farmland in the United States every day, forty acres per hour. Almost 60 percent of America's farmers are older than 55 years of age and likely to retire in the next two decades. So, like Pelster, we once again need to adapt.

First of all, the Pelster Housebarn and Missouri's German agricultural heritage need and deserve greater appreciation to encourage their preservation; living history offers one vital approach to foster that appreciation. Few of us, especially young Missourians, know and appreciate the great challenges that Missouri Germans faced in creating lives and livelihoods from the land itself. Even though living history farms cannot recreate and communicate the relentless daily demands of farm life, they offer one obvious way to preserve this heritage within the German Heritage Corridor.

For nearly forty years, Deutsche Country Days took place each October at the *Luxenhaus Farm* (loghouse farm) near Marthasville. The event was a living history festival celebrating early German farm life in Missouri. The farm consists of nearly twenty historic structures rescued from demolition throughout the German Heritage Corridor and then restored by original construction methods. During Deutsch Country Days, artists and artisans in period costumes demonstrated traditional techniques such as tin smithing and candle dipping. The Missouri Humanities Council is now partnering with the Luxenhaus Farm Foundation to preserve the unique site and build upon its living history programs. No festival was held in 2018, but a few classes were planned for 2019.

Education always represents a gamble, so Jim Dierberg and members of his staff at the Hermann Farm and Museum bet the farm. Dierberg's involvement in Hermann began in 1971, when his family-owned banking firm acquired a bank there. Three years later, he revived Hermannhof Winery. Deeply influenced by his visits to living history farms in Germany during the 1960s, Dierberg recognized the vital importance for stewardship of the unique landscape of central Missouri and the history layered upon it. Hermann Farm and Museum celebrates the

Hermann Farm

A SELF-GUIDED WALKING TOUR of a typical village of early settlers takes you though several buildings. A tram tour takes you through the two-hundred-acre farm, where you'll see the hills and valleys typical of farms in this area, the Shire draft horses, and a pair of white Missouri mules. Check before you go to see when the tram tours run by calling 573-486-3276 or visiting HermannFarm.com.

geh und erforsche!

importance of farming to Missouri's German heritage with a livestock farm, stables, wagon works, a forge, a heritage garden, and historic houses. Each season offers living history programs about how rural Missourians in the German Heritage Corridor lived, worked, and shaped the land. The farm features several kinds of livestock, including the massive and popular Shire draft horses. Hermann Farm and Museum offers a portal to the region's unique rural heritage but transcends nostalgia by promoting pride of place along with its strong land stewardship ethic.

Secondly, conservation of a landmark like the Pelster Housebarn and more broadly of our Missouri German agricultural heritage requires active planning. Farmland is not just empty space awaiting future development but a crucial economic and cultural resource for all of Missouri. The state of Missouri has the second-largest number of farms in the country behind only Texas. Not only do Missouri farms play a vital role in our economy, the farms along the Katy Trail help make the world-renowned Katy Trail such an inviting landscape, as well as an essential part of Missouri's important and growing tourism industry. Farmland and open space also help to address fundamental human needs for green space and parkland, described by Nobel Prize-winning biologist E. O. Wilson as "biophilia."

The Katy Land Trust, an organization dedicated to preserving the rural landscape between St. Charles and Jefferson City, assists landowners in designating all or part of their land for permanent forest, agricultural, or recreational usage. Through private and voluntary land protection, the Katy Land Trust helps to preserve lands in and around the Katy Trail. The Katy Land Trust works with local landowners to support their personal goals for their land and seeks community support in preserving the special character of its unique cultural region with its rich resources, history, and proud traditions.

> *Many operators of new farms work off-farm like Missouri's German farmers once did.*

The Peers Store

The Katy Land Trust has restored Peers Store, which now serves as somewhat of a headquarters for the trust. Formerly Glosemeyer's general store, Peers Store is located on the Katy Trail between Treloar and Marthasville; it reopened in 2015 and also serves as a gallery, featuring artists who have spent a lifetime painting and photographing the beauty of the Missouri River area. The artists include painters Bryan Haynes, Gary Lucy, Billyo O'Donnell, Julie Wiegand and photographer William (Bill) Fields. The Missouri Humanities Council, in partnership with the Katy Land Trust, is also planning public programming about Missouri's German Heritage Corridor at the Peers Store—maybe not exactly barn again, but certainly a new life for the Peers Store.

Like Wilhelm Pelster and his old housebarn, niche agriculture offers another adaptive approach to conserving the agricultural heritage of the German Heritage Corridor. Nearly 300,000 new farms have begun operations since 2002, according to recent Agricultural Census data. They are adapting to changing markets by filling local niche markets with specialty produce and value-added products. Compared with all farms nationwide, these new arrivals tend to have more diversified production, fewer acres, lower total-dollar sales, and operators who also work off-farm like Missouri's German farmers once did with their furniture, wagonmaking, or blacksmithing specialties. Interestingly, many of these new operations now take place in urban and suburban areas rather than remote locations.

Some Missouri farmers are adapting traditional agriculture by embracing this new agricultural model. For example, Slow Food St. Louis has made the Biodiversity Microgrant Program its priority. Recognizing the importance of small farms to local food production, the program has awarded more than $77,000 to more than fifty farmers since 2009, supporting cultivation of numerous heirloom varieties and heritage breeds. These grants fund projects submitted by small farmers and other food producers that reflect the Slow Food ideal of good, clean, and fairly priced food. They fund projects that result in healthy, delicious food produced in an environmentally conscious way and made accessible to the community at large. This sounds ideal for a diverse new breed of young agriculturalists, like Wilhelm Pelster, "traditional farmers with a creative spark."

Building, Dwelling, and Thinking

German philosopher Martin Heidegger argued that the modern world had forgotten the traditional relationship between building and dwelling. He looked at the origins of the German word *bauen* (to build) and claimed that it had lost its original meaning of "being" in a certain place. Heidegger said the way in which we dwell reveals our identity, who we really are.

"Building, dwelling, thinking" sounds like heavy conceptual lifting, until we look again at the Pelster Housebarn. With its handcrafted, half-timbered structure for early Missouri German farm life rooted in the very earth itself, the relationship of building and dwelling in Missouri's German cultural heritage finally falls into place. In Howard Marshall's elegant words, "The Pelster Housebarn is the embodiment … of the good fit between an artifact and the land that is so radiant a feature in traditional rural culture."

But does it still fit? Is the Pelster Housebarn a romantic relic, the site of future subdivisions and shopping centers, or does it contain the seeds of a renewed relationship between us and the natural world, especially agriculture? Since dwelling relates so closely to how we exist, our "being in the world," Heidegger maintained that dwellings should nurture things, both natural and human. Building, in other words, is not just a matter of real estate. Building as dwelling enables a person, family, or community to know our historical past, deeply experience the present, and anticipate a meaningful future—to help us feel at home in the world, like we really fit.

Katy Land Trust and Peers Store

FOUNDED BY Dan and Connie Burkhardt, the Katy Land Trust aims to help landowners preserve lands in and around the Katy Trail through private and voluntary land protections from St. Charles to Jefferson City. The trust raises funds to assist landowners in these measures. Find more information and several interesting videos about The Peers Store on the Katy Trail between Treloar and Marthasville at KatyLandTrust.org.

geh und erforsche!

Another Fine Mash

You don't really have to be an anthropologist to know that beer figures prominently in German culture. It is literally and figuratively steeped in tradition. Monks regarded it as "a gift from God" and devoted themselves to its perfection. Beer was considered much healthier than ordinary drinking water as Abbess Hildegard von Bingen pointed out in her scientific studies in AD 1150 to 1160 in Disibodenberg. The beloved beer stein originated as a hygenic measure during plagues to keep flying insects out of the beer. The German *Biergarten* grew out of 16th-century laws restricting when beer could be brewed. Passed in 1516, the still-operative German beer purity law called the *Rheinheitsgebot* mandates that beer may contain only water, barley, and hops. The *Auswanderung* brought these German bier traditions to Missouri along with their other family heirlooms.

Marc Houseman, Executive Director of the Washington, Missouri, Historical Society, smiles broadly when he tells visitors, "You may know about John B. Busch's younger brother Adolphus." Most Missourians already know about the world-famous Anheuser-Busch brewery in St. Louis, but very few know about the earlier, smaller Busch brewery located fifty miles west in Washington, Missouri. This other Busch brewery, also listed on the National Register of Historic Places but well off the beaten tourist path compared to its famous relative, actually reveals a much more typical story of Missouri's German beer heritage.

The John B. Busch Brewery, also known as the Washington Brewery, was established in 1854 or 1855 (historical records differ) by German immigrants John Baptiste Busch, Fred Gersie, and Henry Busch and continued in operation for nearly one hundred years. Prohibition ended beer production at the John B. Busch Brewery in 1918, but the brewery continued to manufacture ice, nonalcoholic or near beer (called Buscho), and soda water into the 1930s. After Prohibition was finally repealed in 1933, the brewery did not resume producing beer but bottled and distributed Budweiser beer until closing in 1954.

The John B. Busch Brewery in Washington, Missouri, was one of three breweries bearing the Busch name in Missouri, founded by brothers George, John B., and Adolphus. John B. was the second oldest son whereas Adolphus Busch, co-founder of Anheuser-Busch, was the next to last of the children by their father's first wife. John Baptiste Busch was born in Hesse/Darmstadt in the Rhineland area of Germany in 1832. Like thousands of other Auswanderung responding to unsettling social and economic forces in the early 19th century, he emigrated to the United States when he was seventeen years old and initially settled in St. Louis with its extensive social networks for recent German immigrants. There John B. learned the brewery business from his elder brother George, then a brewer at what was probably the first Busch Brewery on Plum Street in south St. Louis. John B. worked two years with George, then moved to Washington and established his own brewery.

The Culture of Beer

Perhaps John B. also learned about the importance of geography and climate from the dozens of 19th-century St. Louis breweries using the city's extensive cave system, like the Falstaff Brewery in north St. Louis. The John B. Busch Brewery is located at the base of the large hill on the south edge of Washington, near a spring along the spring-fed branch of DuBois Creek, now often referred to as Busch's Creek. It was built on Missouri River valley limestone and carved into the hillside. The larger west ice house is set into the hill, while the smaller east ice house is located at the top of the hill. Ice was important for the production of traditional,

The John B. Busch complex of brewery buildings had been serving as an event center for weddings, events, and such, but sold in 2018 and is closed for renovations. You can drive by the buildings at 108 Busch Avenue in Washington, Missouri.

John B. Busch House

THE JOHN B. BUSCH HOUSE was purchased about 1947 by the Washington VFW group. The VFW added a large auditorium hall to the rear of the house, and that hall can be rented. With advance notice, tours can also be arranged.

You can see the house at 813 Jefferson Street, in Washington, Missouri. Call 636-239-6311.

geh und erforsche!

cold-brewed German lager beer because it needs cold storage, especially in the summer. Later the Washington Brewery would create its own lagoon to serve its growing need for fresh water as well as to produce ice for refrigerating the beer.

In *Built in the U.S.A.*, architectural historian Dianne Newell notes that "the breweries of the Northeast and Midwest were frequently expressions of the German origins of their owners and workers." That certainly applies to the dozens of sturdy red-brick, Romanesque buildings at the Anheuser-Busch Brewery in St. Louis, which was built by Adolphus and which is on the National Register of Historic Places. That brewery features elaborate details like a chandelier cast in the form of a hops plant, but the smaller sibling brewery in Washington was equally decorated.

Although some of the original buildings of the John B. Busch Brewery in Washington have long been demolished, those that remain also express their German origins but on a much smaller scale. Their thick brick walls, stone foundations, and arched windows and door openings clearly indicate that these were early Missouri German buildings in Washington and the German Heritage Corridor.

The brewers as well as the breweries revealed that fundamental German heritage. Most of the men like the Busches, who would come to rule the brewing industry—and amass personal fortunes in doing so—rose from typically humble beginnings. One observer painted a less than romantic picture of early 19th-century German immigrant brewers:

The German artisan who founded the American beer industry was a kind of special cook with a trade recipe he had learned in Germany. He began by boiling beer in small quantities in family kettles or wash-boilers, and often, with his wife, retailed it to a German trade in a small saloon. The man and wife were typical Germans of the working class—industrious, frugal, honest, and rather unsophisticated. The old-time brewmaster worked in necessarily unclean underground cellars, full of the drip of great ice-houses overhead, and of quantities of carbonic acid gas, sufficient to smother small animals, below; with floors saturated with the organic matter of former brews, and slippery with the molds that grow under such conditions. In this place he tramped—a heavy figure in a slouch hat, course workman's clothes, and high leather boots. But for his special cook's knowledge of brewing, he dominated the brewing industry.

While his much more ambitious younger brother Adolphus aggressively pursued industrial expansion, the John B. Busch family in Washington operated in old German style by simply taking care of the local Washington community and surrounding Franklin County. The brewery's total output never exceeded ten thousand barrels a year, usually closer to six thousand. Houseman estimated that the Washington Brewery employed about two dozen workers at its peak at the turn of the 20th century, compared to the thousands employed at the Anheuser-Busch brewery in St. Louis. However, beer brewing sent working-class waves rippling throughout their communities to local farmers, teamsters, builders, and tavern owners.

For German immigrants like John B. Busch at the top of that pecking order, the Washington Brewery offered a great deal of social status. Particularly within German American urban settlements like Washington, German lager beer pulsed at the beating cultural heart of daily life for many German immigrants, and its makers took great pride in their craft tradition. Brewmasters commanded unmatched respect, while brewery owners and civic leaders like John B. Busch epitomized the success story of Missouri Germans. For example, the once

das Tagebuch

One of my grandfathers was a teamster in the early part of the 20th century, who, according to family lore, moved the brewery's precious cargo across city streets. I remember entire south St. Louis neighborhoods filled with brewery workers living near their massive workplace, as well as the pervasive aroma of brewing beer accenting a morning jog, as late as the mid-1970s.

Arsenal Street German Architecture

Arsenal Street in St. Louis provides many examples of untouched German architecture. It runs east-west from Broadway to the River Des Peres in the Lindenwood Park neighborhood. The street was named after the St. Louis Arsenal, a storage depot on the east end of the street.

geh und erforsche!

stately Busch mansion in Washington overlooks the brewery from the surrounding hillside. Like a good German *burgermeister* (mayor), John B. Busch founded the Bank of Washington and was deeply involved in his church, local Turnverein (German gymnastic society and occasional site of beer drinking), and not surprisingly, the town waterworks. John B. Busch Sr. died at age 62 in 1894 of congestive heart failure. At a *kraftigen* (hefty) 375 pounds, he did not drink beer, according to Houseman.

Over the years, the John B. Busch Brewery in Washington sold beer under many different brand names: Washington Lager Beer and Busch Beer in the early years, later Culmbacher and Busch's Pilsner. A May 1877 announcement in *Die Washingtoner Post* noted that the brewery was selling its usual bock beer. The Busch Beer name was used at the Washington brewery for many years before Prohibition. Major changes happened to beer brewing during the late 1800s as industrialization, and industrial innovators like Adolphus Busch, introduced mechanical refrigeration. John Baptiste's son, John B. Busch, moved back to Washington in 1894 to became company president. John B. Busch served as president during the Prohibition ordeal until his death in 1937, when Ulrich W. Busch Sr. took over.

The post-World War II years also caused huge changes in making beer. Major consolidation of the industry occurred; breweries like Anheuser-Busch got much bigger while smaller ones failed to compete. By the 1950s that growth, coupled with mass marketing to consumers, crushed small, regional brewers like the Washington Brewery. The John B. Busch Brewing Company closed in 1954, the same year Anheuser-Busch introduced its popular Busch Bavarian beer. Houseman recounted the brewery's final days:

> *On the day the plant closed for good … there were five employees who lost their jobs. Ulrich Busch Jr. had been at the helm for several years but his heart was never in the brewing business. He was schooled as an architect and kept plenty busy designing schools, commercial, and residential structures. The brewery, for him, was*

just an annoying sideline. It was a Friday afternoon, and as Busch and the five workers walked out that day, Busch turned to lock the door. As they started walking toward their respective vehicles, Busch simply said, "Well, today was your last day." And that, as they say, was that.

Topping the Heritage Off

In 2000 the John B. Busch Brewery was named to the National Register of Historic Places, but the key question for Missouri's German Heritage Corridor remains: What is the future of our Missouri German brewery heritage? Perhaps the answer lies in the continuing changes shaking up the brewing industry.

The 2008 sale of American brewing titan Anheuser-Busch to Belgian InBev concluded yet another wave of consolidation within the beer industry. InBev and its rival SABMiller, both products of mergers during the early part of the 21st century, have led intense global efforts to increase distribution channels. The rising cost of key beer ingredients like grain has also driven brewers to increase their scale and purchasing power. Unlike John B. Busch Sr., however, some contemporary brewers have mounted strong and innovative challenges to this increasing consolidation.

In 2008, when InBev purchased Anheuser-Busch for $52 billion, it ended the dominant role of the Busch family in the American beer business. But William K. (Billy) Busch, a great

Anheuser-Busch Brewery

LOCATED IN THE SOULARD neighborhood of St. Louis, the Anheuser-Busch Brewery offers tours. Opened in 1852, the brewery was ideally placed to take advantage of natural caves along the Mississippi River. These caves had the cool temperatures required to brew lager-style beers, introduced to St. Louis by German brewers. The site was also near a large German immigrant population, who could both work at the brewery and consume its products. A free, 45-minute tour explains the 7-Step Budweiser brewing process by taking visitors through the Beechwood Aging Cellars and Brewhouse. The Beer Museum Tour focuses on the company's history and architecture. Guests visit three buildings registered as National Historic Landmarks, including the Clydesdale Stables Brewhouse and the Old Lyon Schoolhouse.

geh und erforsche!

Urban Chestnut

URBAN CHESTNUT Brewing Company in St. Louis has a co-founder who grew up in Bavaria, where he apprenticed at a local brewery. Florian Kuplent spent time in Germany, England, New England, and finally at Anhueuser-Busch in St. Louis before helping launch Urban Chestnut in 2010. Kuplent points out that while Urban Chestnut doesn't focus exclusively on German-style beers, they are definitely part of the company's roots. On their beer tap handles are names such as Dorfbier, Oachkatzlschwoaf, and Stammtisch. The Urban Chestnut Brewing Company offers a free self-guided tour of the Grove Brewery and Bierhall. The tour takes visitors through the production process. You can also purchase a tasting with the self-guided tour, or you can book a free guided tour on Saturdays. Reservations are required because there are only twelve spots on the Saturday tours. The Urban Chestnut Bierhall is at 4465 Manchester Avenue, and the more traditional Biergarten is at 3229 Washington Avenue.

geh und erforsche!

das Tagebuch

Urban Chestnut opening a brewery in Germany is a textbook example of what Austin Loignon, one of my amazing colleagues in the Missouri Humanities Council Scholars symposium for the German Heritage Corridor initiative, refers to as intercultural transfer, this continuously evolving interchange of ideas, people, and products between Germany and Missouri.

grandson of Adolphus Busch, was not among the family members forced to agree in the takeover not to compete. He then partnered with a St. Louis investor and assembled a veteran management team, including former Anheuser-Busch executives, to found the William K. Busch Brewing Company and write the next chapter of the Busch family brewing legacy.

The William K. Busch Brewing Company clearly indicated from the outset of the venture that they are not a micro-brewery, but intend their Kraftig beer to compete directly with popular lagers like Budweiser, Coors, and Miller. Kraftig draws heavily upon its German brewing tradition and famous family name as competitive advantages. Unique heritage resources or connections like that might (or might not) also apply to historic sites in the German Heritage Corridor, such as the John B. Busch Brewery.

American beer culture may now even be influencing the venerable German beer tradition. Urban Chestnut Brewing in mid-town St. Louis taps into the rapidly growing craft brewing phenomenon centered in cities like Boston, Denver, Portland, Seattle, and St. Louis. These small-scale artisan and local breweries, often located in old abandoned industrial areas and sites, are experimenting with an incredibly wide range of styles and flavors not found in mass-produced lager beers like Budweiser.

While embracing the craft beer movement, Urban Chestnut also honors Old World brewing traditions symbolized by the chestnut, long associated with the German *Biergarten* and *Bierkeller*.

Another intercultural transfer is also taking place. In January 2015, Urban Chestnut opened its Urban Chestnut Hallertauer Brauerei of locally sourced Bavarian *Bier* in Brewmaster Florian Kuplent's homeland of Bavaria, within the world's largest hop-producing region. Just as Missouri and America transformed traditional German beer at the turn of the 20th century, new opportunities may be brewing for small-scale sites like the John B. Busch Brewery in Washington, Missouri. Maybe that sad day when Ulrich Busch Jr. locked the doors wasn't the end after all.

Lemp Brewery

JOHANN ADAM LEMP arrived in this country in 1836 and came to St. Louis in 1838, where he started a family grocery and sold vinegar and his popular lager recipe, which he brought with him from Eschwege, Germany. He then opened the Western Brewery, built above natural underground caves. Lemp died in 1862, and his son, William J. Lemp, took over operations and bought the property that would become the Lemp Brewery Complex in 1864. By the 1870s, Lemp's Western Brewery was the largest brewery in St. Louis in a field of thirty, with Anheuser & Company's Bavarian Brewery coming in second. During Prohibition, the brewery made a near-beer product known as Cerva, but it was unprofitable and the property was sold to a shoe company. Today, the historic Lemp Brewery Complex consists of twenty-nine buildings standing on more than thirteen acres, and tenants include artists, commercial offices, and industry.

geh und erforsche!

Schlafly Brewery

CALLING ITSELF "The Saint Louis Brewery," the maker of Schlafly Beer is Missouri's largest locally owned independent brewery. It brews more than sixty styles of fresh beer. The Schlafly Tap Room in midtown St. Louis opened in 1991 and was the first new brewpub to open in Missouri since Prohibition. It is housed in a restored wood and brick building on the National Register of Historic Places. You can take free tours of the Tap Room at 2100 Locust Street every Sunday and Schlafly Bottleworks at 7260 Southwest Avenue from noon to 5 PM every half hour on Fridays, Saturdays, and Sundays.

geh und erforsche!

das Tagebuch

Beer also became an essential part of my Missouri German heritage: sharing beer with friends while listening to Cardinals' baseball back in the 1980s after long, sweaty hours renovating old houses; watching the intense rivalry of the St. Louis Hawks against the Boston Celtics on our boxy black and white television set with my father while he slowly enjoyed Busch Bavarian beer after a long day's work; begging (or sneaking) a kinderbier from the adults staying up late on a Saturday night watching old movies like "Gaslight" on the Falstaff Circle Theater on television. Today's beer connoisseurs can spend hours passionately debating the relative merits of their favorite new discoveries. It's much more than the hops, you see.

This photograph taken with a glass negative is labeled, "Prof. George Husmann of the Ag Depart. in grapery." Husmann is on the right.

die Weinstrasse

A major photographic exhibit entitled *What Wondrous Life*, on display at Deutschheim State Historic Site's Feldman-Stark House, depicts the remarkable life story of Missouri German horticulturist and winemaker George Husmann. The exhibit follows his truly amazing life from Meyenburg, a village near the North Sea in the Kingdom of Hanover, Germany, to Hermann as a youth, through the course of his education and development as one of the true founders of the American wine industry. He even became and remains a national hero in France, no small feat for someone of German descent. As a cultural artifact, *What Wondrous Life* epitomizes the winding *Strasse* (road) to excellence that the Missouri wine industry followed through the German Heritage Corridor under the leadership of Husmann.

Husmann arrived with his family in 1839 at the age of eleven in a brand-new settlement in a frontier state that was then justifiably called the Far West. At age nineteen, he planted his first vineyard and strongly advocated for hardy native American grape varieties, including Norton's Virginia Seedling and Concord, throughout his distinguished horticultural career. His many career achievements include: his steadfast opposition to slavery, including military service in the Union Army and authoring Missouri's ordinance abolishing slavery; publishing articles, a magazine, and several classic books about all aspects of the wine industry; founding a wine cooperative in the village of Bluffton; helping to save the French vines and its wine industry from phylloxera, a devastating aphid; teaching horticulture and wine-making at the University of Missouri; playing a vital leadership role in developing the Napa Valley and California wine industries; and finally, bringing American wines to world-wide attention.

The Catalog

THE 32-PAGE CATALOG for *What Wondrous Life* showcases Missouri humanities. It includes an outstanding biography of George Husmann's life by winegrower, food writer, and Husmann scholar Linda Walker Stevens; a background article about German immigration to Missouri by the late Adolf E. Schroeder, a distinguished University of Missouri professor of Germanic Studies, which provides invaluable cultural context for Husmann's biography; marvelous archival photography of Husmann and Missouri German communities; and a valuable research bibliography of Husmann's voluminous writings about grapes and wine in a museum exhibit characterized by outstanding graphic design.

So why doesn't everyone in Missouri know about this wondrous life of Husmann? Like Missouri's German heritage in general, the story of Husmann and his beloved Missouri wine industry depicted in this museum exhibit suffered a phylloxera of forgetting in the 20th century that nearly destroyed this amazing heirloom of Missouri's cultural heritage, until we eventually found our way back to Missouri's *Weinstrasse*.

Roots

Missouri Germans like George Husmann provided the rootstock of our state's wine industry. Nostalgia caused these German immigrants to Missouri, like immigrants everywhere, to value and cultivate their heritage, which included a German wine-making heritage reaching far back through medieval cloisters to Roman settlements. In 1836, the German Settlement Society selected some land on the south bank of the Missouri River, west of St. Louis, and founded Hermann with the intention of establishing a new *Vaterland* (Fatherland) in America. To that end, the planners laid out the town of Hermann with some plots originally sold as wine plots. One of those idealistic young members of the German Settlement Society was Martin Husmann, George Husmann's father.

As a rural schoolmaster in Germany, Martin Husmann had been allotted a plot to garden and a field to cultivate, as well as a pasture and meadow to support his livestock. All of nature became a classroom for his studies. The family of Martin's wife Johanna counted Johann Wolfgang von Goethe as a close friend. Like his good friend Alexander von Humboldt, Goethe believed that everything in nature was connected. Not surprisingly, then, Goethe's nature poetry, his botanical interests, and fondness for wine from Franconia, a region in Germany, seem to

das Tagebuch

I had the opportunity and privilege of interviewing George Husmann expert Linda Walker Stevens at the "What Wondrous Life" exhibit during Deutschheim State Historic Site's 2018 Maifest celebration. Her knowledge of and devotion to the life and work of Husmann model the kind of interpretation many of us hope to have for the entire German Heritage Corridor. As a former California winegrower herself, she values and communicates the ongoing value of this unique heritage.

Mechanical grape harvesters bring in the crop in a Stone Hill Vineyard near Hermann.

have found connections through George's parents and their extended family to the aspiring young horticulturist.

Martin Husmann encouraged his children—he called his students his children, too—to accompany him on a daily ramble to view the changeable beauty and fitness of the earth's forms. Young George noted that "of the fruits then plentiful in the forest and prairie we had wild strawberries, black-eye raspberries, wild plums, huckleberries, the Virginia bird cherry, summer and winter grapes, and persimmons, many of them of very good quality." If ice prevented them from walking through the countryside, the Husmanns skated along the country trails.

Reflecting upon his life in an address to the Normal Institute in Columbia in 1880, Professor George Husmann happily recounted those family adventures exploring the natural world. Those precious meanderings with his father, he recalled, gave his soul an abiding love for the beauties of the earth "and a habit to look from nature up to nature's God."

Friedrich Muench—"Papa Muench" to early Missouri German immigrants who valued his leadership, including for winegrowing—considered Martin Husmann one of the first grape growers at Hermann. Only a year after the first Hermann settlers arrived in late fall 1837, Martin Husmann had remarked upon the challenges of traditional agriculture as well as the considerable potential for grape culture in the hilly Hermann region along the Missouri River. He thought that the wild grapes abundantly growing in the woods indicated favorable soil and climate for well-chosen species. George Husmann also documented that his father had championed winegrowing at Hermann from about 1841, promoting the local wine industry despite intense ridicule from some fellow residents.

In the spring of 1847, 19-year-old George Husmann obtained cuttings of Catawba and Isabella grapes from Cincinnati and planted a vineyard on the family farm. That same spring, Saxon immigrant Carl Teubner purchased two hundred acres, including a high bluff on the Missouri River. Teubner also brought eight thousand fruit trees and vines from Cincinnati, introducing the Herbemont grape to Missouri in the process. He formed what Husmann later termed "the nucleus of fruit growing and winemaking around Hermann" and initiated the first reliable nursery in the state.

These Missouri German pioneers showed great awareness and appreciation of the region's natural history and geography by intelligently adapting their ideals and wine heritage to the Far West territory of central Missouri, grafting the ideas and inspiration of Goethe and von Humboldt onto the New World.

The course of Husmann's life experienced considerable turbulence in the late 1840s. His mother had died on his thirteenth birthday, then a terrible accident claimed the life of his father when Husmann was nineteen. With no one left at the Husmann farm, he joined his sister Josephine under the roof of her new husband Teubner. George began working as an apprentice at Teubner's growing nursery business. Echoing his memory of nature walks with his father, he wrote that he "imbibed the love for all choice fruits, but especially for the noble grape, the finest of all, which has clung to me during good and bad fortune all my life."

Like many young Americans during the late

das Tagebuch

I still recall with awe a bouquet of wild grasses that my wife's father gathered for us in his fields where he raised grass-fed beef. He named each type of grass and described its characteristics and benefits for the animals. It was the most beautiful bouquet I had ever seen. Like George Husmann, I was also blessed with a wonderful mentor in how to explore the natural world. But educators now talk about "nature-deficit" disorder among children in books like "Last Child in the Woods."

1840s, young Husmann "lit out for the territories" and tried gold prospecting during the California Gold Rush. Perhaps he wanted to try his luck, change his luck, or simply escape bad memories. However, he rushed home when his beloved brother-in-law Carl Teubner suddenly died in a pandemic so typical of mid-19th-century frontier America.

Husmann cared devotedly for his widowed sister Josephine and her two young daughters while managing Teubner's growing nursery, including the grape vines, of course. When his sister Josie herself died during an 1854 cholera epidemic, Husmann quietly assumed guardianship of her children. After reviewing the challenges posed by the lack of experience among Hermann's eager but untrained winegrowers, Husmann educated himself in order to improve the craft of his fellow wine enthusiasts. His father had helped persuade his fellow Hermann citizens to grow grapes; now Husmann resolved to teach them how to turn those grapes into excellent wines. Throughout his career, Husmann always insisted his fellow vintners offer only the best possible wines to the marketplace, just as he gave his best to his family.

First Fruits

By the end of the 1840s, Hermann settlers were producing their first wine from locally cultivated grapes. By 1848 the town's wineries produced a thousand gallons, and by 1855 over five hundred acres of vineyards were in production. Wine from Hermann was now being shipped to St. Louis and beyond. Master baker Jacob Rommel recognized that the Norton's Virginia Seedling variety adapted well to the bio-region and began planting it commercially.

In 1847, German immigrant Michael Poeschel, a wool-spinner by trade, began building Stone Hill Winery. He is credited with holding the first winefest in Hermann in 1848. By the end of the 19th century, Stone Hill had become the second largest winery in the United States and the third largest winery in the world, with annual production exceeding a million gallons of wine. Its signature wines, such as Black Pearl, Hermannsberger, and Starkenberger, won eight gold medals between 1873 and 1904 at the highly competitive world's fairs of the period. (See page 44 for more about Stone Hill and Hermannhof wineries.)

Railroads extended the markets available to the young Missouri wine industry, but completion of the first transcontinental route in 1869 also made it possible to sell California wines in the eastern and midwestern United States.

Stone Hill Winery won gold medals at world fairs in the late 1800s. Prohibition closed it but it reopened as a winery in 1965.

California wines quickly became very popular throughout America because they more closely resembled traditional European wines. Nevertheless, Missouri's wine production trailed only California's until the onset of Prohibition.

Husmann served with distinction in the Union Army during the Civil War. At the onset of the war, both Husmann and his business partner Charles Manwaring left their highly profitable Hermann nurseries and joined the Union Army. In May of 1864, during a trip home to Hermann to visit his wife and young son, Manwaring, by-then Provost-Marshal for the Second District, was killed by Confederates while he was attempting to capture rebel bushwhackers on the Hermann wharf. He was buried at the cemetery near the graves of Charles and Josephine Teubner.

In October of 1864, General John Sappington Marmaduke's Confederate forces then camped on the Husmann farm, destroying thousands of fruit trees and vines on their march to Jefferson City. After the war, as a delegate to the State Constitutional Convention, the undaunted Husmann proudly drafted "An Ordinance Abolishing Slavery in Missouri."

In 1866 Husmann dedicated his first

By the end of the 19th century, Stone Hill had become the second largest winery in the United States and the third largest winery in the world.

Blumenhof Winery

LIKE STONE HILL WINERY and Hermannhof (on page 44), this winery deserves a special mention for its German heritage. Blumenhof means "Court of Flowers." The winery takes its name from the Blumenberg family's ancestral farm in northwestern Germany, and that German heritage is expressed in the winery's architecture. Three generations of the Blumenberg family have been involved in producing its wines, made from grapes grown in its own vineyards and from other nearby independent Missouri grape growers.

Blumenhof is in Dutzow, settled in 1834, which makes it the first German settlement west of the Mississippi. Dutzow is between Augusta and Marthasville on Highway 94, a scenic *weinstrasse* itself. While you can no longer visit the nearby original farms of Friedrich Muench or Gottfried Duden (see Chapter 3), you can absorb a bit of their culture here. The winery is open every day of the year except Thanksgiving, Christmas, and New Year's Day.

geh und erforsche!

book, *The Cultivation of the Native Grape, and Manufacture of American Wines* "to the grape growers of our country, one and indivisible, as their friend and fellow-laborer." He not only provided enormous technical detail on American grapes and the wine-making process itself, but also a careful cost-benefit analysis in what quickly became a standard reference book for American winegrowers. Like Walt Whitman in literature and James B. Eads, the builder of the bridge spanning the Mississippi River, Husmann also articulated a vision of a truly united United States:

> *I firmly believe that this continent is destined to be the greatest wine-producing country in the world. America will be, from the Atlantic to the Pacific, one smiling and happy Wineland, where each laborer shall sit under his own vine, and none will be too poor to enjoy the purest and most wholesome of all stimulants, good, cheap, native wine.*

In true Missouri German fashion, Husmann also emphasized that the southern states would need to free themselves from the continuing evils of slavery in order to achieve that vision. In 1869 he established *The American Grape Grower*, the only journal of its kind in the United States at that time, in order to further cultivate his vision of the American wine industry.

During the 1870s, Husmann and other Missouri wine experts shipped grape cuttings to France, Germany, and other countries

das Tagebuch

On my way to an interview in Washington, Missouri, I stopped for lunch at Blumenhof Winery on Highway 94 in historic Dutzow, the promised land of Gottfried Duden. A chance encounter with owner Mark Blumenberg beneath a canopy of grapevines revealed his deep appreciation of and care for the genius of the place, an unspoken homage to George Husmann that our visionary hero would surely have anticipated and appreciated.

devastated by the deadly phylloxera infestation. The Old World vines had zero resistance to this aphid, and French wine production dropped a catastrophic 75 percent. Husmann, by then a Professor of Agriculture at the University of Missouri, suggested French winegrowers graft their vines onto the phylloxera-resistant Missouri vines. By the winter of 1872, working with the St. Louis firm Bush and Sons and Meissner, he sent nearly 400,000 vine cuttings to Montpellier, France. Despite some initial French resistance to using American rootstock, *la défense* began and quickly took root.

Husmann noted in *American Grape Growing and Wine Making* that:

> *I put an exactly fitting graft of two eyes on the cuttings, having them first shortened for the uppermost knot, and winding around it, all along the graft-cut, a suitable twine. In this wise one can finish about 175 grafts in a day, sitting snugly at home. ... I have not heard any complaints from France.*

In fact, two monuments still stand in Montpellier, France, honoring Husmann and his colleagues credited with saving the French wine industry.

In 1879 Husmann was appointed the first Professor of Pomology and Superintendent of Forestry at the University of Missouri, where he established a nursery, orchards, and vineyards to advance viticultural knowledge. Just as his father had inspired his own studies of nature, Husmann's son and two daughters studied agriculture and horticulture there, too.

Like the blossoming career of gifted Husmann, Missouri German winemakers also assumed a leading role in the nation's wine industry by the end of the 1800s.

And the circle of life continues. According to

These two monuments in Montpellier, France, still honor George Husmann and other Missouri grape growers for helping save the French wine industry.

George Husmann's gravestone at Tulocay Cemetery in Napa Valley, California, honors him as both a pioneer and a promoter of American viticulture.

Elbert Pirtle of Pirtle Wineries:

> *A few amateur viticulturists in France and Germany decided that grafting might not be necessary if they could cross their vines with ours and get what they called "direct producers." … In the early 1930s, some of the resulting vines were imported into the United States. It was discovered that their American blood had given them the winter hardiness needed for Eastern and Midwestern winters. So now, in Missouri, a region that has the summer climate and soils equal to the best winegrowing regions in Europe, we now have the vines for good wines. After nearly one hundred years, the French have unwittingly repaid us.*

Prohibition

However, two World Wars and especially Prohibition undermined that world leadership role and nearly destroyed Missouri's German wine heritage. Before the 18th Amendment and Volstead Act prohibited the manufacture and sale of alcohol in the United States, nearly fifty Missouri counties boasted wineries. Missouri's *Weinstrasse* region along the Missouri River had grown to include more than one hundred wineries before being abruptly ended in 1920. This amendment, animated by anger toward America's German immigrants, crushed some families, local economies, and Missouri's entire wine industry. Owner Ottmar Stark of Stone Hill Winery ordered all of his vineyards destroyed in the town where the Husmanns had worked so hard to bring them to life.

In Missouri, only St. Stanislaus Novitiate (Society of Jesus) in Florissant survived Prohibition and continued to make sacramental wine. Following repeal of Prohibition in 1934, a few wineries did reopen, but many Missouri counties remained legally dry. High liquor taxes and license fees discouraged the industry's rebirth. Missouri's wine industry lived only in memory, and then just barely so.

Once vines were torn up because of Prohibition, owners converted the land to other crops and even nonagricultural uses. After Prohibition ended, vineyards couldn't easily be returned to grape production. As Husmann made abundantly clear to anyone who would listen, quality wine requires grapes that need specialized conditions and care to create decent wines, as well as several years to start producing in sufficient quantity and quality. Vineyards throughout Missouri and all across America that once produced a wide variety of grapes and wines lost their pride of place in agriculture, and Husmann's vision receded back to the 19th century.

Late harvest

Brett Dufur, author of *Exploring Missouri's Wine Country*, noted one ironic result of Prohibition's ill-fated public policy:

In fact, the survival of many historic buildings in Hermann is largely attributed to the economic downturn caused by Prohibition. Instead of destroying older homes and building new ones, the old buildings were continually lived in and kept up, which allows us to appreciate early German construction even today.

And it was not just the historic buildings that found new economic and cultural life. Toward the end of the 1900s, the rediscovery of Missouri's German wine heritage by producers and wine enthusiasts helped catalyze a renewal of the Missouri wine industry.

Winegrower, food writer, and Husmann scholar Linda Walker Stevens recounts the status of wine pioneer Husmann in Hermann when she first undertook her *What Wondrous Life* research:

When I moved [mid-1980s] from Napa Valley to Husmann's former Missouri hometown, the small German wine village of Hermann, I expected to learn a lot about George Husmann. … I quickly realized the truth of the old folk wisdom that says no one can be a hero in his hometown: Hermanners knew less about their former fellow citizen than did wine enthusiasts elsewhere. Fortunately, however, my research—begun in 1986—yielded a treasure trove of previously untapped material. Gradually, George Husmann grew as real and as known to me as any of my living neighbors.

The region once known as Deutschheim received the first certification by the US government as a distinct American Viticultural Area (AVA). This certification recognizes the qualities of soil, climate, and other unique characteristics that help create identifiable wines. The Augusta AVA, on the north side of the Missouri River in southwestern St. Charles County, was recognized in June 1980, eight months before Napa Valley, California's first AVA. The Hermann AVA, on the south side of the river, chiefly in Gasconade County, was designated by the federal government in 1983. Missouri itself now features over 1,700 acres of grapes and more than 130 wineries, a major Missouri industry on its way to "a smiling and happy Wineland."

George Husmann showed grapes to E.T. Meredith, right, who later served as Secretary of Agriculture for President Woodrow Wilson. Husmann spent his career developing American wine.

"However, grapes and vineyards are often overlooked when people consider what [agricultural] commodities are produced within the state," said Jim Anderson, Executive Director of Missouri Wine and Grape Board. "Vineyards and wineries are unique, in that unlike many other traditional farms, they are able to more directly connect their end product to consumers."

Anderson noted that the grape and wine industry's economic impact shows up in areas of Missouri that most other agricultural industries do not immediately and visibly affect. "The Division of Tourism advertises wineries in many television markets because of their appeal to the same demographic group that tends to travel the most," Anderson said. "When wineries are built, bed-and-breakfasts, restaurants, motels, craft shops, and other tourist attractions soon follow. As the industry matures, these clusters of tourism are developing statewide."

As the Missouri Humanities Council has anticipated with the German Heritage Corridor initiative, wineries are key cultivars in the new Experience Economy taking root in Missouri.

Also, according to Anderson, research about wine grapes reduces production costs and increases the market value of both grapes and wine, thereby increasing grape production in a kind of virtuous cycle. "New grape varieties that produce high-quality wines will likewise augment production and sales," he said. "These efforts will promote a long-term increase in industry profits and boost national recognition of Missouri vineyards and wineries."

Husmann's inspired teaching about nature and the noble grape hasn't really ended. Dean Volenberg of the University of Missouri Grape and Wine Institute said growing Missouri's wine industry involves expertise in many dimensions. As the Viticulture and Winery Operations Extension Specialist, Volenberg helps growers solve problems, as Husmann did. Research specialists at the Institute include enology research leader Misha Kwansiewski, whose work primarily involves characteristics of grapes that affect the quality and taste of wine.

Research collaboration also includes Saint Louis University and Missouri State University. A $4.6 million grant to Saint Louis University from the National Science Foundation is helping researchers understand how the root systems of grapevines affect the vine's stems, leaves, and fruits. Meanwhile, Missouri State University's viticulture program produces and bottles wine from grapes grown at the Missouri State Fruit Experiment Station.

Volenberg said new grape cultivars help continually revitalize Missouri's wine industry. Missouri can exhibit extreme weather such as hot, humid summers and freezing winters, so winegrowers depend upon finding resilient cultivars. If cultivars are identified, they are grown in experimental patches, observed, researched, and evaluated to determine if they yield quality wine that meets high standards.

Besides the normal challenges of growing grapes like the venerable Norton in the humid Missouri River valley bio-region, when Missouri winegrowers plant new cultivars, there is little traditional knowledge upon which to rely. Each of these diverse species exhibits unique growth patterns, specific windows for ripening and harvesting, physical characteristics, and distinctive flavors. For example, Stone Hill Winery in Hermann is growing grapes specifically chosen for them. "All grape varieties are chosen to perform well in our climate, on our specific farms, and on our soil types," said Nick Pehle, vineyard manager.

The always challenging and often extreme weather found here in the heart of the country poses the biggest challenge. "Our biggest way to overcome frost and cold weather is site selection," Pehle adds. "All of our farms are above nine hundred feet in elevation and are on well-drained slopes and mostly irrigated." It is a reign of terroir, if you will, of cooperating with and coaxing what the Romans called the genius of the place. Such awareness and sensitivity sustains the wondrous life of Missouri wine.

That cultural lesson still remains at the heart, still beating erratically, of die Schone Seele *(the beautiful soul) of the landscape throughout the German Heritage Corridor.*

Trace elements

All wine essentially and ultimately comes from the earth. As Husmann learned throughout his *Bildungsroman* (education) from wide-eyed child explorer to international wine expert and legend, you can spend a lifetime learning about soil types and how they impact grape growing and the flavor of the wine produced. In fact, that's what wine experts—vintners, importers, master sommeliers, and even writers—have to do, because soil type is the fundamental, but not the only, element of the genius of the place. The most amazing thing about soil, relative to wine-making, is how much variation exists within a single region. A single vineyard can vary significantly from its neighbors, and even one single parcel can vary widely from the bottom of the slope to the top.

It can therefore be a humbling experience for winegrowers to partner with rather than overpower the land. The term "humility" comes from the Latin word *humilitas*, a noun related to the adjective *humilis*, which is sometimes translated as "humble," but also as "grounded," or "from the earth," since it derives from the word *humus*, or earth. George Husmann absorbed that lesson in humility at a very early age from his parents, then passed it on to everyone interested in wine who was willing to listen. That cultural lesson still remains at the heart, still beating erratically, of *die Schone Seele* (the beautiful soul) of the landscape throughout the German Heritage Corridor.

Like the wondrous life of Missouri German wine pioneer Husmann now celebrated at Deutschheim State Historic Site, Missouri's German wine heritage once again represents a highly valued cultural resource that raises the quality of our Missouri life. The more seriously winemakers, sommeliers, connoisseurs, and consumers understand and appreciate the natural and cultural heritage of Missouri wines, the better these wines will taste. The best vintners and sommeliers insist that they can taste trace elements from the soil of the grapes in the flavors of the wine. At its best and our best, then, you can still savor the wondrous life of Husmann in a glass of Missouri wine.

The Deutschheim Historic Site in Hermann shows how ordinary Missouri Germans lived in the 1800s.

THE ENCHANTMENT OF EVERYDAY LIFE

Alltagskultur

die Deutsche Kuche

Grow your own organic food. Eliminate chemicals on your plants and produce. Waste nothing, especially water. Eat foods grown locally.

Today, many people, especially those of younger generations, have become "foodies," embracing all or most of the above principles. This trend holds tremendous implications for thoughtful place-making and for Missouri's German heritage.

A *Huffington Post* blog dealing with the highly popular local food movement in America on June 5, 2015, called kitchen gardens the latest, must-have kitchen tool. Today's foodies could learn a lot from the kitchen gardens of German immigrants. They drew deeply upon their unique cultural heritage both as a matter of survival but also to add interesting variety to their everyday diets. And today, anyone can visit an authentic kitchen garden at Deutschheim State Historic Site in Hermann.

Although the four-square garden there illustrates many of the historic German foodways that washed up in Missouri during the wave of trans-Atlantic German immigration that took place during the 19th century, the basic principles and practices still hold value for people interested in the local food movement or simply in good food and gardening.

A Restored Garden

The four-square garden, long buried and forgotten for decades, has been identified, excavated, and restored to a highly productive working garden, and it is now used extensively as an entertaining and interpretive tool about 19th-century Missouri German culture. The Deutschheim gardens are open daily, 10 AM to 4 PM, April through October.

The rectangular garden plot is subdivided into equal sections by wide paths that cross in the middle, just as they were in Germany dating back to the Roman occupation and medieval monasteries. Heirloom varieties like those used by German immigrants grace the carefully tended plots of Deutschheim's four-squares. Here you will find flowers such as harlequin marigolds or sweet alyssum planted among the garden vegetables; the flowers offer both beauty and practicality. Studies have shown marigolds discourage nematodes, for example, and sweet alyssum provides nectar for hoverflies, which feed on aphids.

The four-square demonstration garden often features a site interpreter dressed in period costume and assuming the identity of a historical figure while answering visitor questions; Hermann's popular annual June garden tour typically features the site as well. If your timing is particularly good, the dulcet tones of a hammered dulcimer or other period instrument might lure you to the four-square demonstration garden. Whatever attracts you there, it's definitely worth finding your way to this highly significant Missouri German artifact.

The Four-Square Garden

A cultural artifact like the Deutschheim four-square garden interprets Missouri's German heritage in its own uniquely valuable way, through historical archaeology, which studies the material remains of past societies such as the German immigrants to discover everyday life in the recent past. Historical archaeology adds to other historical evidence they left behind, such as archival records.

Unlike classical archaeology (think *Raiders of the Lost Ark*) conducted on legendary sites of antiquity, such as lost Troy that lay buried under layers and millenia of desert sands, historical archaeology like the reconstructed Deutschheim four-square garden represents one valuable part of a much larger mosaic of artifacts depicting Missouri's 19th-century German heritage. For example, public records clearly indicate that German immigrants settling in Hermann

Hermann Garden Tours

ON THE FIRST FULL WEEKEND of June, the Hermann Garden Club sponsors annual garden tours to help raise money for scholarships and beautification projects in Hermann. The tour usually includes a walking tour of gardens in downtown Hermann and a driving tour to several country gardens. The tour may include some public but also several private gardens, both cottage gardens and river-view gardens. This active garden club has been sponsoring tours since 1995. For more information, vist HermannGardenTours.com.

geh und erforsche!

The Deutschheim Historic Site

preferred property lines with long plots of land and homes that fronted public sidewalks with gardens behind the homes. These long plots behind the homes, typically about 60 by 120 feet, were large enough to accommodate cisterns, generous gardens, and even small livestock. The Deutschheim State Historic Site's 1840 Pommer-Gentner House is a perfect example of the home fronting public sidewalks with the gardens behind.

Private records such as letters, journals, and cookbooks provide first-hand accounts of German food traditions, as well. The autobiography of Henriette (Jette) Giesberg Bruns, *Hold Dear, As Always, Jette, A German Immigrant Life in Letters,* edited by Adolf E. Schroeder, University of Missouri Press, is one record. She lived in Westphalia, then Jefferson City and St. Louis in Missouri, but in her letters, she recalls the family house on Neubrucken Street in Oelde, Germany in the early 1800s:

To the left in front of the windows of the living room there was a little garden with dwarf fruit trees and strawberries. Straight ahead you came to the bridge over the Aa and only then came the big garden, which covered the space along the water for the length of four of the houses on the street. There were magnificent high fruit trees bordering it. And to the left, in the rear, were shrubs down to Dr. Roer's garden, high bushes, hedges, winding and sand-covered paths, then currant bushes in long rows, and several arbors with stone tables.

There were beds of asparagus and vegetables surrounded by the flowers. To the right there was a little gate in the hedge leading out to the promenade and the city. This was used only by the two uncles, but almost every day, so that Uncle Bernhard should not always be alone.

Small, personal artifacts also tell the story. Wooden garden shoes on display at Deutschheim State Historic Site were used for mucking around Missouri mud.

Historical archaeology, archival records, and personal artifacts at the restored four-square demonstration garden help create a much more fully developed picture of Missouri German immigrant "foodways" for visitors.

'Foodways'

When you think of a holiday, do you recall certain special foods? Most of us still fondly recall celebrations with revered (or possibly reviled) food traditions like anise-flavored springerle cookies, with their elaborate designs that were only prepared around Christmastime. Special foods like the springerle cookie can imaginatively connect us to a cultural heritage handed down across generations. It's also an especially satisfying branch of the humanities.

However, foodways, the eating habits and culinary practices of a people, region, or historical period, extend well beyond those special holiday traditions.

For anthropologists, all the activities associated with food in our daily lives make up our foodways. They include customs involving the production and preparation of food, its buying and selling, even folklore about food. Foodways

A guide at the Deutschheim Historic Site in Hermann explains how the four-square garden worked.

connect people to a geographic region, a climate (think Mediterranean cuisine), a time period, or ethnic or religious groups. Like historical archaeology, foodways help anthropologists and scholars from other social sciences understand past cultures like Missouri's German heritage.

New foodways, such as the renewed interest in canning and preserving or the growing popularity of farmers markets, are being created or revived all the time. Vintage cooking tools, such as a ceramic mixing bowl, and cookbooks offer additional insights into the foodways of these cultural groups. Considering foodways can increase awareness and appreciation for the role and importance that food still plays in our lives, holding up yet another important anthropological mirror for humans.

Missouri German Cuisine

Now available in a fiftieth-anniversary edition, *The German Cookbook* by renowned *The New York Times* food writer Mimi Sheraton is widely considered to be the definitive authority on German cuisine. What better mirror, then, to begin reflecting upon Missouri German foodways? As Sheraton writes, "The German motto *"gut Essen, gut Trinken,"* (good eating, good drinking) belongs on the national coat of arms, along with the before-meal wish, *Gesegnete Mahlzeit* (blessed be your meal). *The German Cookbook* offers some serious food for thought (or vice versa).

At the outset of *The German Cookbook*, the author notes few countries in Europe have more varied or beautiful landscapes than those of Germany, ranging across virtually every kind of temperate zone terrain. Missouri also falls in the so-called temperate zone, although the term clearly masks our extreme summers and winters. Like its art, architecture, dialects, and customs, German cuisine relates to its cultural regions and its surrounding countries, such as France, Denmark, central Europe, and Italy. Very often the names of the same dishes will vary according to regions and dialects, such as German potato pancakes or Swiss rosti.

das Tagebuch

Some of the church cookbooks from congregations throughout the German Heritage Corridor are legendary. Only the most naïve anthropologist would risk highlighting one church cookbook and not the others.

Missouri Germans planted cabbage in their four-square gardens, but they usually also planted larger plots or even entire fields of cabbages elsewhere.

Longstanding German traditions of trade and travel dating back to the Middle Ages have also contributed to the variety of its cuisine. German immigrants to Missouri, who founded towns like Frankfort, Hamburg, Munichburg, Rhineland, Swiss, Vienna, and Westphalia, brought their appealing regional varieties of foodways with them to their New World settlements and to their kitchen gardens.

In her series *The Historical Gardener*, former Deutschheim State Historic Site Administrator Erin McCawley Renn identified and examined another important German foodway those *Auswanderung* brought to Missouri: the practical gardens that abounded in Germany. As one venerable German gardening adage wryly noted, "Prayer and manure will not be in vain; manure will help for sure." Just as they were in Germany, "the garden was right outside the house door if possible, with the house forming a fourth side of the fencing which protected the plantings." Kitchen gardens like the four-square garden were also called *Nutzgarden* (useful gardens), indicating their vital household function.

Middle class gardens shared this attitude of usefulness. In this respect they distinctly differ from the English middle-class model of the cottage (or cutting) garden primarily as a beauty spot. The further down the economic ladder one goes, the more yard space served utilitarian purposes.

Renn also noted that in a country like Germany where certain cherished foods could only be obtained during certain, limited seasons, traditions evolved with the annual natural cycle when foods taste their best. For example, Germans treasure their cherry trees, their strawberry beds, and asparagus patches. Even upper-class Germans wanted their own fruit trees and berry bushes scattered around the lawn. For everything there was a season.

The Menu

We still typically think of German food as rich and hearty fare emphasizing meat and potatoes —and sweets—even though the dishes can be defined by different regional styles. The growing season in Germany limited crop production to grains such as wheat and barley, although oats and rye eventually were added as staple grains. Herbs such as parsley, celery, and dill were used and are still featured in German cuisine. The combination of sweet and sour flavors, such as vinegar, sugar, and fruits, popular in its sauces since medieval times, also characterizes German food. Sheep, cows, and goats provided cheese,

milk, and butter. Smoking and salting meat preserved food, a continuing practice easily evident in the thousand plus varieties of German sausages available today. Preserving the harvest was essential to cuisine and to survival itself on the isolated Missouri frontier. The four-square garden played an important culinary role within those foodways.

At the simplest level, the garden or other green spaces provided key herbs for preparing German foods. In Germany, Maiwein (a spring tonic) is served in conjunction with Maifest. It combines dry white Riesling wine, sometimes fruit, and Waldmeister (an herb known in America as sweet woodruff). Although *Waldmeister* grows wild in German forests, as do other culinary and medicinal herbs, it could also be cultivated in the kitchen garden, as it is at the four-square garden at the historic site.

In addition to culinary herbs, the four-square garden went "green" long before that became trendy. Despite their rather starchy reputations, Germans and Missouri Germans actually loved spring greens and early summer vegetables. Many regions of Germany would feature cooked mixed greens during Easter week, almost like offering the first fruits (or greens) of the season. The Spring 1996 issue of *Der Maibaum* (The Maypole) had a recipe for cooked mixed greens that illustrates that practice, as well as the Missouri German foodway of not wasting anything in the garden.

Gather about 2 pounds of tasty greens, such as purslane, watercress, parsley, dill, sorrel, Guter Heinrich [Good Henry, a wild spinach], and tender young dandelion leaves. Wash them thoroughly, then finely chop the greens. Sauté a diced onion until it looks transparent and then add the cooked onion to the warm greens. Season to taste with salt, pepper, and a pinch of sugar, then add 4 to 5 tbs. of crème fraîche or sour cream to the mixture and toss the greens. Serve the cooked mixed greens with new potatoes and pork chops or hard-boiled eggs and crusty bread.

Throughout history, pickling was essential for preserving food during cold German (or Missouri) winter months. The word "pickle" comes from the Dutch *pekel* or northern German Pökel (salt or brine), an important component in the pickling process. Immersing fresh fruits or vegetables in an acidic liquid or saltwater brine until they are no longer raw or vulnerable to spoilage is fundamental to pickling. When

The Magic Chef Mansion

CHARLES STOCKSTROM was a German who came to St. Louis in 1880 and made his fortune in the Quick Meal Stove Company, which was later renamed Magic Chef. This company was the largest stove maker in the world at one time, employing two thousand people. The mansion, completed in 1908 by architect Ernst Janssen, was modeled after the Schloss castle in Schwerin, Germany. The exterior reflects French Renaissance, while the interior is more German. Stockstrom died at age 83 in 1935, but his daughter, Adda Ohmeyer, lived there until her death in 1990. The mansion is open for tours, and private group tours may be arranged. Some of the original furnishings have been returned to the home. Call 314-664-3400 or visit magicchefmansion.com/tours.

geh und erforsche!

das Tagebuch

I had the pleasure of sampling Maiwein punch at the fortieth anniversary celebration of the Deutschheim Verein, which is a support group for the Deutschheim State Historic Site. Linda Walker Stevens, creator of an important exhibit about Missouri wine producer George Husmann, prepared this traditional spring tonic for the adult visitors to the site.

Special events at the Deutschheim Historic Site demonstrate the Missouri Germans' self-reliant life, including growing their own herbs, like the rosemary below, and making their own baskets.

we think of pickles, cucumbers—another mainstay of the four-square garden—most commonly come to mind. Missouri German cooks would often make cucumber pickles from the kitchen garden with a salt and vinegar brine. Microbial organisms develop during the pickling process, which turn the naturally occurring sugars of foods into lactic acid. In turn, the liquid quickly becomes acidic, making it impossible for any spoiling bacteria to multiply—very *gut* for the gut. Garden herbs like dill and mustard add flavor and interest.

Germans of all social classes loved fresh fruit. In the early 19th century, Missouri German families grew many fruit trees in their kitchen gardens from seed. Besides fresh fruit for immediate eating or prepared as pies and fruit cobbler, fruit from the garden could also be used to flavor the ever-present vinegar.

They also customized the flavor of vinegar with herbs and spices cultivated in the garden. Vinegar results from bacteria fermenting alcohol to produce acetic acid. The vinegar can be created from any number of sources, such as apple cider, beer, honey and water, whiskey and water, or vegetable juice. Homemade vinegar could then be used in that essential pickling process. Many people believed homemade vinegar tasted better than bottles purchased from a store, if a store was even available during that early historical period of Missouri life.

Root crops such as potatoes, turnips, carrots, and especially cabbage were also important household crops, although the four-square garden might contain only small amounts of those vegetables. The bulk of the household's root crops might be cultivated in farm fields located at another site. Archival photos of 19th-century Hermann actually show vacant lots planted entirely to cabbage. The general rule of thumb was to provide one hundred head of cabbages per person annually as a winter food allowance. A sturdy root cellar often supplemented the four-square garden.

How did they cook all those root vegetables from the garden and beyond? Here's a traditional recipe for potato pancakes from the August 1993 issue of *Der Maibaum*:

Scrub about 2 pounds of potatoes, peel and boil until cooked. Rice or mash the potatoes, then let them cool to room temperature. Beat 4 eggs thoroughly, add 3 tablespoons thick sour cream and stir into the potatoes. Sprinkle with about 2 tablespoons of flour and blend in thoroughly to the potatoes. Dice 1 or 2 onions to add to the potato mixture. Heat a small amount of fat in a cast-iron skillet until a drop of batter sizzles on contact, then fry dollops of the batter until brown and crispy. Top and serve with applesauce.

A Swiss variation called rosti not surprisingly adds grated cheese to the potato mixture.

Erin Renn concluded that the list of items grown in a "useful" garden like the Deutschheim four-square garden included much else:

Rhubarb, onions, leeks, garlic, chives, shallots, white cabbage, red cabbage, kohlrabi, kale, broccoli, peas to be eaten fresh and to be dried for winter soups, runner beans, sorrel, cresses, various lettuces, radishes, brussel sprouts,

Certain flowers were often planted with the kitchen garden, as they seemed to repel some pests.

celery, celeriac, and tomatoes.

And there you have the four-square garden: varied and practical, just the cultural reflections you might expect to find there.

Lessons from the Garden

Renn concludes her series in *The Historical Gardener* with this statement:

> *Anyone familiar with current organic or "green" gardening practices will recognize the wisdom of the German gardeners of the 19th century. We are rediscovering the value of heritage seeds, locally produced food, organic fertilizers, companion plantings for pest control, and the value of naturally enriched soil from crop rotation and composting. The collection of rainfall in rain barrels for our gardens follows the tradition of cisterns so essential to the survival of the settlers in 1840. The value of these long lost traditions has been recognized, and "useful" gardens are again the source of both good health and pleasant recreation.*

They can be, if we are willing to converse once again with our Missouri German heritage through key cultural artifacts such as the Deutschheim four-square garden. For example, paths of mulch or brick separate the planting squares of the garden to make it much easier for a conscientious gardener in his or her wooden shoes to weed and harvest the varied crops without compressing the all-important and constantly enriched soil.

Missouri Germans rotated their crops each year from one plot to the next in order to disrupt or break pest cycles and to enhance the fertility of the soil by restoring vital nutrients depleted by certain crops. They employed companion plantings to bolster each individual plant and as a form of organic pest control; planting one crop after another in succession also kept the garden fully productive and "useful" in their way of thinking. Recalling cisterns, many local gardeners now collect rainwater in wooden or recycled plastic rain barrels. Early Missouri Germans did not waste that precious natural resource on chemically treated lawns.

However, many visitors to the four-square garden may wonder: "Why keep digging around in the past?" Deutschheim State Historic Site Administrator Cynthia (Cindy) Browne, a key participant in the Missouri Humanities Council German Heritage Corridor initiative, replies, "So much of today's organic methods are very old traditions that were abandoned in the 20th century." Those old traditions remain alive and well at the four-square garden.

Browne notes the critical importance of German foodways in Missouri to both their physical and cultural survival back in the 19th-century Far West. Pickling and preserving produce helped them survive life-threatening winters, not just dinner parties. Equally important but especially for us, those German food customs and traditions enriched and transformed American culture in the process. The hipness of the four-square garden today suggests that the process hasn't really finished and there might be new life in this heirloom.

Gesegnete Mahlzeit (Blessed be your meal)!

Authentic German Eats

Photo Credits: G&W Sausage Company, the Bavarian Smoke Haus, Hermann Wurst Haus, Gus' Pretzels, and the Vintage Restaurant.

THE BAVARIAN SMOKE HAUS in New Melle opened in 1996. Owners Jim and Karen Joerling have perfected a number of bratwursts and other specialty and smoked meats. It's a genuine German meat shop, offering German-style sausage, smoked pork or poultry, and different bacons and smoked hams.

THE FEASTING FOX HISTORIC RESTAURANT, PUB, AND BANQUET CENTER promises German fare, German drink, and German fun. Anheuser-Busch built the Bavarian-style Busch Gretchen Inn at South Grand and Meramec Street in St. Louis in 1913. It was built before Prohibition because Adolphus Busch wanted to show that beer could be served in a respectable family establishment. Anheuser-Busch continued to operate the Inn and Bevo Mill during Prohibition. But after the repeal of Prohibition, breweries could not operate a drinking establishment. So it was leased and operated by various people over the years, suffering a fire in 1968 but being refurbished. It sat vacant from 1986 until 1993, and Anheuser-Busch was preparing to sell the property when the Dutchtown South Neighborhood Association began a successful campaign to save the landmark. Today, you can dine on authentic German food in the traditional restaurant and pub or enjoy a traditional big German party in two on-site event facilities that maintain the historic charm of the main floor. Try the Weiner, Holsteiner, Jaeger, or Huhn schnitzels, or perhaps Hackbraten, sauerbraten, or Black Forest sweet and sour pork. For dessert, there's apple strudel, Black Forest torte, or what else, German chocolate cake. The Feasting Fox is at 4200 South Grand.

G&W SAUSAGE COMPANY in St. Louis is another real deal. Run by two cousins, Bob and Gerhard Wanninger, they are descendants of two brothers who emigrated from Regensburg, Germany, to St. Louis in 1965. These two brothers were sons of a second generation German sausage meister in Bavaria. They used the family's secret recipe for Bavarian-style sausage and served immigrants in the German-influenced South St. Louis neighborhoods. Their products are sold in their own store, at many St. Louis restaurants, and at many grocery stores. They make thirty different kinds of Bavarian-style sausage. Try the Landjager beef stick, a local favorite.

GUS' PRETZELS is a family-owned business that has been using the same recipe and twisting each

pretzel by hand since 1920. You can view the entire pretzel-making process in a viewing area. Pretzel bakeries could be found throughout St. Louis's strong German communities in the early 1900s. One of these pretzel bakers was Frank Ramsperger, who had been a riveter until he was injured and started baking pretzels to support his family. When his daughter Marcella married, her husband saw the potential and bought the business in 1952, naming it Gus' Pretzel Shop. The pretzels are still sold at the shop and in grocery stores. The shop is at 1820 Arsenal Street.

HERMANN WURST HAUS not only offers forty-seven kinds of bratwurst and German sausages, but it also will teach you how to make sausage and bacon in classes. The Wurst House has a market and deli, so you can sample flavors, enjoy a deli lunch or early dinner, and then shop for home. The market sells other Missouri-made products and sausage-making supplies. The business also offers catering and custom butchering and processing of beef, lamb, and pork, as well as offering several deer sausage processing options. Owner Mike Sloan has been in the meat processing business for forty years, first working with his parents at their meat processing plant in Swiss, Missouri. He ventured on his own in 2011 and throughout his career has won more than four hundred state, regional, national, and international awards for his sausages.

SCHNEITHORST'S HOFAMBURG INN in Ladue likes to tell *die Geschichte*, or its story. The present-day Schneithorst's made its way to Lindbergh and Clayton Roads in 1956. But the story really starts in 1917, when Arthur Schneithorst started Benish's Restaurant in downtown St. Louis at Eighth and Olive Streets. His son, Arthur Junior recalls dining there until the Depression years forced its closing. His father started another restaurant, a grill, until 1937, when the family took over Bevo Mill operations and Arthur Junior got a taste of real Bavarian dining. Arthur Senior passed away in 1947, and then in 1956, Arthur Junior bought the land where Hofamberg Inn was born. Schneithorst's still offers a Bavarian atmosphere and menu, but also serves new, lighter dishes as well, at 2600 South Lindbergh.

THE VINTAGE RESTAURANT at Stone Hill Winery in Hermann is in the winery's former carriage house and horse barn and serves German specialties along with contemporary cuisine, paired with their wines.

geh und erforsche!

The Washington Historical Society has an impressive exhibit on zithers and Franz Schwarzer, the man who made Washington, Missouri, famous for zithers.

An die Musik

das Tagebuch

If not quite a piece of the True Cross, the zither is truly extraordinary. My wife reverently remarked, "So unique", as we gazed upon it. As modern architect Mies van der Rohe, himself a product of that proud German crafts tradition, famously declared, "God dwells in the details."

"So unique" seems like the only way to characterize this fantastic 19th-century zither manufactured by the Franz Schwarzer factory in Washington, Missouri, deep in the heart of the Missouri German Heritage Corridor. Not only is it obviously an extraordinary musical instrument, but its hand-crafted woodworking of the beautiful rosewood and its inlays of turquoise and mother-of-pearl make it a work of art. Viewing a unique object like the Franz Schwarzer zither immediately raises so many questions, about its origins, manufacture, owners, and subsequent use.

The Washington Historical Society has anticipated these questions and attempted to address them with an outstanding exhibition on the second floor of the museum. This highly engaging museum exhibition about zithers and Franz Schwarzer, the Washington, Missouri, native known world-wide as the self-styled "King of Zither Manufacturers," provides much valuable cultural context that enables interested viewers to answer the many questions raised by such an exceptional cultural artifact.

The exhibition displays zithers ranging from Schwarzer's regular models designed for family use to highly personalized ones for outstanding performers or connoisseurs of fine art and music like Schwarzer himself. A wealth of archival photos and an excellent exhibit brochure enriches your museum experience of the Schwarzer zither. A small display depicting a zither manufacturing workbench at the factory with its variety of tools and materials, such as silver German frets or mother-of-pearl, helps you imagine the instrument from the entirely different perspective of the artisan.

The Washington Historical Society has produced an excellent video to accompany the exhibit, drawing richly upon vintage historical photographs. One section of the video features master players bringing the zither's unique sounds to life. Knowledgeable museum guides like Washington Historical Society Executive Director Marc Houseman personalize the experience even further. He can tell you about the beloved place of Schwarzer within Washington's community.

Recently, the Washington Historical Society helped sponsor a national zither festival that

A national zither festival brought enthusiasts from all over the country to the home of the Zither King.

brought zither enthusiasts from all over the United States to the *Heimat* (home) of the Zither King to once again celebrate this unique instrument. Like music itself, this noteworthy artifact works at many levels of meaning that affect an observer in many different ways.

So what does this unique artifact and its accompanying exhibition show us about Missouri's German cultural heritage? An old German proverb holds that "music washes away from the soul the dust of everyday life." Many observers have long considered music itself the soul of Missouri's 19th-century German culture. From that perspective, this elaborate and elegant zither manufactured by the Schwarzer company signifies the changing course of its musical tributary within the flowing cultural heritage of Missouri Germans.

A Typical Immigrant

The origins of Schwarzer zithers clearly illustrate the now familiar pattern of the Missouri German immigrant experience. Although of educated, middle-class origins, Schwarzer embodies the 19th-century American Dream of Missouri's immigrants from German-speaking Europe. Schwarzer was born in the town of Olmutz, Austria, in 1828. The son of a building contractor, he attended the Polytechnic Institute of Vienna where he studied both architecture and woodworking. After completing his degree, he then studied zither under highly regarded composer Ludwig Ritter Von Ditrich.

Schwarzer moved to America in 1864 where he quickly discovered his speculative plot of land was not utopia, and farming was not in his future. He and his wife eventually moved to the bustling town of Washington, Missouri. With the vital support and partnership of his wife Josephine, a former Austrian stage actress, the Schwarzers prospered during the so-called Gilded Age at the end of the 19th century by literally carving out a unique niche in American manufacturing that was created by the musical heritage of Missouri's German immigrants.

The origins of the Schwarzer zither provide a classic case study of intercultural transfer. To meet the growing local demand by these Missouri German immigrants for their coveted national instrument, Schwarzer turned his woodworking craftsmanship and musical background toward building better zithers. The New World of Missouri offered an ample supply of beautiful wood for his instruments, but he imported the silver German frets, mother-of-pearl inlay, ivory, and wood veneers from the Old World. In 1873, Schwarzer entered three of his zithers into the International Exhibition in Vienna. Against competitors from all over the world, this recent immigrant to the Missouri frontier, itself just emerging from a highly contested Civil War, won the coveted Gold Medal of Progress.

Was this a musical instrument or a work of art? Those boundary lines were blurred even in the very beginning of Schwarzer's zither manufacturing. According to an October 1965 *Missouri Review* article about Schwarzer's life and work by Thomas M. Davis and Franz R. Beinke:

> *Schwarzer designed, often with the help of his wife, the inlay patterns on the top and edges of the instrument[s]. In the early years of the factory he did all of the finer work. ... The veneer for the top of the zither was cut from rosewood,*

Beethoven Conservatory

THE FIRST CONSERVATORY in St. Louis started as a music school in 1871 under Director August Waldauer, who in 1880 founded the St. Louis Musical Union, the predecessor of the St. Louis symphony orchestra. The Beethoven Conservatory was named for the famous German composer, Ludwig van Beethoven. The conservatory building was designed and built by August Beinke, born in Missouri, and John Ludwig Lees, an 1879 immigrant from Alsace-Lorraine. The building still stands on the northwest corner of 23rd and Locust Streets. It is now a commercial photography studio.

geh und erforschel

das Tagebuch

As I have with Marc Houseman of the Washington Historical Society, I've enjoyed the great privilege of collaborating with the since deceased Dr. Anita Mallinckrodt on the Missouri Humanities Council German Heritage Corridor scholars symposium. Like many people, I have also been inspired by her curatorial (from a Latin word meaning "to care for") devotion to Missouri's German heritage over the course of many decades.

tulipwood, mahogany, or some other finish wood. The design for the inlay was then carefully traced, one section at a time, on the veneer. With small knives, usually made in the factory, the design was cut out of the veneer; the tiny pieces of mother-of-pearl were "laid in" the appropriate places in the open area, matching not only the cut edges of the veneer, but also creating the pattern in the open area. Then glue and ebony sawdust were mixed together, smeared over the inlay, and allowed to dry. After the glue had set, the total surface was slowly sanded, removing the excess glue, and leaving the polished inlay in the black ebony background.

Because of the tension created by fitting the small pieces together, and the strain on the eyes, only short periods at one time could be spent on the inlaying process. … On the more complicated designs, the inlaying might take several months; and on the intricately patterned models which sold for over $600, a full year was necessary to complete the inlaying. After the inlaid patterns were completed, the veneer was glued on the face of the instrument, leaving only the ivory trim and tulipwood burl to be fitted and glued to the edges of the instrument.

Employing up to twenty-five skilled workers at the peak of its fame around the turn of the 20th century, the Schwarzer factory in Washington, Missouri, produced zithers that were already legendary during his lifetime, as well as a dazzling variety of both bowed and plucked stringed instruments. One highly favorable article in *The Music Trades* (December 6, 1902), observed:

Franz Schwarzer established his plant in 1864 and has supervised the output personally ever since. Such long experience guarantees the zither he produces, signed by his autograph—like an Amati violin—to be what they should be. Some day, in the 25th century, perhaps, Schwarzer zithers of 1864–99 may be as much sought after as 17th-century Cremona fiddles. His own aim is to make good ones, not merely

Four German Singing Groups

THE KANSAS CITY LIEDERKRANZ (at left) sings locally, and you can call 816-358-4056 for more information. The Liederkranz Singing Society of St. Louis was established in 1860, and still persists, as do two other St. Louis singing groups, the Deutscher Mannerchor St. Louis, and the Chor des Deutschen Kulturvereins.

cheap ones, and they can last as long as the violins of the old masters.

For whom did Schwarzer manufacture such exquisite musical instruments? Museum director Houseman displayed two volumes of Schwarzer factory records that included identification numbers for instruments, a valuable Schwarzer innovation both for business and research purposes, as well as information about buyers.

Although local band leaders and others from Washington, Missouri, definitely purchased his zithers and other instruments, the market for Schwarzer zithers extended throughout America, and indeed the world. A New York instrument dealer, Herr Lohr, regularly purchased Schwarzer instruments in large quantities, as did Benedictine nuns and the Sisters of Notre Dame. Houseman traced the sale of some instruments to one particular convent, then showed a document from that same convent years later that banned the sisters from their over-indulgence in playing the zither.

Like his contemporary John B. Busch in the brewing industry, Schwarzer enjoyed high social status in Washington, Missouri. An excellent employer as well as businessman, it was said that no one who worked for Schwarzer ever voluntarily left his employ. He joined the local *Turnverein* and, appropriately enough, became the first director of the *Liederkranz* (literally "wreath of songs," or singing society). He helped form the Washington fire brigade in 1873 and served in the highly prestigious role of Fire Chief.

By the turn of the century, the Schwarzers had built a beautiful estate near his factory and turned the estate into a park with walking paths, a greenhouse filled with tropical plants, and a pet alligator, about ten feet long. Schwarzer Park remained open to everyone in Washington, Missouri. Schwarzer converted his first small factory into a small museum, or "cabinet of curiosities," as they were often called back then, which he called his Relic House.

An Obsession

However, Schwarzer zithers were no such anachronistic relics or curiosities. His zithers were jewels crowning the incredibly rich musical life of Missouri German communities. While relatively little research in English exists on Washington's musical life, an excellent cultural history of nearby Augusta's *Harmonie-Verein* by the late noted local historian and German Heritage Corridor scholar Anita M. Mallinckrodt provides a much-needed comparative perspective. The late Ralph Gregory, himself a highly respected historian of Washington's German cultural heritage, strongly endorsed Mallinckrodt's valuable case study of Missouri's German American musical heritage.

Recalling that venerable German maxim about music, Mallinckrodt wrote, "It was sung and played music that most refreshed body and soul at Augusta. In fact, a future observer looking back on Augusta's culture would call music its 'obsession.'" She mentions outdoor picnics and concerts featuring Mozart choruses as well as evening dances in large residential ballrooms or in local drinking establishments. In her 2005 book *Augusta's "Harmony"* about Missouri German music in Augusta around 1875, she reported that "music … remained the heart of most festivals. They frequently included parades and almost always a dance that stretched into the early morning hours." These dances were inevitably called balls.

This "obsession" with music reached well beyond the city limits of little Augusta and its *Harmonie-Verein* to the entire Deutschheim region:

> *In fall 1880 the Verein organized a big Musikfest that echoed up and down the river valley—the Hermann Band and Choral Society came down-river, as well as Washington's Coronet Band. (Not present that day, but also a favorite visitor to Augusta, was Vollrath's Orchestra, of St. Charles. A Gert Goebel photo of it "at Augusta on the steamer* Colorado, *June 1893," showed thirteen musicians gathered on deck around the steamship's bell.) Despite "the terrible heat" of August,*

Musikfest guests paraded through Augusta to the popular tune "Five Leather Stockings" and later danced until 2 AM.

That "obsession" with music within Missouri's German musical heritage extended all the way to the lofty status of Schwarzer zithers. In 1912 the American Zither Congress convened its first Congress in Washington, Missouri, with delegates attending from all parts of the United States. They held their meetings in the beautiful and beloved Schwarzer Park, where the elderly widow Mrs. Josephine Schwarzer, seated like royalty in the arbor of her beloved park, was crowned with a laurel wreath. Speaker A. W. Schwepp called the site "the very shrine of all devout and enthusiastic American zither players." He also talked enthusiastically of the importance of the Congress as a "move in the right direction" for the future of zither playing, but history had already changed course in exactly the wrong direction for Schwarzer zithers.

This photo is from the collection of the late Albert Hesse, who worked at the zither factory his entire life. People who bought zithers or had them repaired would often send an image of themselves with their zither, as a thank you to him.

Back to the Future

The zither had already lost its pride of place as the main musical instrument among Missouri Germans by the time of the 1912 American Zither Congress held in Washington, Missouri. Sale of Schwarzer zithers used as family instruments had already steeply declined by that time, to be replaced by these elaborate, handcrafted instruments used mainly by professional musicians, who were already skilled at playing them. Second- and third-generation German Americans for whom German was no longer their first language became less and less willing to master this challenging instrument, and the subsequent pressures to "Americanize" because of the First World War drove musical traditions like the zither even further from the mainstream of Missouri German culture. The popular 1949 movie *The Third Man,* starring Joseph Cotton and Orson Welles, featuring its haunting zither theme by Anton Karas, temporarily revived interest in the instrument, but the Schwarzer factory permanently closed its doors in 1953. The factory and the enchanting Schwarzer house were demolished in 1964, and the park that was beside the house no longer exists.

Today, cultural artifacts like this Franz Schwarzer zither have now entered the challenging but highly meaningful realm of Missouri folk arts, with its concern for preserving valuable cultural traditions.

One such effort was spurred a few years ago by zither enthusiast Rich Krueger from Illinois. He visited Washington, Missouri, to encourage a zither revival in the town the zither helped make famous back in the 19th century. Like the fascinating emergence of an heirloom seed, a small group of people interested in learning to play the zither gradually formed throughout the Deutschheim region. According to Houseman, emergence of the local Schwarzer zither ensemble helped attract the April 2018 national zither concert to Washington, Missouri.

This national concert included two days of zither workshops as well as top national performers and zither master Tomy Tomerson

The Schwarzer Zither Ensemble

TWICE A WEEK, at least when performances are planned, a dozen members of the Schwarzer Zither Ensemble gather at the Washington Historical Society for practice. This is the largest ensemble of zither players in the country, and players come from Washington, Union, Eureka, and Marthasville. They range in age from teenagers to a woman in her eighties. The group has performed and shared zither history with local and state organizations and at Washington Historical Society events.

Playing a zither has been described as playing three guitars at one time because the right hand uses a thumb pick on five strings on the fretboard that the left hand is holding down while fingers except for the pinkie are plucking the other twenty-nine or more open strings. It's even more complicated than this, but you get the idea.

geh und erforsche!

from Germany. The April 2018 concert proved well-attended despite the relative challenge for a national audience to get there.

The Washington concert also differed in quality from other national zither concerts. Many observers remarked about the enormous enthusiasm on the part of concert participants and audience members to experience the authenticity of the concert venue near the site of what A.W. Schwepp had called over a century earlier "the very shrine of all devout and enthusiastic American zither players."

Houseman described how the event took on some of the characteristics of a pilgrimage to view sacred relics and how that enthusiasm in turn has energized the local Schwarzer zither ensemble. That group is now forming a beginner's group to better ensure the future of this unique cultural heritage. In the words of an old hymn, the life of the Schwarzer zither "flows on in endless song that hails a new creation."

However, time and memory do not always flow in a straight course. Many groups and associations like the Schwarzer zither ensemble have emerged that seek meaningful alternatives to contemporary trends like globalization and digital technology. Renaissance festivals or Civil War reenactments offer prime examples of this trend. Even Steampunk, a very post-modern, contemporary movement, is an example of this trend. Steampunk incorporates technology and designs inspired by 19th-century machinery, often highly imaginatively portrayed in an alternative history of the late 19th century or a pretend future for today.

These passionate pretenders might profitably take another look at the award-winning zithers of Franz Schwarzer: a brilliant inventor of that period also gifted with a strong design aesthetic, his beautiful and artistic actress wife Josephine, their enchanting estate at Schwarzer Park with its horticultural specimens and exotic animals, and their small but devoted guild of musical artisans. After 150 years, could that unique musical artifact of Missouri's German heritage inspire a "vintage tomorrow" of its own? Maybe at this very moment, a new movement is already being composed for the score of Franz Schwarzer zithers.

An die Musik [To Music]

BY FRANZ VON SCHOBER
Music by Franz Schubert
Translated by Tom Potter
Translation donated to the public domain, Tom Potter, 2008

Oft hat ein Seufzer, deiner Harf' entflossen,
Oft comes a sigh, a holy chord from your harp strings,
Ein süsser heiliger Akkord von dir,
That sparks in me a vision, one I clearly see,
Den Himmel bess'rer Zeiten mir erschlossen,
A glimpse of heaven, and the sight of better times before me,
Du holde Kunst, ich danke dir dafür,
I thank you for these things, you dear sweet Art,
Du holde Kunst, ich danke dir!
For these things, my thanks to you.

Cole Camp's German Music

A small town in Missouri, population about 1,200, although not part of the German Heritage Corridor, has made a big effort to preserve its German heritage through music. Beginning in the 1830s, a wave of immigrants from across Europe but primarily from northern Germany came to this area and settled here on the edge of civilization to find new opportunities and make new homes at the junction of Benton, Morgan, and Pettis counties. The majority were Lutherans from the north German province of Lower Saxony, with the majority coming from the area between Bremen and Hamburg. They brought with them their *Plattdeutsch* (Low German), which is still spoken here today.

In 1989 as part of the town's Sesquicentennial celebration, a German Club was formed, and in 1990 a singing group began, too. This group of singers became very popular and soon grew to fifty members.

In 1992, the St. Louis Maennerchor was invited to help the Cole Camp singers perform their first annual *Saengerfest* (singer festival). This festival is held annually on the second Saturday in June and has included singing groups from St. Louis, Kansas City, Concordia, Tulsa, and Omaha.

In October, the singers perform at the annual Oktoberfest.

On the first Sunday in December an annual German Christmas program of German carols is performed at St. Paul's Lutheran Church. Anyone is welcome.

The Cole Camp singers are members of a national organization, the *Nord-Amerikanische Saengerbund* (the North American Singers Association).

The German Club recently constructed an Immigrant Memorial, and at the beginning of the annual *Saengerfest* in June, there is a wreath-laying ceremony at the memorial. This memorial is unique in that it contains two icons recovered from the rubble of Berlin and brought back by a local soldier. The memorial consists of two areas, one made up of numbered bricks containing the names and place of origin of original immigrants. The other area contains bricks engraved with the names of descendants of the immigrants. For more information, message Neil Heimsoth through the German Immigrant Memorial Facebook page.

geh und erforsche!

From left and top: The Cole Camp singing group sings carols in German at Christmas at St. Paul's Lutheran Church. The German Club erects a traditional Maypole during Maifest. Singers perform at *Sangerfest* in June, after laying a wreath at the German Immigrant Memorial.

The Friedrich Jahn Memorial in Forest Park honors the founder of gymnastic education.

One Good Turner

The Friedrich Jahn Memorial below and east of Art Hill in St. Louis's Forest Park honors the Prussian gymnastics educator and German patriot. Jahn founded the *Turnverein* international gymnastic and social society in 1811 Berlin. *Turn Vater Jahn* (Father Jahn of the Turners) was known as the father of modern gymnastics and systematic physical culture. He especially promoted the use of parallel bars, rings, and the high bars in international competition, and he helped advance the modern Olympic movement. The history of physical education in the United States intersects with the history of the American Turners, but Turnverein played an even more important role in Missouri's German heritage.

This 41-foot-long monument takes the shape of a welcoming bench but features a colossal bronze bust of the imposing Jahn in the center. A youth putting the shot and a young woman gracefully dancing with a wand flank Vater Jahn. Six polished black granite informational plaques, which replaced the original 1913 bronze plaques, now line the granite and limestone base. The Friedrich Jahn Memorial was sculpted by Robert Cauer in Krueznach, Germany, for $14,000, then shipped to St. Louis.

The North American Turn Bund–St. Louis Chapter donated the Friedrich Jahn Memorial to the city. It occupies the site of the 1904 World's Fair German pavilion, appropriately enough near a running path. At the time of its 1913 installation, almost 15 percent of the population of St. Louis claimed native German origin. The city was home to more than 150 German cultural societies, such as the dozen influential Turnverein located throughout various neighborhoods of the city. The monument was restored and rededicated by the American Turners in 1972 and again in 1989 by the American Turners and Forest Park Forever; additional restoration work was completed in late 2013 and 2014.

Gymnastics to Resistance

The stability and permanence of the Jahn memorial belie the dynamic forces that shaped his life. In 1813 Jahn helped found and lead the Lutzow Free Corps, a volunteer force of fellow Prussians fighting Napoleon Bonaparte's advancing army. Prussia was a German state. After returning from the fighting, he was promoted to state teacher of gymnastics in 1816.

His Turnverein movement, organized to prepare German youth to defend their country in the early part of the 19th century, grew out of a larger response to the defeat of Prussia and other German states by Napoleon. The Turnen Gymnastic Physical Culture organization was founded with clear political objectives to liberate Prussia or Germany from French occupation and to create a democratic Germany by dismantling its repressive feudal kingdoms. Vater Jahn encouraged young gymnasts to develop a spirit of patriotism and *Deutschheit* (Germanness) in addition to physical strength and determination.

The physical training program Jahn created and advocated in his books came to be practiced throughout Germany, in small towns as well as in large cities. In the Romantic style of the early 19th century, traditional German games, songs, and *Bier* helped foster this sense of national pride and unity. Jahn's philosophy and attitude toward physical training became deeply rooted in German culture. Physical culture as a mass movement came to be looked upon not only as a source of national pride, but perhaps more importantly, as a source of national strength.

Like any strength training program, however, Turnerism had to overcome a great deal of resistance. The Turnverein not only promoted *Turnen* (gymnastics) but also threatened to turn German politics and society upside down. Following the defeat of Napoleon, aristocratic leaders of the traditional small German states reacted nervously to the rising spirit of German nationalism by young leaders like Paul Follenius and Friedrich Muench (see Chapter 3) that the Napoleonic Wars had unleashed.

Jahn similarly aroused the suspicion of authorities for his outspoken nationalistic views and strong influence on youth. He was arrested and imprisoned for almost a year, and his gymnastics club was closed. After his release he was confined to the city of Kolberg until 1825. He was forbidden, however, to live in a city with a university or a secondary school, so he moved to Freyburg an der Unstrut for the rest of his life.

Then German politics and history turned once again. Jahn received the Iron Cross for military bravery in 1840. The ban on gymnastics, in effect since 1819, was finally lifted in 1842, and Jahn served in the national parliament during the revolutionary 1848–49 period. The Turner movement in Germany remained liberal democratic in nature; many Turners took part in the Revolution of 1848. After its defeat, though, the movement was suppressed, and a tidal wave of nearly one million emigrants swept many of Vater Jahn's Turners into the United States and many into the Far West of Missouri.

Turnverein Exhibit

WASHINGTON, MISSOURI, has an excellent display about the Washington Turnvereins, and quite by accident. Emily Schmidt, the widow of Elmar Schmidt the Younger, as he was called, moved a whole bunch of old papers to the curb for trash. A neighbor happened to be going by and noticed what appeared to be German posters and records. She got permission and rescued this treasure trove for the Washington Historical Society, which has built a display based on these old photographs, posters promoting plays, theater performances, or the appearances of politicians coming through the area. Other artifacts include juggling clubs used to train for hand-eye coordination and furniture stamped with WTV (Washington Turnvereins). This tremendous archive includes the last entry into the Turnverein's minutes, which noted the society was donating its large seal as scrap metal to aid efforts to collect metal during World War II.

The Washington Turnverein was founded by Franz Wilhelmi, a major in the Civil War in Company G of the 17th Missouri Infantry, or what became known as the Western Turner Rifle Regiment, or more simply, the Turner Brigade. The exhibit includes his pistols and swords.

geh und erforsche!

The Battle Cry of Freedom

Like the classical Greeks so admired in early 19th-century Germany, Jahn emphasized a balanced approach to physical fitness in order to achieve "a sound mind in a sound body," as the Latin motto urged. The stated ideals of the Turnverein sounded a similar theme of balance regarding political liberty:

> *Liberty against all oppression. Tolerance against all fanaticism. Reason against superstition. Justice against all exploitation. Free speech, free press, free assembly for the discussion of all questions so that men and women may think unfettered and order their lives by the dictates of their own conscience.*

As you can probably imagine, the American experience of chattel slavery and Civil War challenged those democratic ideals like a call to arms. The Nord-Americka Turnbund sprang into action like Vater Jahn had envisioned nearly half a century earlier.

Although German Americans comprised much of the Union Army corps, the Turnverein movement established by Jahn formed its very core. The following text from *The Union Cause in St. Louis in 1861: An Historical Sketch*, by Robert J. Rombauer, published in St. Louis, 1909, clearly illustrates the vital military role of the Turnverein in the Camp Jackson affair.

> *The Third Regiment of the United States Reserve Corps, Missouri Volunteers mustered for home service on May 8, under President Lincoln's order of April 30, with ten Companies establishing Headquarters and Armory at the St. Louis Turner Hall (in German, "St. Louis Turnverein") on Tenth and Walnut streets, where many of its members had been drilling before. Company A was formed of St. Louis Turners, who also largely entered into the formation of other Companies, as their numbers exceeded the original quota, which was rapidly filled up by the first four Volunteer Regiments. The Regiment marched out to Camp Jackson. It chiefly garrisoned in the city until July 1, when three of its Companies joined the Southwest expedition, while on the 16th of July six Companies marched, via Jefferson, into Callaway County and defeated a Secession troop under Harris, after a short engagement, and took possession of Fulton, from where the Companies returned to St. Louis, to be mustered out at the expiration of service. The Regiment had among its members many prominent business men, whose offices in the center of town made Turner Hall a convenient place of assembly. The Regiment held 20 per cent Americans, 5 per cent other nationalities and 75 per cent Germans.*
>
> *The Fourth Regiment Infantry, Missouri Volunteers, was organized with twelve Companies towards the end of April, 1861. It was originally a hunting society of longer standing called "Die Schwarzen Jaeger" (The Black Hunters), equipped with the usual outfit of a hunting society. This and the Schuetzen Section of the St. Louis Turnverein were the first armed Union volunteer bodies in St. Louis, even before President Lincoln's call for 75,000 men. The German word Schuetze (plural: Schuetzen) literally means "shooter," and with the appropriate prefix, was used to denote everything from an archer (Bogenschuetze) to a rifleman (Gewehrschuetze) to a sharpshooter (Scharfschuetze). A more general English term for Schuetze would be "marksman." The organized movement of Schuetzen (originally archers, later riflemen) began in Germany during the middle ages. This movement gained new momentum during resistance to the occupation of Germany by Napoleon in the early 1800s, and again during the 1848 revolutions. Eventually, the Schuetzen movement grew into shooting and hunting clubs, comparable in German culture to American country clubs. Alcoholic beverages became a big part of the Schuetzen clubs.*

This 1860 photograph shows the St. Louis Turnverein rifle club.

German immigrants had brought their Schuetzen traditions, as well as Bier and democratic ideals, to Missouri with them. Numerous Turnverein gymnastic or athletic clubs had Schuetzen groups or sections within them. For example, the 17th Regiment, Missouri Infantry, another German immigrant unit, was known among Missouri Germans as the Westliches Turner-Schützenregiment. These German shooting and hunting clubs had been established in Missouri as far back as the 1830s and were in place all over the state when conflict erupted.

A ladies' bar drill class at the South St. Louis Turnverein, circa 1910. Although the society closed in 1940, its building still stands today and has been converted to apartments.

According to Rombauer:

> *Soon after the organization of the society a rifle section was formed with about fifty members, who were pledged to military obedience when in service; they elected their officers and instructors and bought their own rifles; took up regular weekly drills, arranged target practices and trial marches to neighboring cities.*

Many of the German Schuetzen clubs in Missouri were the first to respond to President Lincoln's request for volunteers to "quell the rebellion." This extreme example of intercultural transfer, rooted in a revolutionary Germany strongly affected by the American Revolution, may well have saved Missouri for the Union.

As the World Turns

Following the Civil War, Missouri Germans put down their weapons and worked for greater respect in American culture. Turnverein emerged all across St. Louis and other urban centers in the German Heritage Corridor as each new German enclave formed a social center for their new cultural matrix. The Turnverein provided valuable job networks, a place to socialize with others who shared a German background (however defined), and a place to remember the *gute alte Tage* (good old days) in *der Vaterland.* For a time at the end of the 19th century, St. Louis featured the largest collection of Turnvereins in the United States. They included:

St. Louis Turnverein, 1850
South St. Louis Turnverein, 1869
North St. Louis Turnverein, 1870
St. Louis Socialer Turnverein, 1872
Carondelet Germania Turnverein, 1872
Concordia Turnverein, 1881
West St. Louis Turnverein, 1887
Schweizer National Turnverein, 1887
Rock Spring Turnverein, 1891
Northwest Turnverein, 1892
Southwest St. Louis Turnverein, 1893
Tower Grove Turnverein, 1906

Outside of St. Louis:

Washington, Missouri, Turnverein, 1859
Hermann, Missouri, Turnverein, 1860

St. Louis even unseated arch-rival Chicago as the executive site of the North American Turnerbund in May 1878.

The American Turnverein movement peaked in 1894. At that time there were 317 societies, with more than 40,000 members and 25,000 children active in National Turnerbund activities. Although Turnverein served as cultural conservatories, they also attempted to introduce Turnen into American public schools. Doing so offered mutual benefits: fitness and health of American society as well as cultural prestige for the Turner movement.

The "German system" of Vater Jahn was restricted mainly to cities with a large German American population like St. Louis because of the cultural perception of Turnen as non-American. However, the Turners influenced the introduction and quality of physical education even in places where their system was not implemented. The American Turners spent much of the first half of the 20th century promoting the addition of physical education to US schools. They also created the first College of Physical Education, which still operates today as a division of the Indiana University in Indianapolis. The American Turners is still one of the oldest continuously operating athletic organizations in the world.

Just as the Turners' patriotic response to the Union cause during the Civil War embodied

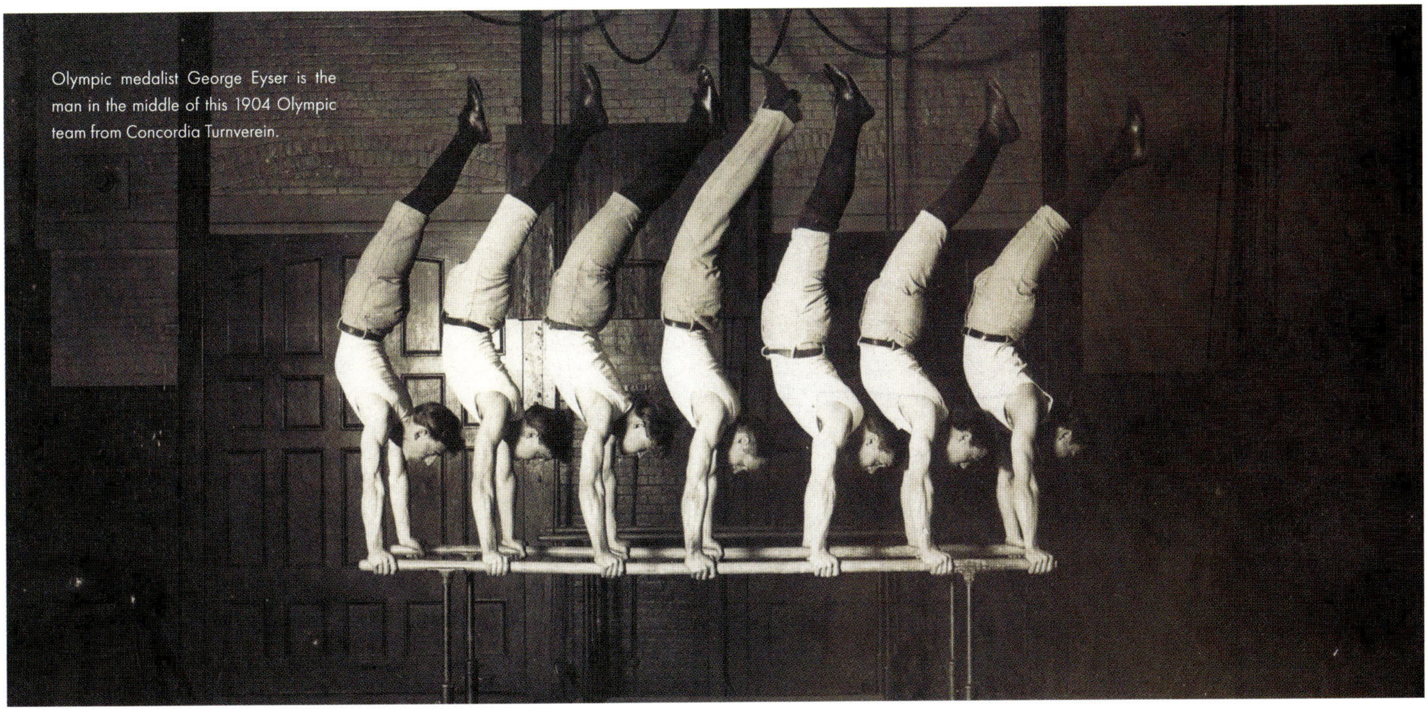

Olympic medalist George Eyser is the man in the middle of this 1904 Olympic team from Concordia Turnverein.

Despite having lost most of his left leg in a train accident, George Eyser won six medals at the 1904 Olympics in St. Louis.

das Tagebuch

My father lost his left leg to cancer, then gallantly taught himself to walk using an artificial limb. When challenges seem overwhelming, I think of Vater Jahn, George Eyser, and my father.

Jahn's liberal democratic ideals, his classical Greek ideals and "German gymnastics" literally sprang to life during the 1904 Summer Olympic Games held in St. Louis. George Louis Eyser (1870–1919) was a German American Turner gymnast who competed there, earning six medals in one day. Eyser was born on August 31, 1870 in Kiel, Germany, and his family emigrated to the United States in 1884.

At some point in his youth, he lost most of his left leg due to a train accident. In its place he wore a wooden prosthesis which allowed him to participate in physical activities such as running, jumping, and especially gymnastics. George moved from Denver to St. Louis sometime around 1902–1903, where he worked as a bookkeeper for a construction company. Like many young German Americans living and working in large cities, he soon joined the local Turnverein. Unlike other young German Americans, though, this Concordia Turner aimed for the 1904 Olympics despite his prosthetic device.

The 1904 Olympics, held in conjunction with the Louisiana Purchase Exposition, were the third modern Olympics and the first in which gold, silver, and bronze medals were awarded to the first three places. On October 29, the only day of the Olympic Gymnastics Championships, George Eyser of the Concordia Turners won a total of six medals: three were gold (parallel bars, long horse vault, and 25-foot rope climbing), two silver (pommel horse and four-event all-around), and one bronze (horizontal bar). Amazingly, he won a gold medal in the vault, which at that time included jumping over a long horse without a springboard and then sticking the landing.

Concordia finished fourth in the team competition, which mainly and not surprisingly featured Turnverein clubs. Along with the Concordia Turners, the South St. Louis Turnverein also represented St. Louis against clubs from cities like New York, Chicago, Cleveland, and others; thirteen Turnvereins participated in the 1904 St. Louis Olympics. Germany and Switzerland competed at the 1904 games—Germany had won the 1896 Olympic gymnastics. Eyser continued competing for Concordia following his 1904 Olympian feats, and the Concordia Turners won the 1908 international meet in Frankfurt, Germany, and

das Tagebuch

My first experience of the Concordia Turners involved following up someone's well-meaning advice to test my emerging volleyball skills back in the late 1970s against the legendary Turners. After having a few volleyballs spiked off my forehead, I recognized there was a "Jahning" gap between my skill level and theirs.

The Concordia Turnverein demonstrates a formation.

the 1909 national meet in Cincinnati, Ohio.

In 2008, *The Times of London* listed Eyser's feats as one of the Top 50 Olympic Games Moments in History.

Old School

Many of St. Louis's Turnvereins, especially in the older, central locations, stopped growing and even started declining around 1910 as German settlement expanded southward and westward throughout the city. Immigration from Germany had already been slowing since the 1880s and German unification. Rather than tightly knit German social networks living in close proximity to their Turnverein, German Americans now began to diffuse across new sections of the city like Marine Villa and the Tower Grove neighborhoods.

As typically happens to immigrant groups in America, those changing demographic trends then turned into an intergenerational culture clash. German-born elders who had faced social isolation, conflict, and even war as they struggled to retain their traditions while forging a new life in America viewed the Turnverein differently from a new generation of German American youth in the early 20th century. These young members had been born and acculturated in America, were often not fully fluent in German, and felt little or no connection to the now-legendary struggles of early 19th-century Germany. Cultural assimilation and two World Wars with Germany as an American enemy further eroded Turnverein membership.

Some halls simply closed their doors while others evolved (or devolved) into dance halls, bars, or bowling alleys. Most Turnverein had closed down by the middle of the 20th century, and the Friedrich Jahn Memorial in Forest Park increasingly oxidized into ancient history—except for George Eyser's Concordia Turners in St. Louis.

While Concordia Turners still maintain their traditionally strong emphasis on gymnastics, they also support a wide variety of athletic and social activities in response to today's needs and demands. Around the time of the German American Tricentennial in 1983, Concordia still dominated the national Turnfest gymnastics competition. It's still a very lively place today.

Concordia Turners Today

STILL SPORTING THE MOTTO, "Sound Mind in a Sound Body," the Concordia Turners remain at 6432 Gravois in St. Louis. They still have a strong focus on gymnastics but also offer youth classes in dance, sports, martial arts, and guitar. Adult members use a weight room and participate in aerobics, volleyball, paddleball, saunas, and the pool in summer. The population of young athletes, including gymnasts, is very diverse today. Other special activities, such as camping and hayrides, are offered occasionally, and the Bavarian-style Black Forest Room and Bar may be rented out for special occasions. Visit ConcordiaTurners.org for more information.

Joseph Pilates

Like Friedrich Jahn, Joseph Pilates had to overcome some enormous challenges. At five years of age, Joseph lost sight in his left eye from bullies throwing stones at him; he also suffered from rickets and asthma. However, a Turnverein Club existed in his hometown of Mönchengladbach.

The Pilates family lived just down the street from this Turnverein, and the name of Heindrich Friedrich Pilates (Joseph's father) appears in the 1892 registry of the Turnverein. Heindrich Friedrich was also a gymnast and owned a nearby gym, so young Joseph Pilates took personal responsibility for his own health and overcame his childhood illnesses. He went from sickly child to becoming so fit he actually posed as a model for anatomy charts as early as the age of fourteen.

In explaining his guiding principle, Joseph Pilates liked to quote German poet Friedrich Schiller: "It is the mind itself which builds the body." He could also have been quoting Vater Jahn.

The Concordia Gymnastic Society, founded in 1875, was named after Concordia Park on the near south side of St. Louis. Like Jahn's original *Turnplatz* in Berlin, Concordia Park was used for the original activities of the Concordia Turners. In 1877 Concordia moved to its first home at 13th and Arsenal, featuring exercise classes and instruction in gymnastics. Most of the members then lived in surrounding neighborhoods like Soulard, Benton Park, and Senate Square. As always, the Turner Hall provided a focal point for the area's culture and entertainment.

The building of Interstate 55 in 1962 forced the Concordia Turners to move to the present location on 6432 Gravois Road. The original portion of the building, The Black Forest Room, had been the popular Black Forest Restaurant. Current facilities include two gymnasiums, a dance/martial arts studio, handball/racquetball court, fitness center, men's and women's locker rooms, kitchen, bar, rental halls, outdoor swimming pool, and sand volleyball court. The purpose of the Concordia Turners remains, as it has always been, to promote the health and well-being of its members and society.

The Core of the Matter

Health and physical fitness, if not gymnastics, now seem like core American values. Near the Friedrich Jahn Memorial in Forest Park, walkers, runners, and cyclists pursue exercise in a magnificent setting. Many probably practice Pilates as well, as twelve million people worldwide do. The hipness of Pilates seems far removed from the *turnplatz* of Vater Jahn, but it's really not.

Joseph Pilates, born in the industrial city of Mönchengladbach, Germany, was a teenager during the first modern Olympics, held in Athens, Greece, in 1896. Around that time, classical Greek civilization attracted widespread cultural interest, and the rebirth of the Olympics illustrated that reverence for antiquity. The German team of gymnasts won a medal at those Olympics and further advanced gymnastics in Germany, as well as in Missouri Turnverein. Many decades later, Joseph Pilates still revered the Ancient Greeks. In his book *Return to Life*, he wrote:

> *Many in the ancient world wisely adopted as their own the Latin motto, "mens sana in corpore sano" (a sound mind in a sound body). The classical Greeks as a people displayed even greater wisdom when they practiced what they preached and thus as a culture came nearest to actually achieving this goal.*

That same Latin motto is engraved into the Friedrich Jahn Memorial.

The similarities of Friedrich Jahn and Joseph Pilates do not end with their philosophies, though. According to Nicole Marcione, a Pilates instructor and doctoral candidate at the University of Southern California's Division of Biokinesiology and Physical Therapy:

> *It is undeniable that Joseph Pilates used the Turnverein exercises of his youth to develop his own method of exercise. The similarities were staggering when making a comparison of exercises found in the various German Turnverein books (from the mid-1800s) that belong to the Los Angeles Turners Club, Joseph Pilates performing similar or the same exercises in his book* Return To Life *in 1945, and modern-day Pilates instructor Benjamin Degenhardt performing the same exercises.*

The international popularity of Pilates shows us how Missouri's German Turnverein heritage has flowed into much larger cultural streams. Sitting at the Friedrich Jahn Memorial offers us a rare opportunity to reflect upon an expanded present while tracing the ripples back to the original stone cast into the pond.

The Pommer-Gentner House, built in 1840, is part of the Deutchheim State Historic Site in Hermann.

REMEMBERING MISSOURI'S
der Geist
GERMAN HERITAGE

Temples of Memory

In classical Greek mythology, the Muses were goddesses who kept watch over the arts and humanities, the basic sources of meaning. The Muses were daughters of Zeus and Mnemosyne, the goddess of memory. Classical Greeks called their temples *mouseion* and treated them as sacred places. In the Middle Ages, Christian pilgrims traveled widely to visit and venerate religious relics.

Museums evolved over centuries into the royal treasure houses of Europe, displaying spoils of war and imperial splendor in the halls of palaces and in the cages of zoos. Wealthy merchant collectors after the Renaissance assembled and displayed priceless relics and exotic specimens in what became widely known as Cabinets of Curiosities.

Early American collectors like Thomas Jefferson attempted to preserve and communicate the incredible natural and cultural diversity of the new American republic revealed by explorers like Lewis and Clark in his own *mouseion* at Monticello. And then there's Graceland in Memphis, Tennessee. Museums have always given place to cultural identity and heritage, however those concepts have been defined.

The missions and collections of museums have evolved significantly from their religious and royal origins. Today they play major roles in civic and economic life such as heritage tourism; over 850 million people now pass through our nation's museums each year. Why? We're still looking for identity and meaning, just like those classical Greeks and religious pilgrims. As the former Metropolitan Museum of Art Director Philippe de Montebello once observed, "A museum is the memory of mankind." Deutschheim State Historic Site in Hermann shares that fundamental mission of cultural memory, and it offers an ideal place from which to consider key issues about how we remember Missouri's German cultural heritage.

Choosing What To Keep

The first key issue any museum must consider is why collect some objects and not others? Deutschheim State Historic Site owes its very existence to the historic preservation efforts of a small but dedicated group of local citizens. The Hermann Brush and Palette Club, a local organization dedicated to advancing the arts in Hermann, began their preservation efforts in 1952 by instituting an annual Maifest celebration to save the historic Rotunda Building in the Upper City Park, as well as to remind people in the Hermann area of their rich heritage.

The Club subsequently saved the historic Pommer-Gentner House from demolition in 1954 and began funding its restoration with proceeds from the Maifest. In 1962 the Brush and Palette Club also acquired ownership of the Strehly House, one of the historic homes featured on the historic house tour during that first Maifest. Riding the currents of interest in heritage fanned in the 1970s by the US Bicentennial,

das Tagebuch

Material culture studies, my field of emphasis within American Studies, explores relationships between people and their things: the making, history, preservation, and interpretation of objects. Anything from buildings and architectural elements like masonry to furniture and garbage can be considered as material culture. Museums and their collections can bring the "stuff" of a culture together in valuable ways, if only by being together in the same place.

Top: The Carl Strehly House in Hermann, part of the Deutschheim State Historic Site, shows how a family of modest means lived. Above: At the Historic Site, you can also view what is believed to be the last carved cask known to exist in Missouri, signed and dated 1875, depicting Bacchus, god of wine.

the Brush and Palette Club donated the buildings, which now comprise Deutschheim State Historic Site, to the state of Missouri in 1978. These splendid survivors both offer regular guided tours of 19th-century German immigration and life in Missouri.

The elegant Pommer-Gentner House, built in 1840, is one of the oldest surviving buildings in Hermann. The Pommers numbered among the original founders of Hermann. Architectural historian Charles van Ravenswaay called the elegant brick dwelling "that interesting house … set apart from the vernacular designs commonly used." It was built in what Germans called Neoclassicizmus style, a more restrained version of the familiar Federal style in the Pommer's original Philadelphia setting.

The Pommers built fine pianofortes back in Philadelphia, one of which is now displayed at the site, before moving to Hermann as part of the German Settlement Society to what they envisioned as a more German community. The interior of the house reflects this early settlement era with its period furnishings in the renowned Biedermeier style, while the Deutschheim State Historic Site honors the family's musical heritage with the Pommer music concert series. A half-timbered barn behind the house displays period gardening tools, right next to the conscientously cultivated four-square kitchen garden displaying its heirloom plants and 19th-century gardening techniques.

Nearby, the historic Carl Strehly house was occupied by the family from 1843 to 1962. It features authentic furnishings and household items reflecting those of a family of moderate means, offering a uniquely valuable perspective on Missouri's German heritage from the mid- to late 19th century. The main part of the Strehly house was built in 1842, then modified and enlarged until the Civil War, resulting in the property as seen today. According to the Historic

St. Paul's Lutheran Church, Concordia

THIS CHURCH HAS ROOTS predating the formation of The Lutheran Church–Missouri Synod. In 1840, the German community of Freedom Township began Lutheran worship led by a teacher, Henry Christian Liever. The first log church was built in 1844, and the first pastor arrived in 1847. The congregation supplied Lutheran education from the beginning, and the first full-time schoolteacher, M. Broening, started in 1858. He had graduated from a school that had been established at Fort Wayne, Indiana, after splitting off from the Concordia Seminary in St. Louis. Rev. Franz Julius Blitz arrived in 1860, when the first brick church sanctuary was dedicated. Pastor Blitz, also a postmaster, gave the town of Concordia in Missouri its name in 1865. The church still provides a school for pre-school through eighth grade and is open to both the unchurched and other denominations if space is available.

geh und erforsche!

das Tagebuch

My wife Sheryl and I have visited the Hermannhof Winery and district regularly since the early 1970s when we began restoring an old house in south St. Louis. Over time that trip back in time has become a barometer of the changes in Deutschheim and in ourselves.

American Buildings Survey, the false aproned chimneys of the winery-tavern, the half timbering and extended facade of the house, and the proximity of these two connected buildings to the front of the lot show us its German building heritage.

The dwelling housed Strehly and Eduard Muehl's printing business, which in 1843 produced the first German newspaper, *Licht-Freund*, west of the Mississippi. Until 1854 they published at considerable personal risk another German-language newspaper, *Hermanner Volkblatt*, strongly opposed to slavery. Visitors to the Strehly House can actually view its printing workshop with original typesetting equipment in order to better understand this vital Missouri German institution.

They also built a winery in 1857 with a vaulted brick cellar. Here you can view what is believed to be the last carved wine cask known to exist in Missouri, signed Bacchus, god of wine, as well as grape vines dating back to the 1870s behind the house, a wine production room, and the short-lived tavern above the house winery. The Strehly House brings to mind and gives place to some basic and highly important elements of Missouri's German heritage.

Hermann Farm Museum

Other Missouri German heritage museums offer interesting and illuminating contrasts to the public mission and collections of Deutschheim State Historic Site. Located not far from Deutschheim State Historic Site, the privately owned and operated Hermann Farm Museum represents a prime example. Jim and Mary Dierberg first came to Hermann during a Maifest in 1971 and fell in love with the town.

"The hills around here really reminded me of Bavaria," Jim Dierberg said. "We thought, 'what a great place for a living history farm.'"

Compared to the lengthy public process for preserving and establishing Deutschheim State Historic Site, Dierberg, the chairman of First Banks Inc., bought a bank in Hermann the following week. "I told Mary we needed a reason to come back," he said. "There was one building in town that was German and was going to be torn down. I bought it and fixed it up. It's like fishing. You catch one fish and you're hooked." The rest, as they say, is history—or heritage.

The Dierbergs bought a winery in Hermann in 1974, complete with cellars that had been built in 1848 but were filled in during the dark days of Prohibition. California winegrowers themselves, they subsequently excavated the cellars and opened Hermannhof Winery. Over the next four decades, the Dierbergs continued buying and restoring historic buildings in and around Hermann, converting them into an entire district of upscale accommodations complete with period furnishings.

The Carl Teubner House at Hermann Farm Museum has been preserved, and the tree is the ginkgo that George Husmann planted.

They also renovated a historic building that had housed an old Hermann car dealership into a Festhalle in order to host special events, converted the 1895 grain mill into a restaurant, and built the *Hofgarten*, an open-air courtyard, which serves as a festive venue. Like Deutschheim State Historic Site, the Dierbergs have contributed mightily to heritage preservation by showcasing Missouri's German heritage in accordance with their unique vision.

Eventually they established the Dierberg Educational Foundation, a nonprofit, charitable organization, to preserve and present the region's cultural history. The mission statement of the Hermann Farm Museum reads:

Hermann Farm Museum is located on 200 acres of rolling hills about 75 miles west of St. Louis, in the heart of beautiful Missouri wine country. Its purpose is to celebrate the importance of German settlement to the development of agriculture in the Missouri River Valley region, and to showcase the home and business establishment of George Husmann, one of the most prominent vintners in the development of the wine industry in America.

Unlike early collections assembled by wealthy entrepreneurs, Hermann Farm is no mere Cabinet of Curiosities. It does, however, engage and educate people of all ages to our Midwestern German rural tradition through living history tours and seasonal celebrations. "The Germans who first came here back in 1837 wanted to keep their traditions," said Jim Dierberg. "I'm following in that tradition."

Although Hermann's Brush and Palette Club helped to halt and reverse the loss of Missouri's German heritage in that important Deutschheim community, sometimes new perspectives as well as additional resources from outside the community can also help us more fully appreciate the cultural heritage right before our eyes. The Hermann Farm Museum established by the Dierbergs not only celebrates the agricultural heritage of Deutschheim but gives it pride of place.

In the spring of 1847, Carl "Charles" Teubner arrived in Hermann from Germany (via Alabama) and purchased two hundred acres just east of town on the scenic Missouri River bluffs. He planted the hillside with thousands of vines and fruit trees. People regarded his nursery operation as the first reliable nursery in the state, and he soon became one of the region's most successful grape growers.

Teubner died unexpectedly in September of 1851 after completing a press house and wine cellar for his business and a grand brick mansion for his family's home; the two historic buildings remain focal points on the Hermann Farm. When George Husmann learned of his brother-in-law's death, he quickly returned from California gold prospecting to assume management of the nursery and winery operation for his sister. Husmann's nursery and fruit tree farm became famous throughout the Midwest, providing grape plants, fruit trees, and more exotic plants and seeds from Europe and Asia to customers all across the United States. A majestic ginkgo tree, one of the largest in America, still standing next to Teubner's grand brick home, bears silent witness to Husmann's horticultural expertise.

Besides its special role in Missouri's German viticultural heritage, the site of Hermann Farm Museum also bears witness to the Civil War in Missouri and the leadership role of Missouri Germans in preserving the Union. In May of 1858, Charles Manwaring, of Geneva, New York, joined with Husmann to form Hermann Nurseries at the site, which by 1860 ranked as the largest, most profitable business in Gasconade County. Despite the obligations of their successful business, both Husmann and Manwaring joined the Union Army at the war's outset. In May 1864, Manwaring was killed by Confederates while he attempted to capture rebel bushwhackers on the Hermann wharf. Manwaring was buried at the cemetery located on the farm, near the graves of Charles and Josephine Teubner.

After the Civil War, the Kallmeyer family acquired and farmed the Hermann Farm site for a century. It first served as a dairy farm, then as an important horse and mule farm and livestock dealership. The Kallmeyers provided working animals to farms throughout Missouri, as well as supplying mules and horses to the US Army in Europe during both world wars. Not surprisingly, Hermann Farm Museum strongly emphasizes animal husbandry. The Kallmeyer family preserved the farm, house, press house, wine cellar, and the surrounding hillside during their tenure. The Kallmeyer's stewardship retained Hermann Farm's historic appearance and sense of place well into the 21st century, so in a very real sense Hermann Farm Museum extends the Kallmeyer's careful stewardship of a cultivated artifact of Missouri's German cultural heritage. The medium is the message.

Religious Institutions

Strong religious institutions of several diverse traditions have also characterized Missouri German life. For example, from its Missouri origins The Lutheran Church–Missouri Synod has collected and curated its cultural heritage. The Lutheran Church–Missouri Synod traces its heritage back to 1847, when Saxon and other German immigrants established a new church body in Missouri to freely practice and follow Lutheranism according to their beliefs. Church leaders incorporated the Concordia Historical Institute in 1927 to preserve church records, then in 1959 the Synod itself designated the Concordia Historical Institute, on the beautiful campus of Concordia Seminary in St. Louis, as its Department of Archives and History. The Institute exists to communicate that unique and highly vital Missouri German Lutheran heritage.

The Institute's facilities include a reference room for patrons to view books, periodicals, parish histories, pamphlets, tracts, and other publications relating to the history of Lutheranism in North America and its European antecedents. It also contains a museum exhibit area and three stack areas for storage of its collections; in accordance with best museum practices, the Institute maintains the stack areas at a constant temperature and humidity to preserve the resources. The Concordia Historical Institute assists districts and congregations of the Synod in preserving their own historical records and also publishes the *Concordia Historical Institute Quarterly*. Its clear religious mission and focus for over a century and a half make it a valuable scholarly resource and model for research about Missouri's German cultural heritage.

das Tagebuch

Like the Church of Latter Day Saints (Mormons), The Lutheran Church–Missouri Synod offers exceptional research for people exploring their genealogy. My cousin Gary, who greatly expanded upon my early genealogical research, speaks very highly of the Institute's resources and staff support for his ongoing genealogical research.

Concordia Seminary, St. Louis

THE SEMINARY'S MISSION is to teach theology and leadership centered in the Gospel to train pastors, missionaries, deacons, deaconesses, scholars, and other leaders for The Lutheran Church–Missouri Synod. The Seminary was founded in 1839 in Perry County by German immigrants. The seminary moved to St. Louis in 1849 to South Jefferson Avenue and Winnebago Street and to its current campus in suburban Clayton in 1926.

geh und erforsche!

Trinity Lutheran Church, St. Louis

THIS CHURCH WAS FOUNDED in 1839 by Saxon immigrants who migrated to St. Louis from Perry County, Missouri. This was the mother church of the Missouri Synod denomination, and the Concordia Seminary and Concordia Publishing House both trace their origins to this congregation, as does the Lutheran parochial school system. The immigrants first began worshiping in the basement of what is now Christ Church Cathedral, on Broadway and Chestnut Streets. The first church on this site was built in 1865 but was destroyed in the great tornado of 1896, which devastated the whole south side of St. Louis. Today, the church continues as a Missouri Synod Lutheran Church, serving the greater St. Louis area.

Saxon Lutheran Memorial

The Institute also maintains the Saxon Lutheran Memorial in Perry County, Missouri. The Saxon Lutheran Memorial village is an outdoor history museum located on the homestead and farm of the former Bergt Farm Complex. Nestled in Frohna, Missouri, the Memorial preserves and presents the migration and settlement of 19th-century Saxon Lutheran immigrants to Missouri.

In the 19th-century German Kingdom of Saxony, Lutheran pastor Martin Stephan and approximately six hundred Saxon Lutherans left for the United States in November 1838 and arrived in January 1839 in New Orleans. Most of those immigrants settled in Perry County, as well as in and around St. Louis. These *Auswanderung* included Christian Adolph Bergt and Caroline Louise Voelker, who married in 1841. In 1847 the Bergts acquired property that would remain in the family until 1957, illustrating once again the frugality and continuity that has long characterized Missouri's German cultural heritage.

The Bergt complex buildings remain conserved in their original locations, unusual in modern America. The Saxon Lutheran Memorial historic village consists of a residential building with frame and hewn log sections, two log outbuildings, a granary, and a timber frame barn, which contains an earlier double crib, hewn log barn, as well as domestic and farming artifacts of 19th-century Missouri German rural settlements in Perry County. A machine shed filled with period machinery was added to the site in 1990. Several buildings connected to the descendants of the Saxons living in the area have also been brought onto the site and restored. These include the Fenwick Cabin, the Hamilton-Goehring Cabin, the Schuppan Haus, and the newest addition, the 1904 Confirmation Room from Concordia Lutheran Church in Frohna.

The Concordia Historical Institute purchased the Bergt complex in 1961, then dedicated and opened it to the public in 1964 as a "walk-in history book" of this special chapter of Missouri German immigrant life. The Saxon Lutheran Memorial is listed on the National Register of Historic Places; in 2009 the Friends of Missouri State Archive Association recognized the Saxon Lutheran Village as the last complete home and farmstead complex of its era. Other buildings have been constructed on the site to depict the customs and way of life of these 19th-century German settlers: a blacksmith shop, a woodworking shop, and a visitors center.

The Saxon Lutheran Memorial hosts numerous events throughout the year, including Community Baking Days on the first Saturday of each month during the outdoor season. Known across Missouri for craft demonstrations and traditional foods at its annual Fall Festival the second Saturday in October, the Saxon Lutheran Memorial continues to attract school field trips, bus tours, and families exploring their Lutheran or Perry County roots. Many museums ask visitors for gifts or donations, but the Saxon Lutheran Memorial is one of the very few that specifically asks for your prayers.

To be a Muse or Amusing

Interpretive activities at Deutschheim State Historic Site also illustrate the challenges of communicating Missouri's German cultural heritage to contemporary audiences. Site interpretation communicates meanings and relationships of our natural and cultural heritage

das Tagebuch

I had the opportunity to help lead a Missouri Folk Arts Community Scholars workshop held in Perry County that included a site visit and wonderful tour of the Saxon Lutheran Memorial village, as well as an incredible meal of traditional German dishes. Let's just say it was a very well-rounded cultural experience.

to visitors through first-hand experiences with objects, historic sites, and landscapes. Site interpretation brings its heritage to light and into focus. Site interpretation shows us the vital difference between cultural heritage and just old stuff.

Unlike general topics such as German opposition to slavery or the Civil War, interpretive themes involve communicating a complete idea with a message. For example, one key theme at Deutschheim State Historic Site is that Missouri Germans had escaped from hated oppression in the Old Country so they strongly opposed slavery here in Missouri. Good museum guides, like good musical composers, create strong themes that provide a memorable melody for their historic sites, which stay with visitors long after they've visited (like the "Ashokan Farewell" in Ken Burns's documentary *The Civil War*). Clear, strong themes give tone value and meaning to museum objects, those notes in the score. The challenge of museum interpretation at Deutschheim State Historic Site mirrors the burden of this book: Why should we remember and value Missouri's German cultural heritage? What's the story here, and how does it relate to me?

Because the mission of Deutschheim State Historic Site to preserve and present 19th-century Missouri German heritage is broad like its Missouri River valley setting, Site Supervisor Cindy Browne said that she and her staff try to thoughtfully respond to particular visitor interests and to personalize their daily site activities. Although their tours for visiting adults and children or school groups tend to be purposefully small in size because of the relatively small size of the historic house interiors, Browne and her specialists try to turn what could be seen as a weakness into a personalized guided tour, more of a conversation really, that relates to the interests of the visitor. Exhibitions at the site, such as one about German immigration, also play an important role. Visitors who can't take the regular tours still find the exhibitions interesting and valuable. Although we live today in a wired world with short attention spans, site visitors will often read all the exhibition text. In addition, everyone loves taking brochures or pamphlets from the site home with them to read. The enchanting four-square heirloom garden offers a different way to communicate German heritage, even through silent contemplation, a valuable message in itself.

Special events at Deutschheim State Historic Site include the annual spring garden tour, the Pommer music concerts, and the December *Weihnachtsfest*. They grow naturally out of the site's unique features yet offer opportunities for more targeted topics and trying on new "frames" of meaning compared to its regular, daily activities. Browne noted that her site specialists can use their special talents to enhance explaining subjects such as music or food while reaching larger audiences than during a normal day.

The annual Deutschheim garden tour during the first weekend in June offers visitors an opportunity to learn firsthand about the gardening practices of Missouri's early German settlers. Visitors enjoy treats such as lavender-flavored

The Life and Works of Rudolph Goebel

RUDOLPH GOEBEL gathered stories and photographs of old-time settlers from before statehood to the 1870s. He has been described as having a keen eye and sense of humor in observing the wisdom and faults of German settlers and the "Old Americans," while shrewdly assessing relations between the two. Two books, *The Life and Works of Rudolph Goebel*, by William Popp, and *Longer Than a Man's Lifetime in Missouri*, by Gert Goebel, provide insight into German settlers. Both books are available from the St. Charles Historical Society store. Visit scchs.org/store

Rudolph Goebel (left) and Robert Benecke (right) were both photographers, and they shared a birthday. Here, they pose for a sixtieth birthday portrait.

Deutschheim Historic Site Supervisor Cindy Browne shares insights with a group interested in historic preservation.

springerle cookies and pink lemonade as they stroll the blooming gardens while artisans demonstrate traditional folk arts. Deutschheim's William H. Pommer Concerts offer visitors an opportunity to experience his music, that of other German Americans, and the German composers who inspired them, while the annual *Weihnachtsfest* at the Pommer-Gentner House quite literally illuminates the lives of Missouri's German immigrants through the special aura of that holiday season.

Finally, public outreach activities, which involve collaborating with interested organizations, enables Deutschheim State Historic Site to reach newer and wider audiences. Browne spoke of several symbiotic relationships for which the site serves as a content provider. She said the site supports the efforts of the Chamber of Commerce and the city by serving as a resource for them year-round, for special events, for group tours like motor coaches, and for festivals, among others. Another important collaborative relationship for the site involves the Deutschheim *Verein* (society), a nonprofit friends organization that supports the mission of the site. The Deutschheim Verein "has their back" by helping Deutschheim State Historic Site build its collections, supporting special events, sponsoring the Pommer concert series, as well as providing other materials and activities needed for excellent site interpretation. The Verein also offers an excellent publication entitled *Der Maibaum* that provides interested researchers a prized venue for their own efforts, as well as enriching the knowledge base for the site.

Site Supervisor Browne and Deutschheim State Historic Site also play a major leadership role in the Missouri Humanities Council's German Heritage Corridor initiative. She believes that the initiative offers an opportunity to involve more people and organizations in preserving and promoting Missouri's German heritage than any single historic site or museum could possibly do by itself. All of these collaborative efforts may ultimately expand awareness of and visits to Deutschheim State Historic Site and its partners throughout the Corridor, as well as creating more meaningful communication about artifacts for visitors.

A Gift from the Past

Browne also observed that what her site specialists most strongly remember and appreciate from their tours is meaningful visitor engagement. Their experiences remind us that the finest interpretive efforts in the world ultimately depend upon the visitors, at least some willingness on their part to engage in a conversation with people

Twillman House

THIS HOUSE, which now provides a home for the Spanish Lake Community Association, was built in 1870 by Johann Heinrich Twillman, an immigrant from the Bielefeld area of Germany. His family arrived in St. Louis in 1842. The original building is made of Mississippi River limestone and handmade brick. When Twillman died in 1882, the house and surrounding 374-acre farm were divided among his family. Descendants lived in the house until 1945, and the association bought it in 2005. It is available for rent for community and other events. Visit SpanishLakeMo.org/twillmanhouse or see at 11840 Bellefontaine Road, Spanish Lake.

geh und erforsche!

from a foreign country called The Past.

Why should we care about objects like a historic building, an heirloom garden, a period piano, or a vintage printing press preserved at Deutschheim State Historic Site? First, museum objects acquire new meaning simply by being preserved. They have become the Chosen Ones, rescued from the dust and decay of ordinary time along with other splendid survivors of their type in a place especially devoted to caring for them, a *mouseion*. Survival of these cultural artifacts helps to authenticate and balance personal memory and written history, but it's only the beginning of this extraordinary communication.

Like other forms of communication such as gesture, speech, and touch, the material culture at Deutschheim State Historic Site and all the special collections within the German Heritage Corridor acquire meaning and value by communicating between people. A material object like a desk, a hairbrush, or a handwritten letter in old Gothic German script can still send messages vibrating across time and space, connecting us to ancestors both different and the same as us. A work of art, for example, can send a message from the creator to the viewer, can share an image, a feeling, or an experience. A museum can contain memories and mutual experiences from across time and distance that can still influence our thoughts and feelings.

Gift-giving in particular seems to be a universal form of communication that naturally involves material culture. As any child opening a birthday present could tell or at least show you, a gift creates a special bond between giver and receiver. In a very real sense, the giver never really leaves the gift but becomes part of the recipient's world through that gift. A valued gift usually leads to a gift in response; that virtuous cycle creates a very special bond between people.

Perhaps we could all start to think of our museums and special collections within and about the German Heritage Corridor as gifts from people with whom we are still connected even after decades and centuries. Imagine receiving a first-class letter from someone we care deeply about—that may be difficult in our wired world of electronic social media—but the best museum experiences feel like such an old-time correspondence. We would study the stamp and the postmark, the hand-writing, the descriptions and stories, even "read between the lines" to wring every last ounce of meaning from that letter and what it possibly means for our future actions. If you can imagine that, then there are some important letters waiting for you at Deutschheim State Historic Site and at other museums and special collections throughout the German Heritage Corridor.

das Tagebuch

When I was a little boy, I used to help my father with his stamp collection. My first role involved soaking stamps off labels, but I later moved up to entering stamps into pages. Later, I could ask my father somewhat intelligent questions about the stamps themselves. Stamp collections are miniature museums of collecting, curating, and communicating. That stamp collection meant the world to me because of the relationship it signified, but after my father's death it also helped to pay for my college education. Museums, like Missouri's German heritage, are not just about the past but also help shape our future.

Other Museums With German Culture Displays

- **THE AUGUST SEHRT HOUSE MUSEUM** in Augusta is a six-room house restored as the town's historical museum. It contains 1880s furnishings, such as a rope bed, and more. The museum is a brick building built in the 1860s by August Sehrt, a town coffin maker. The Augusta Historical Society conducts programs there the first Sundays of months May through September.
- The log **GRABS HOUSE AND STORE** buildings in Rusche Park were restored and relocated for use as a local museum in 1990. The museum is usually open from 1-4 PM the first Sunday of every month from March through December, weather permitting. Visit at 6th and Main Street, or Highway D, in Marthasville. Call the city at 636-433-5554 for more information.
- The **MISSOURI MEERSCHAUM COMPANY** in Washington, Missouri, is the world's oldest and largest manufacturer of corn cob pipes. The word "meerschaum" is derived from a German word meaning "sea foam" and was a Turkish clay used in high grade pipes. Missouri Meerschaum corn cob pipes are known for being cool, sweet-smoking pipes. It was actually a genuine Dutch—not Deutsche—immigrant and woodworker, Henry Tibbe, who began production of corn cob pipes in 1869. A local farmer had whittled a pipe out of corn cob and liked it so much he asked Tibbe to turn some on his lathe, and before he knew it, Tibbe was working less with wood and manufacturing more pipes. There is no doubt that many of Tibbe's managers and employees and also subsequent owners of the company were German immigrants or descendants. The company has a fine museum and retail shop, one open every day except Sunday. Visit at 400 West Front Street, Washington, Missouri.
- The **TOWNLEY HOUSE MUSEUM**, at 304 South Market Street, Chamois, is probably the oldest building in Chamois and was built in 1856 by Charles Phelps. In 1864, one of his daughters married Alvah W. Townley, and the house remained in the Townley family until 1991, when it was donated to the Osage County Historical Society. The last person to own the house was Viola Hartwig Townley, who had German heritage. The museum contains many artifacts beyond those of the Townley family, including a reversible rug, clothing, and a confirmation certificate in German from St. John's Evangelisch Kirche (Evangelical Church, but now St. John's United Church of Christ), donated by area families with German heritage. The museum is actually a complex that includes a barn, a smokehouse, and more. The museum was transferred to the Chamois Historic Preservation Commission in 2012. The museum is open by appointment only by calling 573-763-5974 or 573-301-5134.

geh und erforsche!

The Friedens German/English Evangelical Cemetery, more commonly known as the Hamburg Cemetery, remains a cemetery even though the town of Hamburg no longer exists.

Volkommen

"Death"
BY RAINER MARIA RILKE

Before us great Death stands
Our fate held close within his quiet hands.
When with proud joy we lift Life's red wine
To drink deep of the mystic shining cup
And ecstasy through all our being leaps—
Death bows his head and weeps.

German poet Rainer Maria Rilke imagined that we carry death within us like the "kernel of a fruit." For Rilke, this elevated idea of *volkommen* (completeness) made possible through death also allows us to fully celebrate life itself.

The Friedens German/English Evangelical Cemetery, located about four miles east of Defiance, Missouri, along US Highway 94 near the Missouri River, provides us with an exceptional vantage point to celebrate Missouri's German cultural heritage. It remains a cemetery for a church and a town (Hamburg, Missouri) that no longer exist except in memory and imagination. In 1940, the US government removed the buildings and residents of this mostly German town, as its name suggests, located in the heart of Missouri's German Heritage Corridor. The purpose of doing so was to build a munitions factory to supply the Allies and, subsequently, US armed forces following American entry into the war in early December 1941.

The oldest gravestone in the cemetery, that of a week-old infant girl, dates back to 1865, while the most recent ones have been added during the past decade. Cemeteries like the Friedens German/English Evangelical Cemetery provide important information and insights into Missouri's German cultural heritage and the lives of the people now buried in this quiet setting. They also help us remember how to remember, to create a more complete understanding.

Controversial Archaeologist

Archaeology is one of the humanities whose primary purpose is to help us remember earlier cultures. Highly successful German entrepreneur Heinrich Schliemann (1822-1890) pioneered in the field of archaeology, focusing his efforts upon Aegean civilization in the Bronze Age. Schliemann argued that the places mentioned in the epic works of Homer were real rather than mythic, so he excavated rather primitively at the Turkish site of Hissarlik, now presumed to be the site of the Lost City of Troy. His ground-breaking work lent considerable weight to the emerging idea that Homer's *Iliad* reflected actual historical events rather than a myth.

However, his excavation of Hissarlik remains highly criticized in the field of archaeology. He blasted through nine levels of archaeological remains in the early 1870s using the new invention of dynamite. In the process of doing so, Schliemann destroyed some significant historical artifacts, including the archaeological level now believed to actually be the historical Troy.

Despite his now obvious mistakes, though, Schliemann helped to create our enduring image of modern archaeology as white Europeans wearing pith helmets while digging under a blazing desert sun among ancient ruins buried

German archaeologist Heinrich Schliemann both discovered and destroyed the Lost City of Troy.

Bellefontaine Cemetery

BELLEFONTAINE CEMETERY AND ARBORETUM is a nonprofit, nonsectarian cemetery located in north St. Louis. It was founded in 1849 during the peak of the rural cemetery movement, as rapidly growing St. Louis restricted cemeteries within the city limits. In addition to the Busch mausoleum (see page 132), the cemetery houses many architecturally significant monuments and mausoleums such as the Louis Sullivan-designed Wainwright Tomb (at left), listed on the National Register of Historic Places. The cemetery contains 314 acres of land and over 87,000 graves, including those of William Clark, Thomas Hart Benton, and William S. Burroughs. Bellefontaine Cemetery also serves as an important landscape arboretum for the St. Louis region.

geh und erforsche!

das Tagebuch

Geneological research is one of the best ways I know to connect with larger communities that we may have forgotten. The first step in researching cemeteries relevant to your questions is to use the FindAGrave.com site online. Be sure to know the name of the township you are researching, find the introductory township map page to locate the precise cemetery, or go to the index to find the family name that you are researching.

Even remote family cemeteries are still considered sacred places throughout the German Heritage Corridor. If you want to visit a family cemetery, be sure to obtain permission from the current landowner. A measure of respect never goes out of fashion.

in the sands. That image, reaching all the way back to Schliemann, was burned into our cultural memories from childhood. It remains very strong in popular culture, as the continued popularity of the Indiana Jones movies clearly indicates.

Archaeology Above Ground

Today, interested explorers with or without pith helmets or fedoras can find much of the information they seek about German cultural heritage by exploring the above-ground archaeology of its old cemeteries.

Archaeology is not just about digging up rather than blowing up funerary remains. Archaeologists interpret material culture, including gravesites, to observe, analyze, and understand cultural systems like Missouri's German heritage. The real purpose of cemetery or funerary studies is to sharpen our understanding of cultural traditions and how they change over time. Like classic archaeology carried out in and among ancient ruins, examining German Heritage Corridor sites like the Hamburg Cemetery can offer insights into historic events and periods, styles and types, as well as change over time. It can reveal socio-economic status, religious beliefs, and aesthetic images, as well as the lives of real people who might otherwise remain completely anonymous to Missouri's German cultural heritage.

Examining material culture like the Hamburg Cemetery illustrates what is now called historical archaeology. Historical archaeology investigates past cultures that have left behind both material culture like gravestones as well as written records like church records, newspaper accounts, or even passenger lists from German ports, like those left by the Auswanderung. Cemetery studies balance more traditional historical research methods.

Genealogists and family historians can also obtain much important information from places like Hamburg Cemetery. County historical societies usually have a listing of their cemeteries organized by townships. These surveys include large city, church, and many small family cemeteries. Historical society volunteers typically

Local blacksmiths fashioned iron crosses, which can still be found in some of the old Missouri German Catholic cemeteries, like this one at the St. Joseph Catholic Church in Westphalia.

conduct much of the background research for these surveys by visiting the county's many cemeteries and recording inscriptions from gravestones. That provides a major resource for anyone interested in Missouri's German cultural heritage.

Cemeteries like Hamburg's are still sacred landscapes. They are both very much of their times and yet timeless. Much of the farmland and open space throughout the German Heritage Corridor, despite the unique sense of place they lend to the region, remain as ordinary residential or commercial real estate subject to the fluctuating development pressures of the marketplace. However, the region's cemeteries possess many legal protections, as well as the power of long-standing cultural traditions. Very few people shiver when they walk on somebody's lawn like they do when accidentally stepping upon a gravesite in the twilight shadows.

Although most cemeteries in the German Heritage Corridor no longer rest in front of the church to remind people of their mortality, even in today's Missouri life they remain closely related to religion, like the St. Joseph Catholic Church landscape in Westphalia shown above.

Cultural Evolution

Cemeteries reveal shifts in the production of gravestones from hand crafted to manufactured ones. An old German funerary tradition exists in some Catholic cemeteries, although there are none in the Hamburg Cemetery. Iron crosses were usually fashioned by local blacksmiths, but few if any demonstrated significant ornamentation. Local artisans also carved a number of wooden crosses for early gravesites, but few of those remain. Most of the early gravestones in the German Heritage Corridor were originally fashioned from sandstone, a material easy to carve but subject to erosion.

By the 1850s, marble had already become highly popular for gravestones among Missouri Germans, and many towns had their own "marble yard." After the Civil War, granite gravestones produced in distant urban centers like St. Louis increasingly found their way into

DOZENS OF SECTS CAN BE FOUND IN THE CORRIDOR

BY MARC HOUSEMAN, *EXECUTIVE DIRECTOR OF THE WASHINGTON HISTORICAL SOCIETY*

THERE ARE DOZENS of cemeteries in the German Heritage Corridor bearing names specifically German, many of which literally have the word "German" in their titles. The corridor's historic churches of the Evangelical, Lutheran, Catholic and German-Methodist faiths most often have their respective cemeteries nearby, if not adjacent to the church itself. Likewise, many of the corridor's Jewish cemeteries are nearly wholly eastern European if not specifically German. Missouri death certificates will sometimes specify "German Cemetery" as the place of a decedent's interment while in fact this is often a corruption of a more formally named congregational or societal cemetery. There are examples, though much rarer than the sects mentioned above, of congregations entirely or primarily German of the Presbyterian faith and even more scarcely, the Baptist faith. Among the immigrant German population there were also the free thinkers or nonconformists who, while not necessarily atheistic, did not join with a particular religious denomination.

Marc Houseman, Executive Director of the Washington Historical Society, was the tour guide for the author to the old Hamburg cemetery.

small cemeteries like Hamburg. Gravestones in the 20th century appear much more streamlined than their older counterparts, with much less ornamentation and far fewer examples of Deutsches language being used.

Although the quality of stonecutting obviously varied, one can find many examples of considerable skill and sophistication from every time period.

The renowned architectural historian Charles van Ravenswaay wrote:

> *By the end of the century, the stonecutters found that even their trade was doomed by the commercial production of gravestones in St. Louis and other centers and that mechanization of the craft had destroyed whatever local market had existed for individual handwork. In the larger towns, the name "marble yards" had been replaced by monuments, and the stonecutters who continued to operate these firms had been forced by changing circumstances into becoming salesmen of mass-produced products.*

Hamburg Cemetery also demonstrates some unique Missouri German landscape practices. The use of evergreen vegetation was an old Germanic tradition that continued after emigration to Missouri in cemeteries throughout the German Heritage Corridor. Here in Missouri, the evergreen used in cemeteries often proved to be the virtually indestructible red cedar; this Missouri native and hardy survivor found ready acceptance and widespread use in places like the Hamburg Cemetery. Vinca (or periwinkle, as it is commonly known) also proved highly popular for the rapidly spreading and easily maintained ground cover that it offered. Although native neither to Germany or to Missouri, the tenacious yucca of the desert southwest also became a landscape favorite in Missouri German cemeteries as well.

Family Values

Cemeteries like the one at Hamburg reveal other interesting and unusual funerary traditions that offer insights into Missouri's German cultural heritage. Some cemeteries, particularly churchyards set in small, rural locations like Ebenezer United Church of Christ in Drain, employed a chronological pattern by date of death in their burial arrangements rather than by families. Whether from deep appreciation for valuable land or an excess of orderliness, reasons for this burial pattern remain unknown. Interestingly enough, though, few if any Missouri cemeteries outside of Missouri's German Heritage Corridor demonstrate this unique pattern.

The German Heritage Corridor also includes hundreds of small family cemeteries, often located in isolated rural landscapes. The Hamburg Cemetery itself also provides clear evidence of many familial relationships among the gravesites. One particularly interesting example of their enduring power involves one family who did not believe that the federal government would ensure perpetual care of the site. The family disinterred all of the family's graves to another site, leaving behind only the coping around the family's former graves as a silent protest.

Other cemeteries within the German Heritage Corridor reveal important social relationships as well as unique funerary styles. The parents of Lilly Anheuser, wife of famous industrialist Adolphus Busch, had built a mausoleum at beautiful Bellefontaine Cemetery, but Mrs.

Adolphus Busch's wife replaced the original Anheuser family mausoleum with this one, much grander in scale.

Busch felt that her husband Adolphus needed something even grander in scale than her family's mausoleum. She therefore had her family's elaborate original structure demolished and the family members reinterred outside.

She then had prominent St. Louis architect Thomas Barnett (who designed the Alexander von Humboldt statue in Tower Grove Park) create a new mausoleum in Bavarian Gothic style. Constructed of stone quarried in Missouri and completed in 1921, the impressive new funerary structure cost $250,000, equivalent to $2.7 million today. The Busch mausoleum features grapevines, representing both Adolphus's birthplace in German wine country and, ironically, his favorite beverage. Over the lintel to the Busch mausoleum, a visitor reads Julius Caesar's words, *"Veni, Vidi, Vici,"* or "I came, I saw, I conquered," but the monument itself was the message.

As the Busch mausoleum clearly indicates, the final resting place can make a powerful statement about the meaning of a person's life. For example, although burials in the Hamburg Cemetery seldom occur now, the cemetery still remains available for new gravesites. The late Richard Scharnhorst, a former member of the Missouri Department of Natural Resources staff, sought a burial site in the farthest corner of the cemetery, as close as he could possibly be placed to the Missouri River. When the leaves fall in late autumn, his gravesite looks peacefully upon his beloved river landscape.

Sometimes less personal considerations factor into the decision-making. Marc Houseman tells about another family considering the Hamburg Cemetery as a gravesite for a family member. They reported discovering the name of the deceased on a sheet of paper blowing around the grounds while they explored the cemetery. The family decided they quite clearly did not need to look any further in their search for a gravesite.

das Tagebuch

My wife Sheryl visited the Amana Colonies in Iowa and discovered a chronological burial pattern like that found in some cemeteries in the German Heritage Corridor. A chronological pattern using exactly the same type of gravesite characterized that communal German colony until nearly the Second World War.

Coping with the Past

The Hamburg Cemetery also reveals important issues about the maintenance and preservation of cemeteries throughout the German Heritage Corridor.

Coping represents an old German tradition found in the Hamburg Cemetery typically used to indicate the boundaries of a gravesite. People such as family members caring for the grave would use the coping to help guide their placement of plants, flowers, and other forms of decoration. Many cemeteries within the German Heritage Corridor and throughout the United

The historic Deutsche Evangelische Graveyard was founded at Femme Osage in 1833 and is part of the German Heritage Corridor.

States reflect this cultural tradition demonstrating high respect and encouraging care of the gravesite. However, many cemeteries today forbid and even remove coping to make lawn maintenance easier for riding lawnmowers.

At a deeper level, Hamburg Cemetery also indicates the constantly changing relationship of cemeteries to communities throughout the German Heritage Corridor. Although few cemeteries have experienced the total loss of their parish and surrounding community like Hamburg did, many of the communities and their residents have grown both physically and culturally distant from the funerary traditions these cemeteries represent. Walking regularly to the gravesite of a beloved family member to maintain the site and to lay flowers within the boundaries of its coping has mainly become a relic of the past. As people increasingly move to all parts of the country and even the world, many gravesites and headstones fall into serious disrepair.

Churches within Missouri's German Heritage Corridor like Friedens German/American Evangelical Church typically took great care with baptismal, marriage, and death records as well as gravesites for their members. Now, however, those traditionally close relationships between Missouri German congregations and these artifacts of cultural memory have considerably weakened if not completely eroded, like some of the headstones themselves.

The Franklin County Cemetery Society represents one meaningful response to such erosion of Missouri German funerary traditions. This nonprofit organization has assisted with research and restoration of more than a hundred Missouri German cemeteries. Caring for the graves of families besides your own enlarges your own sense of community. If tradition is "the democracy of the dead," in the words of G.K. Chesterton, curators of Missouri's German cemeteries like the Franklin County Cemetery Society have extended to our ancestors full voting privileges in Missouri's German heritage.

A German Requiem

Many 19th-century German Romantics like the poet Rilke embraced the idea of death as *vollkommen* (perfect or complete, the supreme climax of life). The 19th-century German philosopher Wilhelm Friedrich Hegel came to think of death as something which should be embraced as part of life; at a very personal level, he focused upon the joy of his infant daughter's birth rather than her brief life. Composer Johannes Brahms wrote his famous German Requiem as a mass for the living rather than a traditional mass for the dead. The Friedens German/English Evangelical Cemetery evokes a sense of *vollkommen*.

In the above-ground archaeology of Missouri's German cemeteries, we find an exclamation point placed upon the story of Missouri's German cultural heritage. As we drink deeply the rich wine of these mystic landscapes filled with stunning creations of wide-ranging religious devotion and masterful artistry, set within great natural beauty and sensitive landscape design, and honoring generations of Missourians with their German surnames and amazing life stories, great Death simply bows his head and weeps.

One German funerary tradition was the use of coping to mark off the boundaries of the gravesites. Coping guided placement of plantings and other decorations.

das Tagebuch

Landscape historian J.B. Jackson has written eloquently on the necessity of ruins in human communities. According to Jackson, we need ruins in order to allow opportunities for restoration and renewal, for retelling the story of the beloved community. As the Academic Coordinator for the Museum of Art and Archaeology at the University of Missouri, I saw first-hand how the ruined columns in the heart of campus played such a vital role in the constantly changing campus community.

Other Cemeteries with Strong German Heritage

- St. Vincent de Paul at Dutzow (above) sits high above the surrounding countryside, providing a breathtaking view. This church dates from 1874 and was originally a German Catholic parish. The cemetery is adjacent to the church.
- Indian Grove Cemetery, also known as Saint Raphaels Cemetery, in Chariton County near the St. Raphael Catholic Church, is another excellent example of an early German cemetery.
- The preservation-minded Brush and Palette Club is seeking help from the community to help preserve the Hermann City Cemetery, a historic landmark for the town. Gravestones remind visitors of some of the people who helped make Hermann such a beautiful town. About three hundred gravesites have been restored but more work remains in the oldest part of the cemetery. Examples of historic gravesites that help us understand Hermann are those of sisters Anna and Theresia Straub, ages 3 and 5, and their grandmother Maria Becht, who died within days of each other, during the cholera epidemic here in 1849. Another is the gravestone of Jacob Eisenhut. It was in pieces and buried in the dirt on the hillside. The marker was pieced together and put up on a new base.

geh und erforsche!

During *Weihnachtsfest* in Hermann, the Pommer-Gentner House is decorated in traditional fashion, and visitors can hear German carols and sample traditional cookies.

der Festspiele

If cemeteries represent the most permanent aspects of material culture for the German Heritage Corridor, then its festivals are certainly one of the most impermanent. However, the fleeting character of our festivals doesn't necessarily mean they are frivolous. All societies sponsor festivals and public celebrations, if not necessarily tailgate parties, to bind people to one another and to their culture. Feasts and festivals such as Maifest and Oktoberfest strongly reflect and still resonate with the natural and cultural heritage of Missouri Germans; many traditional Missouri German festivals have now become a regular part of Missouri life. And then there's the food!

Feasts and festivals, whether religious or secular, national or local, meet many important psychological and social needs while strengthening cultural identity. Celebrating a religious holiday or the Fourth of July with family and friends publicly declares your allegiance and reinforces your sense of community. During transitional periods of history like the Protestant Reformation, however, feasts and festivals like All Saints' Day may have lost some of their traditional value and binding functions.

Those of us living in the dramatically changing 21st century have therefore come to expect new, more modern iterations of traditional feasts and festivals, maybe going a bit easier on personal sacrifice and penitence. Reinterpreting feasts and festivals can reflect or even stimulate cultural changes, which generally occur in such periods of cultural transition and even crisis. For example, the US Bicentennial celebration offered a welcome respite for the country following the turbulent 1960s and the Watergate crisis and stimulated considerable interest in historic preservation and genealogy. Today, many festivals involve renewing cultural heritage, including its economy, as well as honoring its venerable traditions.

For example, as any viewer of Rick Steves travel shows must know, nearly every German burg sets up a *Kristkindlmarkt* (Christmas market). A winter festival gives you a genuine reason to go outside and directly into the cold winds of winter. At a Kristkindlmarkt, hardy visitors and shoppers can explore historic sites; browse through the colorful stands selling handicrafts, wooden toys, and glass ornaments; sample the *glühwein* (hot mulled wine), all kinds of fantastic cookies, and various hot nuts in a paper bag; or just savor the festive atmosphere and good spirits of all sorts. These fairs have proven so popular that other parts of the world have started copying, or reviving, the tradition, and the annual *Weihnachtsfest* (Christmas) in Hermann offers an excellent example of how such a festival can reflect and renew our Missouri German cultural heritage.

Pelz Nichol, a German St. Nicholas, appears at the Deutschheim State Historic Site in Hermann during the first two weekends of December, during the festival.

Frohliche Weihnachten

Deutschheim State Historic Site holds its annual Weihnachtsfest, a traditional 19th-century German Christmas celebration, during the first two weekends in December; it is one of three special events that the historic site features each year. Although Site Supervisor Cindy Browne loves all her children equally, she admits that "Weihnachtsfest really is the best special event we host." During the festival, the historic Deutschheim Site decorates its historic 1840 Pommer-Gentner House with seasonal greenery and lamplights. Weihnachtsfest also features traditional German music of the Christmas season in the piano-making workshop, which displays the beautiful 1830s pianoforte built by owner Charles Pommer back in Philadelphia before he emigrated to Missouri. You may also find musicians dressed in period costume performing traditional holiday music throughout the historic house.

Its historic rooms feature Christmas trees decorated with authentic German ornaments. An early type of artificial tree called *Federbaume* (feather trees) were made to resemble European firs, the preferred German Christmas tree symbolizing eternal life. On the practical level, their open shape makes displaying their ornaments much easier. Feather trees are made from goose quills that have been dyed green and then wrapped with

das Tagebuch

Here's my big chance to thank all the cooks at Zion Lutheran Church in old north St. Louis when I was growing up for the fabulous sauerbraten, green bean casseroles, and fruit pies they served at the annual Harvest Home (homecoming) church dinners all those decades ago.

Decorations at Deutschheim State Historic Site include a hanging tree, blown-glass ornaments, and authentic *Scherenschnitte*, which are paper ornaments. Springerle cookies are served.

wire around wooden dowels so that the sheared feathers resemble pine needles. Feather trees were first made in the 1860s when the unlimited cutting of firs for Christmas decorating was outlawed in Germany.

However, not all Christmas trees stood on floors or tables. In some parts of Germany, Christmas trees actually hung from the ceiling (with care, of course), a custom that some immigrants brought with them to Missouri, which is recreated at Weihnachtsfest. A "tree" of boughs affixed to a framework creates the image of a lovely hanging tree, decorated with ornaments made of ribbons, straw, gilded walnuts, painted eggs, and paper ornaments or "scraps" that you would have found in the 19th-century. *Scherenschnitte*, paper ornaments artfully cut by hand with scissors, also decorate the glamorous feather trees.

During Weihnachtsfest, Deutschheim State Historic Site specialists explain how the Christmas customs of Missouri German immigrants became Missouri and American traditions that are still celebrated today. Maybe it's the sense (or scents) of the season, but during Weihnachtsfest, the site specialists seem especially animated. One highlight of Weihnachtsfest includes sampling the delicious culinary custom of traditional German Christmas cookies, including springerle, *Lebkuchen*, and *zimmerschied*. The site's Weihnachtsfest gift shop not surprisingly offers springerle molds and rolling pins, recipe books, imported German pop-up cards, and books for visitors looking for unique Christmas gift-giving opportunities.

On one of those two early December weekends, the Hermann Kristkindlmarkt adds a medieval marketplace atmosphere to the Weihnachtsfest. In addition to the displays and museum guides at Deutschheim State Historic Site, other venues such as the Festhalle, The Mill, and the outdoor *Hofgarten* of the local Hermannhof district all hold festive activities involving this annual holiday celebration. According to *German World* magazine, the Hermann Kristkindlmarkt offers one of the most authentic German Christmas markets in North America. Every year, visitors from all over the Midwest explore its fifty vendors and their traditional German crafts and trades. Spirits of Christmas Past and Present mingle easily together, making it almost impossible to separate one from one another.

Festivals as Mirror Image

In his classic work *Mirror for Man*, anthropologist Clyde Kluckhohn called anthropology a mirror for humans, so perhaps we can better understand Missouri's German cultural heritage by considering how feasts and festivals such as Weihnachtsfest mirror cultural and personal changes. As Site Supervisor Cindy Browne observed, Weihwnachtsfest to a considerable degree reflects its time as well as each site supervisor's vision. It also reflects the local community and the larger Christmas festivities that have also changed over time. She noted that she and her staff "try to tell of traditions from the past that may have slipped away as well as those that continue."

Weihnachtsfest was originally held at the house winery in the site's Strehly House; residents told her it was regularly attended by locals who enjoyed sampling traditional cookies only available each year at the event. Residents sampled a local cook's famed *Schokoladenlebkuchen* in tiny pieces in order to ensure enough to go around. A long-time resident portrayed *Pelz Nichol*, a German St. Nicholas, and the Christmas exhibits occupied their traditional places. "It was," she said, "very charming and enjoyed each year as a local tradition."

Today Deutschheim State Historic Site hosts the event at the historic and elegant Pommer-Gentner House. Browne noted that she chose the Pommer-Gentner House specifically because it directly and elegantly links Philadelphia and its German Settlement Society to Hermann. Philadelphia was where the first Christmas tree in the United States was cut, decorated in the German tradition, and displayed by Dr. Constantin Hering, brother-in-law to Hermann's own George Husmann. The Deutschheim display shows Weihnachtsfest festival visitors how the family brought German Christmas traditions like the tree with them when they moved farther west to Missouri.

In addition, the Pommer-Gentner House has been renovated since those early days at the Deutschheim Site in the 1970s to 1980s; it can better accommodate the larger crowds that now come to Hermann for the event. The festival has also changed in that a second weekend involving a Kristkindlmarkt in Hermann has attracted more visitors from outside the community, while residents tend to attend the first weekend at Stone Hill. However, as Browne emphasized, "The site hosts Weihnachtsfest both weekends," holding up a mirror for residents and visitors.

Festivals and events also vary widely in authenticity, that Holy Grail of modern heritage tourism. To be defined as authentic in terms of tourism, the product or experience should still exist, express the true identity of the host community, and communicate properly the content and meaning so that the visitor can fully appreciate its value. Authenticity is critical for the success of Weihnachtsfest, Browne said. She specifically cited the authentic feather trees with their original blown-glass ornaments, period "scrap" ornaments, and wax candles on counterbalanced antique candleholders. Although she and her staff display the feather trees (the first artificial Christmas trees), they decorate the site only in cut greenery. The historic site also displays Victorian-era toys, as did the Strehly

Noteworthy Oktoberfests

- **ANHEUSER-BUSCH BREWERY OKTOBERFEST** features German music and entertainment, plus German-style beer and food. Games include barrel rolling and stein relays.
- **JEFFERSON CITY'S OKTOBERFEST** (above) is an annual event hosted by the Old Munichburg Association. Live music, a beer and wine garden serving authentic German food, demonstrations, and other activities are on West Dunklin, Washington, and Broadway Streets.
- **OKTOBERFEST IN COLE CAMP**, a town that has preserved its unique German heritage, includes traditional German food and beer, a wine and beer tasting, and antique farm machinery displays. It is held in conjunction with a Prairie Day event, which includes hayrides, nature exhibits, kids games, and evening star gazing.
- **SOULARD OKTOBERFEST** takes place in the oldest continuously run farmers market west of the Mississippi, founded in 1779. Authentic German fare, a wine garden, and live German bands complement the *bier* hall.
- **ST. CHARLES OKTOBERFEST** is one of the city's largest annual festivals. In Frontier Park along the Missouri River and next to the historic district, the festival features German music, vendors, and of course food and drink. *Gemütlichkeit* for the whole family!

geh und erforsche!

Other Hermann Festivals

- **WURSTFEST** is the fourth weekend of March and features all things sausage, German music, dancing, and a Wiener Dog Derby.
- **MAIFEST** is the third weekend of May and is a traditional spring celebration, with German music, Maypole dancers, children's games, and *bier gartens.*
- **OKTOBERFEST** (right) celebrates German Heritage throughout the entire month.

geh und erforsche!

House decades ago, and shares the traditions of both Catholic and Protestant families. *Pelz Nichol* still visits all the Hermann Christmas venues throughout the weekend.

Browne observed that most visitors to Weihnachtsfest have no idea these traditions actually originated in Germany and that our Missouri traditions are in fact German ones. We've lost sight of their origin. For that matter, she admits she did not know their origins before coming to Deutschheim as site supervisor. Carols sung in German provide beautiful background music, and occasionally visitors will sing along—some even in German. Many visitors know that *"Stille Nacht"* ("Silent Night") is German, but nothing else about it except perhaps its being sung during the First World War by German and American soldiers one Christmas Eve.

And then there's the great food. According to C. Michael Hall and Liz Sharples in their book *Food and Wine Festivals and Events Around the World*, "What is on the plate or in the glass at an event says much about the area, the community, the landscape, and the host. It may also say something about the individual who is consuming it."

Sharing of food and drink forms powerful emotional connections with a place; think of a first date or homecoming celebration. The renewed importance of food and drink in local culture and related tourism, perhaps related to the local food movement, has also encouraged the rapid growth of local heritage festivals. Rather than undertake a pilgrimage to find "a piece of the true cross," modern heritage tourists travel on their stomachs searching for a truly good croissant.

According to Site Supervisor Cindy Browne:

The Weihnachtsfest would not be the same without traditional German cookies, baked here in Hermann, most from Deutschheim's Midwest German Christmas *cookbook, which sells very briskly during the Weihnachtsfest.*

The festival still features a local legend's famous Schokoladenlebkuchen, but Deutschheim is now more likely to introduce it to new visitors each year. One traditional cookie that I've not yet learned to make is Ilse's marzipan, always made from scratch, formed into little potatoes with "eyes" indented, just as her mother made for her in Hamburg, Germany, as a little girl. Ilse always blanches the almonds herself and grinds them to make this wonderfully authentic cookie.

Most guests have never tasted marzipan.

We always serve delicious springerle cookies, beautiful creations made by Linda Walker Stevens [author of Most Wondrous Life *about*

> *Sampling bite-size cookies is a tradition Deutschheim State Historic Site has kept for many decades of Weihnachtsfest. It would not be the same without them.*

George Husmann], with anise flavor, the traditional German way. Many, many visitors remark that this reminds them of those their grandmother once made; sometimes they just called them anise cookies, not springerle. It is a delight to see smiles spread across their faces as they savor the taste of Christmas from their past. Some wrinkle their nose at the mention of anise (so we have lemon-flavored, too) and others love it.

A personal favorite that I bake is the zimmershied cookies, adapted to be made with Missouri black walnuts by German immigrants from Lower Saxony in the 1840s, always a visitor favorite and very easy to make. Many remember these as "refrigerator cookies," and the cookies do spend a night in the frig before they are sliced and baked. Rich with butter and chopped black walnuts, we always run out and I bake more.

Other cookie selections vary each year but sampling cookies, bite size so you can try multiple kinds, is a tradition Deutschheim has kept for many decades of Weihnachtsfest. It would not be the same without them.

Festivals as Heritage Tourism

Travelers and tourists apparently like to gaze deeply into the mirror of culture. Cultural heritage tourism is a branch of tourism oriented toward the cultural heritage of the location where the tourism is taking place. The National Trust for Historic Preservation defines it as "traveling to experience the places, artifacts, and activities that authentically represent the stories and people of the past," and "heritage tourism can include cultural, historic, and natural resources."

According to a Geotourism Study conducted by *National Geographic Traveler* in 2002:

- 61 percent of American travelers who took at least one trip the past three years agreed their experience is better when the destination preserves its natural, historic, and cultural sites and attractions.
- 52 percent are very or extremely likely to take trips to places that have authentic historic or archaeological buildings and sites.
- 49 percent are very or extremely likely to take trips to places where they can experience people, lifestyles, and cultures very different from their own.

Cultural heritage matters greatly to travelers and tourists in our new Experience Economy.

Festivals like Weihnachtsfest can play a vital role in bringing such resources dramatically to life. Browne observed that many visitors comment on "the smell of Christmas" upon entering the Pommer-Gentner House, especially if they grew up on a farm and remember cutting cedar boughs or a cedar tree for Christmas. "They breathe it in and usually share a story, with us or with their family." That potential for multigenerational storytelling makes community festivals and cultural heritage tourism important dimensions of Missouri's German cultural heritage in relation to the Missouri Humanities Council German Heritage Corridor initiative.

Caitlin Yager, the Heritage Programs Coordinator for the Missouri Humanities Council, views cultural heritage tourism for the Corridor as important for three main reasons:

- to encourage visitors to explore and experience a cultural heritage different from their own;
- to assist in exploring and understanding our own heritage, either for the first time or from a new, different perspective;
- to use cultural heritage and the experiences of those people as ways to impact local community and economic development.

However, cultural heritage tourism, sometimes referred to as "sense of place," can become just another consumer commodity if not cautiously calibrated. One too many T-shirt shops can tip the highly delicate balance; townspeople can feel like bit players on a stage set. The community's sense of itself and its outward image occasionally collide in festivals.

Browne is aware of that delicate balance, so she emphasizes preserving that old

The *Christmas Truce* is an illustration originally published in *The Illustrated London News*, January 9, 1915. The caption reads: "Saxons and Anglo-Saxons fraternising on the field of battle at the season of peace and goodwill: Officers and men from the German and British trenches meet and greet one another—A German officer photographing a group of foes and friends."

das Tagebuch

Some people collect baseball cards or dinnerware; I seem to collect museum experiences. Writing an article for Missouri Life magazine several years ago, I was profoundly moved by the National World War One memorial in Kansas City. Although it doesn't fit neatly in the German Heritage Corridor, in my view the World War I memorial seems essential for understanding Missouri's German cultural heritage.

memory of Christmas in Hermann for residents as well as sharing it with visitors. Festivals like Weihnachtsfest have involved the coevolution of people, landscape, food, drink, community, and culture. Community planning for festivals and special events needs a comprehensive approach and considerable involvement instead of just branding, to maintain authenticity and sustain that sense of place for future generations.

In regard to preserving heritage to understand the past but also shape the future, Yager with the Missouri Humanities Council said:

> *You cannot hope to shape a healthy future unless you understand your culture, your heritage, very simply, where you "come from." Brunswick, for example, knows that a big part of its heritage is the fact that they are known for growing pecans. While that might not scream "culture" or "economic development opportunity," the community got creative and decided to create a festival dedicated to it. An important facet of their past is guiding their future by bringing in money and tourism, while also educating people on and celebrating something significant from their past. With the German Heritage Corridor, we hope to use a similar tactic when promoting and celebrating the German cultural heritage of individual communities, asking them:*
>
> - *What is your unique natural and cultural heritage?*
> - *How can we use that today to help you tomorrow?*

Maybe history does repeat itself, and not always as farce. Yager's questions call to mind many young 19th-century idealists like Paul Follenius and Friedrich Muench hoping to revitalize their German cultural heritage in the Far West of Missouri (see Chapter 3). Now, however, what Follenius and Muench, among many others, created here has also become part of that heritage, to be transformed in the alchemy of cultural heritage tourism.

Stille Nacht

While heritage tourism and festivals like the Weihnachtsfest grow out of the core discipline of history, they also draw upon a wide variety of the humanities, how humans tell their stories and create meaning in their lives. Instead of iron chefs competing for prizes and status, the culinary arts help us share traditional foods with our ancestors and descendants. Instead of flipping houses for a quick profit, the decorative arts enable us to enter rooms and past lives.

The National WWI Museum and Memorial

SITTING ATOP A HILL in Kansas City, this complex is impressive as a public memorial as well as a museum. Its poppy field display may take your breath away. As the Memorial dramatically reveals, the First World War swept away the preindustrialized world. In the process, the war transformed Missouri cultural heritage, too, almost like reversing the polarities of an electrical battery, by making Missouri Germans hide rather than celebrate their unique heritage. Visitors will also learn why "the war to end all wars" wasn't the last.

Festivals in particular possess many aspects of drama and theater, telling the community's story to a wandering and wondering audience. In festivals, "the play's the thing by which to capture the conscience" of residents and visitors.

Music is also one of the humanities that tells our stories and creates meaning. It can also help explain the role of festivals in preserving and enriching Missouri's German cultural heritage. Fleeting as a festival, the music of Christmas can nevertheless remain with you forever. On the other hand, in Richard Wagner's opera *Die Meistersingers*, Hans Sachs, the Meister (master) of the town's music festival, sings plaintively and prophetically about the Wahn (madness) that sometimes possesses individuals (think Elvis singing "Blue Christmas") and perhaps even the entire heritage of a culture.

Sometimes, though, the better angels of our nature organize the festival and choose the music. In December 1914, one of the most unusual events in all of human history, a spontaneous Weihnachtsfest, took place on the bloody battlefields of Flanders. Following a fierce battle by German troops with British and French armies, both sides were dug in, relatively safe in muddy trenches dug six to eight feet deep along lines that seemed to stretch forever. Then German troops quite unexpectedly began placing small Christmas trees, lit with candles, outside of their trenches and started singing Christmas songs. Across the way, British and French troops responded with carols of their own. Many of the Germans who had worked in England before the war were able to speak enough English well enough to propose a Christmas truce.

According to Stanley Weintraub in his book, *Silent Night:*

> *Signboards arose up and down the trenches in a variety of shapes. They were usually in English, or—from the Germans—in fractured English. Rightly, the Germans assumed that the other side could not read traditional gothic lettering, and that few English understood spoken German. 'YOU NO FIGHT, WE NO FIGHT' was the most frequently employed German message. Some British units improvised 'MERRY CHRISTMAS' banners and waited for a response. More placards on both sides popped up.*

Soldiers left their trenches and shook hands in the middle of No Man's Land. They buried the dead who had been unreachable because of the recent fighting. Then they exchanged gifts: chocolate cake, cognac, postcards, newspapers, and tobacco. In a few places along the trenches, soldiers laid down their rifles and picked up soccer balls, turning No Man's Land into a lively football pitch. A Scottish poet of that era, Frederick Niven, writing of the miracle in "A Carol from Flanders," wrote:

O ye who read this truthful rime
From Flanders, kneel and say:
God speed the time when every day
Shall be as Christmas Day.

At its best, Weihnachtsfest becomes our own "Carol from Flanders." Maybe it's the holiday season that makes this festival appeal so widely to so many people. It almost seems as though the *Wahn*, the dark clouds of war with Germany during the 20th century that have often darkened Missouri's German cultural heritage, momentarily lift to reveal a bright vision of the Holy Grail. In the special glow of Weihnachtsfest, we catch a fleeting glimpse of *E Pluribus Unum*, Missouri's German cultural heritage proudly and happily enriching Missouri and American life. While festivals like Weihnachtsfest inevitably reflect and change with the times, they also give us a rare opportunity to stop time altogether and to gather ourselves into whole people once again.

Frohliche Weihnachten!

EISWEIN

Ice Wine

Savoring German Heritage

Over thirty years ago, I spoke at the University of Tubingen in Germany about Missouri's German cultural heritage and actually believed I knew something about this important topic. This new exploration of Missouri's German cultural heritage that you have in your hands clearly exposed that illusion for what it was: an exciting, early chapter in the story of my *Bildungsroman* (life education). What I've learned from this chapter of the Bildungsroman is how much remains to learn about this incredibly rich cultural heritage.

On his deathbed, the great German poet and scientist Johann Wolfgang von Goethe is supposed to have whispered the words "more light" to those attending him. Goethe may simply have wanted someone to draw back the curtains in the room, but in the light of his life those words came to mean "enlightenment." The end of this journey into Missouri's German cultural heritage also calls for "more light" in the form of additional perspectives from others on this brave old world. A glass of very fine wine might also prove illuminating.

Late Harvest Wine

Vintners like those in Missouri's German Heritage Corridor sometimes make *Eiswein* (ice wine) from grapes picked very late in the harvest season, ripened well past the sugar levels required for ordinary *Tafelwein* (table wine). This extra ripening time, which can often last for weeks, creates residual sugar in the remaining grapes. The high sugar content of the selected grapes can become a wine that's sweet or a wine high in alcohol—or preferably both.

In order for the grapes to freeze, they have to remain on the vine well into the winter months, whenever that takes place along the German Heritage Corridor. Waiting for them to freeze adds significant risk for both grower and vintner from rain, rot, and ravens. If the weather doesn't cooperate and the grapes don't freeze, the entire crop of selected grapes can be lost. Harvesting of the grapes typically takes place by hand in the early and thus cold morning hours when acidity levels peak. Pressing these hardy survivors produces only tiny amounts of juice, which is one key reason Eiswein is valuable and commands extremely high prices.

Grapes for late-harvest wine may be picked in November—it all depends on the weather. Eiswein, by contrast, is an extreme version of the late-harvest style; the grapes are usually picked in December or early January during the first sustained drop in temperature. Shriveled berries are harvested and gently pressed while still frozen. Water, which accounts for roughly four-fifths of the fluid volume, remains trapped inside the skins as ice and gets discarded. The flavorful, super-concentrated juice, the other one-fifth of the volume, stays fluid; it seeps into the fermenting vat to yield Eiswein.

A Special Reserve

I have come to think of this publication about Missouri's German cultural heritage as a kind of Eiswein. Like Eiswein, it distills some of the best artifacts of Missouri's German cultural heritage. These hardy survivors endured the bitter frosts of two world wars and Prohibition as well as the pervasive blight of much thoughtless modern development. I also regard it as a special reserve

wine that required considerable care in its preparation and preservation. That's because it's made from a small supply of heirloom grapes, cultivated from the priceless and irreplaceable rootstock of Missouri's German cultural heritage.

Well over thirty years ago, all of the following offered me ample evidence of the endangered status of these heirloom grapes: genealogical research stimulated by the US Bicentennial in 1976; Charles van Ravenswaay's 1977 book, *The Arts and Architecture of German Settlements in Missouri: A Survey of a Vanishing Culture*; the German-American Tricentennial (1983) celebration; and my American Studies program and related research at Saint Louis University during the 1980s. Now, decades later, the surviving "vineyards" of this heritage across the German Heritage Corridor have experienced even more losses. However, I firmly believe this endangered species of cultural diversity, especially when distilled into a precious Eiswein, can still enlighten and delight Missouri life.

That's because Eiswein pairs very well with nostalgia. The term "nostalgia," of Swiss origin, is a composite of Greek words *nostos* (homecoming) and *algos* (longing) meaning "mourning for the lost home" (think of Odysseus struggling for decades to get back home to Ithaca and his family). The *die Heimat* (home) of Missouri's German cultural heritage dwells in the very heart of Missouri life, offering us a taste of home. Nostalgia can be debilitating if it keeps us "bottled up" and dwelling solely in the past, or it can help us healthily carry our heritage forward into the future, just as we would transport our precious family heirlooms. Such a potent potable definitely has to be enjoyed in moderation, sipped slowly, and savored to maximize its health benefits, as George Husmann recommended during his wondrous life.

However, nostalgia is history without the pain. Many winegrowers and vintners believe that everything that goes into the land eventually reveals itself in the grapes and the wine. Not surprisingly, then, this vintage of Eiswein contains several predominant flavors as well as a bracing acidity:

- ***Natur***: The German Heritage Corridor is Missouri's own Romantic Road. It still reveals an awareness and appreciation of the natural world that blends deep knowledge of nature with a preindustrial ethos of reverence revealed in its farms, wineries, and its very location in the heart of Missouri.
- ***Landschaft***: Along with *Natur*, in this Eiswein one can detect and savor a deep-seated desire to respectfully shape that living landscape for beauty and permanence in its streetscapes, buildings, and even cemeteries.
- ***Freiheit***: German immigrants in the 19th century brought a revolutionary love of *die Freiheit* (liberty) to America, where it had first been planted in the late 18th century and spread to Europe. Just like Missouri German wine experts helped rescue European vineyards in the 19th century by grafting their rootstock onto European vines, German immigrants like Friedrich Muench grafted *Freiheit* onto the Far West

of Missouri to help it withstand the blighting influences of slavery.

- ***Gemutlichkeit***: Maybe the Eiswein is just too heady for me, but I really believe you can still hold it up to the light and catch sparkling reflections of food, festivals, and wine gardens, even the faint echo of a zither, the *Gemutlichkeit* (coziness) of a German home.
- ***Schmerzen:*** This Eiswein is not all sweetness and light, however. You can still detect hints of *der Schmerz* (the pain) of transatlantic voyages and burials at sea, fierce frontier conditions, and soul-crushing cultural challenges during World War I and Prohibition. Even its own high standards occasionally demanded far too much of ordinary people, as George Bayer, one of the founders of Hermann, unhappily learned.

Eiswein definitely represents an acquired taste, and its appreciation requires "more light." Enjoying its many flavors benefits greatly from patient exploration, as well as thoughtful mentoring from the many dedicated stewards of Missouri's German cultural heritage. It can be enjoyed alone, but it really sparkles when shared *mit Freunde* (with friends), special companions who also savor its special qualities and the great care that goes into making it. I have tried throughout this publication to acknowledge their many written and spoken contributions to this project. Cheers!

Because classical Greek culture meant so much to German cultural heritage, it seems especially appropriate that the Eiswein of Missouri's German cultural heritage should enliven and enrich a contemporary symposium about that heritage's current meaning. The leader of a symposium in classical Greek culture was charged with balancing its quality, amount, and flow of wine in order to ensure that the conversation functioned at a high level of lively intelligence, rather than deteriorating into drunken drivel (or dribble, if you will). The German Heritage Corridor initiative has been and will continue, I hope, to serve as such a symposium.

Eiswein represents the perfect toast to this monumental journey, to my friends and colleagues in the Missouri Humanities Council German Heritage Corridor initiative, and to my own *Bildungsroman* occasionally sketched here in the pages of *das Tagebuch*. Despite my very clear awareness of its considerable limitations and incompleteness, I also take considerable comfort in knowing that even the incomparable Alexander von Humboldt, Goethe's great friend and inspiration for this project, could not complete his *Kosmos* lifework.

This publication is by no means a *Kosmos*, an encyclopedia, or the last word on Missouri's German cultural heritage. Previous generations of Missouri Germans would probably call it a "hotch-potch." However, I do hope this hotch-potch offers you a small window with a good view on that remarkable world, preferably on a hill overlooking a vineyard with the Missouri River in the distance, with more light and a clear vantage on this unfolding new chapter in the German Heritage Corridor's exploration, preservation, and interpretation.

Acknowledgments

THE SHEER SIZE of Missouri's German Heritage Corridor (see page ix), not to mention its lengthy history and cultural complexity, requires multiple perspectives. With her longstanding and widespread statewide advocacy for Missouri's German cultural heritage, public historian Dorris Keevan-Franke provided *Missouri Life* the overview perspective that helped us build a solid foundation for this uniquely multilayered publication about that rich heritage.

Then *Missouri Life* asked me to offer an ethnographer's perspective on Missouri's vast German cultural heritage because of my previous *Missouri Life* essays about Missouri's special places, my expertise in American material culture studies, and my own Missouri German heritage.

My interpretations of Missouri German cultural artifacts draw heavily upon the humanities such as literature and cultural geography, as well as the people and resources of the Missouri Humanities Council's German Heritage Corridor learning community, with special thanks to Dr. Steve Belko, Executive Director of the Missouri Humanities Council, and Caitlin Yager, the Humanities Council's outstanding Heritage Program Coordinator. I sincerely hope that my essays and this multilayered publication return value to that vital initiative and learning community. I would especially like to acknowledge the scholarly insights I gained at our State Historical Society conference panel on Missouri's German heritage from Dr. Petra deWitt and Dr. Cathie Schoppenhorst, as well as celebrate the endless and essential support of museum directors Cindy Browne and Marc Houseman.

The incredible array of visual images displayed throughout this publication depicting Missouri's historic and contemporary German cultural heritage offers another, invaluable perspective into that heritage. Documenting that expansive heritage and illustrating key features of the interpretive essays required high levels of due diligence from Kath Teoli, Edward Lang, and Casey Vroman.

As always for *Missouri Life*, your perspective remains the most important one of all. To help you enrich your own perspective, we have included an exploration layer of this publication, as well as my field notes *(das Tagebuch)* to perhaps prompt you to go explore and further reflect on your own about Missouri's German cultural heritage.

—W. Arthur Mehrhoff

CURT DENNISON

Discover Hermann's German Heritage

Above: The Gasconade County Courthouse stands proud atop a bluff overlooking the Missouri River Valley below. *Photo by Ken Kunstmann* • Below: Many trails surround Hermann.

The city of Hermann welcomes thousands of visitors each year, showcasing a distinctive German experience right here in Missouri. Harkening Old-World charm, buildings of Hermann have been restored to their former glory in addition to housing businesses unique to the town itself, including German cuisine and beverages.

Visitors can experience a piece of Germany in an authentic way in a community founded by German immigrants almost 200 years ago. Before prohibition, Hermann was one of the largest wine producers in the world. The hilly and rocky terrain make the area perfect for growing grapes.

Continuing with traditions that began all those years ago, Hermann is known for its many festivals throughout the year. From events that spotlight the area's wine industry, food, and Christmas traditions, celebrations take a cue from their beginnings in the Old County.

There is plenty to do and see, even when a festival is not in full swing. Surrounded by vineyards, rolling hills, and the Missouri River Valley, the town boasts many attractions for the adventure seeker. Not only do hiking enthusiasts have much to appreciate while in Hermann, but the bicyclist will be able to take a ride on the nationally acclaimed Katy Trail nearby.

Hermann has a plethora of event venues, hosting weddings, special occasions, and business gatherings each year. With a picturesque setting, it is no wonder Hermann is a memory maker.

Being a small community, Hermann has a dedicated art scene. The art council has a mission "to encourage and sponsor a variety of musical, theatrical, dramatic, and other visual and performing arts programs for the advancement of cultural awareness and the arts within the city and surrounding area of Hermann."

Visitors can get to Hermann by bicycle, car, hiking, or by train. Amtrak brings guests either from St. Louis, which is one hour away, or Kansas City via the Missouri River Runner. While the Katy Trail runs on the opposite side the river, there is a dedicated walkway to the town along a route that crosses the Missouri River bridge. Of course, there are several routes into Hermann for the driving enthusiast, making it is easy to discover Hermann if you have never been here before.

Quaint inns, charming B&Bs, and a historic hotel welcome guests every day. Hermann is more than a day trip, it is a destination. Find more information at VisitHermann.com.

Hermann boasts German charm along the Missouri River, one hour west of St. Louis.

Hill of Peace Church in Friedenberg

Apple Creek Grotto

German Journey to Perry County

Baden, Bavaria & Saxony

In the early 1820s, German Catholic immigrants from the Baden area were among the first to settle in Apple Creek. These immigrants left Europe from the nearest ports, Le Havre, France, and Antwerp, Belgium, and arrived in Perry County through New Orleans. The settlement's first Catholic church named St. Joseph was built in 1828. Between 1881–1884, a third church was constructed for the parish. Our Lady of St. Joseph shrine was built in 1857 and incorporates a natural cave spring with stonework and the Via Dolorosa walkway.

More Baden immigrants came in the 1840s to Biehle Station, named after an early German immigrant, Maurus Biehle. They, too, constructed a church, cleared the land for building homes and businesses and left their unique German traits behind with their descendants. You can still find this heritage today in food, speech, writings, and way of life.

Friedenberg was founded in 1838 by Lutheran immigrants from Bavaria, Germany. These Bavarians came from the Upper Franconian region, some from the city of Langenstadt near present-day Kulmbach. They worshiped in members' homes until a log church was built in 1846 north of Cinque Hommes Creek. From 1852 until 1885 the congregation worshiped at their church at Frankenberg overlooking the Cinque Hommes Bottoms. In 1885 the congregation moved to its present site named Friendenberg by the Bavarians, meaning "Hill of Peace" and built a brick church which serves today as a historical site documenting their journey, faith, and aspirations to start a new life in a new country.

In 1838, approximately seven hundred German Lutherans from the Saxony Region left their homes, farms, businesses, and all that they knew, to embark on a dangerous sea voyage to America. They traveled by steamboat from New Orleans to St. Louis, later claiming their settlements in Perry County named Paitzdorf, Seelitz, Dresden, Frohna, Johannisberg, Wittenberg, and Altenburg. Eventually, the leadership from these settlements joined to form the Lutheran Church-Missouri Synod denomination. Several of these communities that were established in 1839 are still thriving today, providing rich cultural experiences that can be found by visiting the Lutheran Heritage Center Research Library & Museum in Altenburg, a German genealogy archive and home of the Log Cabin College, the first Concordia University site. Enjoy the nearby Saxon Lutheran Memorial log cabin village, a living history German settlement, and an amazing Fall Festival.

Countless German descendants in Missouri and beyond can trace their roots back to Perry County. To plan a trip to this authentic early Missouri region, or for more information, visit VisitPerryCounty.com.

Concordia Log Cabin College

Urban Chestnut Brewing Company

Urban Chestnut Brewing Company (UCBC) is an unconventionally minded yet traditionally oriented brewer of craft beer. Founded in 2010 by Florian Kuplent and David Wolfe, Urban Chestnut operates three breweries in St. Louis. Kuplent is a German-born-and-trained Brewmaster with extensive experience at small breweries worldwide and with the world's largest brewery, Anheuser-Busch. Wolfe is a twenty-year brewing industry member. Their breweries are:

- The Midtown Brewery & Biergarten at 3229 Washington Avenue in Grand Center
- The Grove Brewery & Bierhall at 4465 Manchester in Forest Park Southeast
- The U.R.B. (Urban Research Brewery) at 4501 Manchester also in Forest Park Southeast, where they brew batches of artisanal, modern American beers (their Revolution series) and classically crafted European styles (their Reverence series).

Urban Chestnut also operates a fourth brewery, the Urban Chestnut Hallertauer Brauerei, in the Hallertau region of Bavaria, where they brew their Hallertauer Serie; small batches of locally sourced, Bavarian bier.

UCBC's German-style beers, such as their flagship Bavarian Lager (Zwickel), as well as Schnickelfritz (Bavarian Weissbier), Stammtisch (German Pilsner) and Dorfbier (Munich Dunkel), reflect Florian's Bavarian heritage, and their excellent reputation stems in part from his education in German brewing, culminating in a master's degree from the prestigious University of Munich's Weihenstephan brewing school. Urban Chestnut also uses German malt and hops in all of their 'old world' offerings to highlight their unique German terroir and to ensure the authenticity of these classic styles.

Urban Chestnut not only supplies the Midwest with traditional German beer, they also seek to bring German culture to the St. Louis beer scene. Their original location in Midtown features a 300-seat Bavarian-style Biergarten (complete with .5L and 1L steins), and their larger production facility in the Grove houses a large industrial beer hall, both of which offer the convivial atmosphere typical of Bavarian beer culture where people enjoy beer and food (such as Schnitzel and bratwurst).

UCBC's commitment to upholding their German roots is at its best during their largest, annual festival of the year: Oktoberfest St. Louis. This three-day celebration of German music, German food, and of course, German bier, takes place each year at the end of September to coincide with Munich's Oktoberfest. The festival's attendance continues to grow each year, and it features a full line up of live music, Masskrugstemmen (stein-holding competitions), and traditional German fare, like bratwursts, pretzels, and Lebkuchen.

The Grove Brewery & Bierhall

Regardless of which brewery you visit, either the Midtown Brewery & Biergarten, the Grove Brewery & Bierhall, The U.R.B., or the Hallertauer Brauerei, all are located in areas with unique histories; areas that are undergoing revolutions of their own, allowing them to be a part of a vibrant culture grounded by their German roots. Visit UrbanChestnut.com for more information.

Florian Kuplent (second from right) with brewery staff at UCBC's Hallertau Brauerei.

The Grove Brewhouse

Bibliography

1. **ein Bildungsroman: The Eye of the Beholder**

2. **die Zeitgeist: Marking the Spirit of the Time**

Ground Zero of a Monumental Journey

- Daum, Andreas. "Alexander von Humboldt, die Natur als 'Kosmos' und die Suche nach Einheit. Zur Geschichte von Wissen und seiner Wirkung als Raumgeschichte," *Berichte zur Wissenschaftsgeschichte*, Vol. 23, Issue 3, 2000, pp.243-268, p.247.
- www.waymarking.com/waymarks WMM8K3_Alexander_Von_Humboldt_Tower_Grove_park_St_Louis_MO.
- Riley, Marianna. "Plaque Honoring Explorer Returned to Tower Grove." *St. Louis Post-Dispatch*, November 13, 1995, p.1B.
- Walls, Laura Dassow."The Passage to Cosmos: Alexander von Humboldt and the Shaping of America." Chicago, IL: University of Chicago Press, 2009.

Incident at Camp Jackson

- "The Camp Jackson Interpretive Sign" *The Civil War Muse*. www.thecivilwarmuse.com/index.php?page=camp-jackson-2.
- Lewis, Peirce F. "Axioms for Reading the Landscape," *The Interpretation of Ordinary Landscapes*. D.W. Meinig, editor. New York: Oxford University Press, 1979, pp.11-32.
- Rowan, Steve. Translated, Wilhelm Kaufmann, "The Germans in the American Civil War." Carlisle, PA: Kalmann, 1999.
- Williams, Scott. "The Role of German Immigrants in Civil War Missouri." Missouri Civil War Museum. www.mcwm.org/history_germans.html.

Sign of the Times

- "Anti-German Prohibition" *History in the City*. www.historyinthecity.weebly .com/prohibition-and-world-war-i.html.
- DeWitt, Petra. "Degrees of Allegiance: Harassment and Loyalty in Missouri's German-American Community during World War I." Athens, OH: Ohio University Press, 2012.
- Geertz, Clifford. "The Interpretation of Cultures." New York: Basic Books Classics, 1977.
- LaFrance, Adrienne. "The Six Main Arcs in Storytelling, as Identified by an AI." *Atlantic Magazine*, July 12, 2016. A machine mapped the most frequently used emotional trajectories in fiction, then compared them with the ones readers like best.
- Leahy, Joseph. "Century-Old War Leaves Lasting Impact on St. Louis German Identity." *St.Louis Public Radio*, August 8, 2014.
- Richardson, Chris. "With Liberty and Justice for All?: The Suppression of the German-American Culture During World War I." *Missouri Historical Review* 90 October 1995: pp.79-89.

3. **die Auswanderung: O Brave New World**

Whoa, Duden

- Burnett, Robyn and Ken Luebbering. "German Settlement in Missouri: New Land, Old Ways." Columbia, MO: University of Missouri Press, 1996.
- Getty Conservation Institute. www.getty.edu/conservation/core_areas /buildings/index.
- Translated by William G. Bek. "Gottfried Duden's Report, 1824-27." *Missouri Historical Review*, Vol. XIII January, 1919: pp.174-180.
- The Library of Congress Teachers Classroom Materials: Immigration. "Immigration...German." www.loc.gov/teachers/classroommaterials /presentationsandactivities/presentations/immigration/german4.html.
- Lowenthal, David. "The Past is a Foreign Country." Cambridge, UK: Cambridge University Press, 1985.
- Parrish, William Earl et. al. "A History of Missouri: 1820-1860." Columbia, MO: University of Missouri Press, 2000.
- Schroeder, Adolf E., "Why Emigrate?" *What Wondrous Life: The World of George Husmann, 1827-1902*. Edited by Linda Walker Stevens. Hermann, MO: Hermann University Press, 2017.
- Swick, Thomas. "The Joys of Travel And Stories That Illuminate."
- Walker, Mack. "Germany and the Emigration, 1816-1885." Cambridge, MA: Harvard University Press, 1964.

Legacy

- Burnett, Robyn and Ken Luebbering. "German Settlement in Missouri: New Land, Old Ways (Missouri Heritage Readers)." First edition. Columbia, MO: University of Missouri, 1996.
- "Fascinated by The Idea of America" *300 Years of Germans in America*. Munich: Verags-GmbH, 1982.
- "Giessen Emigration Society," Missouri Germans Consortium. www.mo-germans.com/members/.
- Noted local historian Ralph Gregory published a full translation of Friedrich Muench's biography of Paul Follenius in the July, 1967 *Bulletin of the Missouri Historical Society*. The version used in this text, from The Deutschheim Association Journal *Der Maibaum, the Deutschheim Verein Journal*, Vol. XIX, No.1 Spring, 2011 has been edited for the 150th anniversary observance.
- LaBarge, Scott. "Why Heroes are Important." Markula Center for Applied Ethics. Santa Clara State University, January 1, 2000. www.scu.edu/ethics /focus-areas/more/resources/heroism-why-heroes-are-important/.
- Mallinckrodt, Anita M., Marc Houseman, Cathie Schoppenhorst, and James F. Muench. *The Historic* "1830s German Immigration to Missouri." Augusta, MO: Footnote Legacies Ltd., 2015.
- Renn, Erin Mc Cawley. "Our German Heritage: Emigrants from Germany, Immigrants to the Midwest, Part I." *Der Maibaum*, Vol. 2, No.2 Summer 1994, pp.1-5 and Part II, Vol. 2, Nos.3-4 Winter 1994, pp.1-3.

Statue of Limitations

- Bek, William G. "The German Settlement Society of Philadelphia and its Colony, Hermann, Missouri." Philadelphia: Americana Germanica Press, 1907.
- Pettijohn, Lee. "Hermann Remembers and Honors George Bayer." Experience Hermann. www.experiencehermann.com /hermann-missouri-news/hermann-remembers-and-honors-george-bayer.
- Stevens, Linda Walker. "Hermann, Missouri: Pearl of Great Price." *Der Maibaum*, Vol. VIII, No.4 Winter, 2001, pp.3, 6-8.

4. **die Landschaften: Shaping the Landscape**

Sense of Place

- Gerlach, Russel L. "Immigrants in the Ozarks." Columbia, MO: University of Missouri Press, 1976.
- Kamphoefner, Walter. "The Westfalians: From Germany to Missouri" (Princeton Legacy Library). Princeton, NJ: Princeton University Press, 2016.
- Marshall, Howard W. and Goodrich, James W., editors. "The German-American Experience in Missouri." Publications of the Missouri Cultural Heritage Center, No. 2. Columbia, MO: University of Missouri, 1986.

The Once and Future Village

- Historic Southside/Old Munichburg district and neighborhood plan..City of Jefferson, MO. August 2017.
- Missouri Department of Natural Resources. National Register nomination for Broadway/Dunklin Historic District. https://dnr.mo.gov/shpo/nps-nr/02001300.pdf. September 25, 2002.
- "Old Munichburg: Jefferson City's historic German 'Southside.'" www.oldmunichburg.com
- Rybczynski, Witold. "City Life." New York: Scribner's, 1995.
- Schroeder, Walter A. "Southside Sketches: Essays on Jefferson City's Old Munichburg." Jefferson City, MO: Old Munichburg Association, 2016.

A Picture Worth a Thousand Words

- The George Engelmann Papers. Missouri Botanical Garden Archives, in the Biodiversity Heritage Library. The Biodiversity Heritage Library (BHL) is a consortium of natural history and botanical libraries, including the Missouri Botanical Garden. www.biodiversitylibrary.org.
- "George Engelmann" in Everipedia. www.everipedia.org/wiki /George_Engelmann/.
- Grove, Carol. "Henry Shaw's Victorian Landscapes: The Missouri Botanical Garden and Tower Grove Park." University of Massachusetts Press, 2005.
- National Academy of Sciences member directory. www.nasonline.org /member-directory/deceased-members/20001821.html.

5. **das Arbeit: Good Work**

Barn Again

- Arendt, Randall. "Rural by Design: Planning for Town and Country" 2nd Edition, Kindle Edition. New York, NY: Routledge Publications, 2017.
- Berry, Wendell. Counterpoint Publishers, 2015.
- Blackwell, Claire. "The Pelster Housebarn A Missouri-German Landmark."

OzarksWatch, Vol. III, No. 1, Summer 1989.

- Heidegger, Martin. "Building, Dwelling, Being," in *Poetry, Language, Thought*. New York, NY: Harper Perennial Books, 1971.
- Marshall, Howard. "The Pelster Housebarn: Endurance of Germanic Architecture on the Midwestern Frontier." *Material Culture*. Vol. 18, No. 2 Summer 1986, pp.65-104.
- Menke, David. "Ravensburg Roots: Life of the Tenant Family." *Der Maibaum*, Vol. XXVI, No. 2 Fall/Winter 2017, pp.4-10. See section on The Housebarn.
- "Object and Image: The German Housebarn in America." An exhibition organized and produced as a joint project of the Missouri Cultural Heritage Center, University of Missouri-Columbia and the Jefferson National Expansion Memorial NHS/National Park Service, St. Louis, MO. 1983.

Another Fine Mash

- Miller, Carl. "The Rise of the Beer Barons." Reprinted from *All About Beer Magazine*, 1999. www.beerhistory.com/library/holdings/beerbarons.shtml.
- Japhe, Brad. "How America Is Shaking Up Centuries of German Beer Tradition." www.eater.com/drinks/2016/2/3/10904398/america-germany-craft-beer-traditions. February 3, 2016.
- National Register nomination for John B. Busch Brewery in Washington, MO. www.dnr.mo.gov/shpo/nps-nr/00001094.pdf.
- Schroeder, Walter A. "Breweries & Saloons in Jefferson City, Missouri." Jefferson City, MO: Old Munichburg Association, 2009.
- Weinberg, David. "Kraftig, not craft beer: the new Busch brewery aiming to compete with Budweiser." January 6, 2012. *St. Louis Public Radio*, wwwnews .stlpublicradio.org/post/kräftig-not-craft-beer-new-busch-brewery-aiming-compete-budweiser#stream/0.

die Weinstrasse

- "The History of Missouri Wine." *Welcome to Missouri Wine Country: Your Guide to the Missouri Wine Experience*. www.missouriwinecountry.com /articles/history/
- Dufur, Brett. "Exploring Missouri Wine Country." Rocheport, MO: Pebble Publishing Company, 2007.
- Robinson, J. editor, "German History" *The Oxford Companion to Wine*. Third Edition, pp.304-308, Oxford University Press 2006.
- "History" Hermann Farm website www.hermannfarm.com/history.
- www.en.wikipedia.org/wiki/German_wine.
- "What Wondrous Life: The World of George Husmann." An Interpretive Exhibit. Missouri Folklore Society June 2003. www.missourifolkloresociety .truman.edu/husmann.html.
- Walker Stevens, Linda, editor. "What Wondrous Life: The World of George Husmann, 1827-1902." Hermann Deutschheim Verein: Hermann, MO, 1917.
- www.missourideutschheimverein.org/husmann.html.
- Stovall, Brittany. "Missouri's Wine and Grape Industry is Booming." *Farm Flavor*, September 26, 2017. www.farmflavor.com/athome.
- Husmann, George. The Project Gutenberg EBook "The Cultivation of The Native Grape, and Manufacture of American Wines." www.gutenberg.org /ebooks/20917

6. Alltagskultur: The Enchantment of Everyday Life

die Deutsche Kuche

- Darnton, Julia. "Foodways: When food meets culture and history." msue .anr.msu.edu/news/foodways_when_food_meets_culture_and_history. Michigan State University Extension. Posted on December 12, 2012.
- "Food History: Midwest Food Customs and Traditions." *Der Maibaum*, Vol. 1, No. 3&4 Winter 1994, pp.2-6.
- Sheraton, Mimi. "The German Cookbook." New York, NY: Random House, 1965.

An die Musik

- Cortinovis, Irene E. "The Golden Age of German Song." *Missouri Historical Review*, 8, Issue 4 July 1974, pp.437-442.
- Davis, Thomas M. and Franz R. Beinke, "Franz Schwarzer: Missouri Zither Maker," *Missouri Historical Review* 60, No. 1 October 1965, pp.24-25:
- Larson, Walt, editor. Franz Schwarzer: "The King of Zither Manufacturers." Washington, MO: Washington Historical Society, 2018.
- Mallinckrodt, Anita M. "Augusta's "Harmony": The Harmonie-Verein Cultural Society, 1856-1922." Augusta, MO: Mallinckrodt Communications, 2005.

One Good Turner

- Collins, Cameron. "George Eyser's Big Day at the 1904 Olympics." www .distilledhistory.com/georgeeyser/. Poster August 12, 2016.
- Friedrich Jahn Memorial. www.forestparkmap.org/friedrich-jahn-memorial.
- Saure, Felix. "Beautiful Bodies, Exercising Warriors and Original Peoples: Sports, Greek Antiquity and National Identity from Winckelmann to Turnvater Jahn", *German History*, Vol. 27, No. 3, July 2009, pp.358–373.
- Wanko, Andrew. "The Glories of Germanhood: A History of the Turnverein in St. Louis." St. Louis, MO.: Landmarks Association of Saint Louis, www .landmarks-stl. org/news/the_glories_of_germanhood_a_history_of_the_ Turnverein_in_st._louis/

7. der Geist: Remembering Missouri's German heritage

Temples of Memory

- Browne, Cynthia. "Deutschheim Turns 40." *Der Maibaum: Journal of the Deutschheim Verein*. Vol. XXVII, No.1 Spring/Summer 2018, pp.3-4.
- Lowenthal, David. "The Past is a Foreign Country." Cambridge, UK: Cambridge University Press, 1985.
- Schlereth, Thomas J., editor. "Material Culture Studies in America." Walnut Creek, CA: AltaMira Press, 1999.
- Mondello, Bob. "A History of Museums, The Memory of Mankind." NPR. www.npr.org/templates/story/story.php?storyId=97377145. November 24, 2008.
- Prown, Jules David. "Mind in Matter: An Introduction to Material Culture Theory and Method." *Winterthur Portfolio*. Vol. 17, No. 1 Spring, 1982, pp.1-19.
- Schieffelin, Edward L. "Reciprocity and the Construction of Reality". Man. 15 (3): (1980-01-01), pp.502–517
- Tilden, Freeman. "Interpreting our Heritage." Raleigh, NC: University of North Carolina Press, 1957.
- Uhlenbrock, Tom. "Dierberg family's Hermann Farm and Museum opens for tours." Special to the *St. Louis Post-Dispatch*, July 3, 2016.
- van Ravenswaay, Charles. "The Arts and Architecture of German Settlements in Missouri: A Story of a Vanishing Culture." Columbia, MO: University of Missouri Press, 1977.

Volkommen

- Butler, Elizabeth M. "The Tyranny of Greece Over Germany: A Study of the Influence Exercised by Greek Art and Poetry Over the Great German Writers of the 18th, 19th and 20th Centuries." Cambridge, UK: Cambridge University Press, 1935.
- Houseman, Marc. "Some peculiarities of predominantly German-American cemeteries in the German Heritage Corridor." Unpublished paper.
- Shepley, Carol Ferring. "Movers and Shakers, Scalawags and Suffragettes: Tales from Bellefontaine Cemetery." St. Louis, MO: Missouri History Museum, 2008.
- Smith, Jeffrey. "The Rural Cemetery Movement: Places of Paradox in 19th Century America." Lanham, MD: Lexington Books, 2017.
- Van Ravenswaay, Charles. "The Arts and Architecture of German Settlements in Missouri: A Survey of a Vanishing Culture." Columbia, MO: University of Missouri Press, 1977.
- Wood, Michael. "In Search of the Trojan War." New American Library, 1987.

der Festspiele

- C. Michael Hall and Liz Sharples. "Food and Wine Festivals and Events Around the World." New York, NY: Routledge, September 2008. "Food and Wine Festivals and Events Around the World" considers the importance to communities of this rapidly growing aspect of the tourism industry.
- Hargrove, Cheryl. "Authenticity in Cultural Heritage Tourism." This article is reprinted in excerpt from the *Forum Journal*, National Trust for Historic Preservation, Fall 2003, Vol. 18 No. 1.
- Kluckhohn, Clyde. "Mirror for Man: The Relation of Anthropology to Modern Life." Routledge Classic Texts in Anthropology, 2017.
- Mehrhoff, W. Arthur. "Cultural Tourism," in *Encyclopedia of Urban America: The Cities and Suburbs*. Edited by Neil Larry Shumsky. Santa Barbara, CA: ABC-CLIO, 1998. pp.225-227.
- Murphy, Peter E. "Tourism: A Community Approach." New York, NY and London, UK: Routledge Publishing, 1985.

Index

Index continued